To my dad Bob Carter, I love you, and I miss you every day. This book is for you.

Contents

Introduction

Chapter 1: Hello world, I'm Amy Kate

Chapter 2: Where it all began

Chapter 2: The high school years

Chapter 4: The big wide world

Chapter 5: Transformation

Chapter 6: The emotional rollercoaster

Chapter 7: Pandora's box

Chapter 8: Was it something I said?

Chapter 9: What would Audrey do?

Chapter 10: Riding the dragon

Chapter 11: Puberty 2.0

Chapter 12: The mid-transition blues

Chapter 13: Operation Foo Foo

Chapter 14: It's like riding a bike

Chapter 15: Objects in the rear-view mirror (are closer than they appear)

How to be a trans ally

Introduction

In June of 1972 I was born at the Leicester Royal Infirmary, much to the relief of my long-suffering mother. The summer of '72 had been a pretty hot one, definitely not the ideal time to be heavily pregnant. Following a fairly uncomplicated birth (I'm her fourth child, shelling peas was mentioned when I asked my mother to recall the occasion), the midwife promptly cut the umbilical cord and pronounced to my mother, 'Congratulations, it's a boy.' That moment, for every child, sparks a chain of events which will shape its destiny. Gender appropriate clothes are purchased or knitted by overly enthusiastic aunts and grandmothers. Names are chosen after many nights arguing whether naming the child after the place of conception will scar them for life (my friend Cannock Chase will testify to this). Nurseries are hastily painted blue or pink unless the parents went for the safe neutral option of yellow. Ceremonial trees are planted as has become popular in recent times, and parents begin to plot their child's future.

But what if that moment was not as it seemed? What if the midwife or doctor's assumption of the baby's gender, based only on their physical assessment, was wrong? From that moment on, the child will be raised and nurtured based on what is between their legs and that alone. Documents will be signed and births registered. Certificates will be issued and put away for safe keeping. Gender appropriate toys will be bought for the child as they grow, like Barbie dolls for the girls and action figures for the boys. The birth of a child is a miraculous thing but it doesn't always go exactly according to the plan. Our birth-assigned physical sex is not always in tune with our brain's subconscious sex, or put simply, our gender identity.

Most people would agree that boys have a penis and girls have a vagina. I don't disagree with that and you'd be hard pressed to find a medical professional to dispute it either. However, science is beginning to unravel the mystery of why some people are born either male or female, but as they grow, it becomes clear to them that this is not right. Instead, there is a deep sadness, the feeling that this is a mistake - and that they are actually of the opposite sex or somewhere in between. I was born with a penis, but it didn't make me a man despite my best efforts to be one. I am the proud owner of a shiny new vagina with very few miles on the clock but that alone does not make me a woman. What makes me a woman is between my ears, not between my legs. This sadness, this feeling of not being comfortable in your own body, which transgender and gender diverse people live with, is called gender dysphoria. I lived with this sadness for forty-two years before I finally had no choice but to confront my demons and deal with them once and for all.

I hate jargon, so I've tried to keep it to a minimum in this book. That said, there are a few terms which need clarity before we go on. Let's start with the difference between sex and gender. Sex refers to whether a person is physically female or male. In our culture this is determined by the presence or absence of a penis. The reality is that it is much more complex than that. Gender is typically used to describe a person's gender identity or subconscious sex, whether that be male, female, neither or both. This can be how they present themselves, their behaviours, (masculine, feminine or neutral) and in some cases, their privileges or restrictions, based on society, culture and tradition. These defined gender binaries of male or female are not always so straight forward either. Take intersex people as an example. Intersex is a general term used to describe a variety of conditions in which a person is born with a reproductive or sexual anatomy that doesn't match the typical binary of male or female. This can be anything from genitalia to chromosomes or even internal organs.

Now that we have the difference between sex and gender all sorted, let's talk about sexuality. It is important to clarify that sexuality and gender identity are not linked directly. After coming out in 2015, one of the first questions I was asked by a colleague at work was, 'so if you're gonna be a woman, does that mean you'll be sleeping with blokes then?' This question made me realise how much emphasis society puts on our physical sex. When a person transitions from one sex to another, they do not typically switch sexuality as well. It can happen and there are exceptions to every rule but generally speaking, if you were attracted to women before transition, the chances are you'll still be attracted to women after. When I explain my own sexuality to curious people who can't help asking, I simply say that my sexuality is who I go to bed *with*, and my gender identity is who I go to bed *as*. Pretty simple really when you think about it.

If like many people, you've never heard the term gender dysphoria, then let me explain. The word dysphoria simply means a feeling of severe dissatisfaction, anxiety or restlessness: a feeling that something is not right. It can lead to deep depression and in many cases suicidal thoughts and self-harm. Gender dysphoria is a sense that despite your birth assigned sex, be it male or female, your subconscious sex (your internal sense of gender) does not match the physical body that you were born with. Most of us, in fact around 98% of the global population of this planet, never question their gender. It isn't something the average person ever really considers. Ask yourself this question: have you ever woken up doubting your internal sense of gender, or your physical sex? Does it feel alien to imagine yourself as the opposite sex? If you are a man who's happy being a man can you easily imagine living your life as a woman? If you're not transgender, these questions may seem very odd and maybe even a little uncomfortable. The possibility that you don't understand or even connect with your own body because your brain feels different causes frustration, anxiety and despair every single day. It must be a terrible mistake, but you're too scared to tell anyone because they won't believe you or they won't understand and may even reject you for telling them. Gender dysphoria is with you from the moment you awake to the moment you go to sleep. It creeps into your thoughts when you should be concentrating on your work, or your exams, or listening to a distraught friend who's telling you their troubles. It occupies your dreams; it offers no escape or respite, it is relentless.

    I do have some good news though, unlike the coronavirus that has ravaged our planet, gender dysphoria, and consequently being transgender, is not contagious. You will be fine. You can't catch it because of an ill fitted mask or because someone coughed on you on the bus. You're either born with it or you're not. I cannot stress this enough – and I'm resisting the urge to write this in bold and underline it – this is not about choice. Nobody chooses to be transgender any more than a person would choose to be asthmatic or diabetic. It's just something some of us were born with, like a third nipple or a birth mark in the shape of Belgium. The only real choice involved in a transgender person's life is whether they decide to transition to their correct gender to ease the pain of dysphoria, or try to find a way to live their life in a way that supresses their gender dysphoria sufficiently. If they choose to transition, will they be safe? Will they lose everything? It's shocking to realise that some people are killed just because they are trans, murdered in cold blood in horrific and brutal ways. In over seventy countries worldwide, it is illegal to be openly gay or present yourself in a gender other than that assigned at birth. In around fourteen of those countries, the penalty can be death. Thankfully, here in Britain, life for the average transgender person isn't quite so extreme but I've had rental agreements cancelled, job applications turned down and offers of help withdrawn once the person became aware that I was transgender. Friends of mine have been verbally and physically attacked in the street while minding their own business, and one was spat at in her workplace by a member of the public in full view of everyone. Society may well be waking up to the fact that transgender people exist, but we are far from seeing widescale acceptance and equal rights and opportunities for trans and gender diverse people. I've heard many people say they've never met a trans person before speaking to me, but don't be so sure. Not everyone who is trans has transitioned. It can be that they just haven't figured it out yet or they have too much to lose if they transition - their children, family, spouse or career. I kept my secret for forty-two years and no one in my life suspected that I was transgender. After years of trying my hardest to fit in, to be a man, I chose to transition because it was that or suicide.

  Why am I writing this? Why now? Transition is in my rear-view mirror and my life has now begun again, and it's a good life. I can't erase the past and I wouldn't want to. It wasn't all bad and the memories I hold are also the memories of my friends, family and former colleagues. To completely obliterate my former life would be sad but also disrespectful to those who shared it with me. Instead, I'd like to take you with me on my journey, to share with you how it felt to grow up knowing I was different, hiding the pain of my lie behind a smile more fake than David Dickinson's tan. I want you to laugh with me, cry with me, feel the array of emotions that I experienced as I grew, matured and eventually transitioned into this beautiful catwalk supermodel (deluded) that I am today. I hope that this book will show that trans and gender diverse people are just like anyone else and not something to be feared or prejudiced towards. Perhaps you have a friend, a relative, or even your own child has come out as transgender. In any case, a better understanding of trans and gender diverse people can only be a good thing.

This book is not a Haynes manual on transgender people. It won't show you how to change a trans person's head gasket or check their oil. It isn't a copy of Practical Knitting either, it won't teach you how to knit one in twelve easy steps. This is my story, in my words, some happy, some sad, some funny, some not so funny. Everyone's transition is different because it is personal to them. I'm not offering advice to those who think they may be transgender, or a guide on how to successfully transition. Frankly, I'm not qualified to do that and there are many people far better equipped to help than I am. This book is an insight into my life, an open, honest account of what transition is really like, what being transgender is really like. At the end of this book, I hope that I will have dispelled many of the myths associated with what being transgender means, because despite what you may have heard, we're not scary monsters.

Chapter One
Hello world, I'm Amy Kate

'I can't be late. Why am I always late?' Despite being on my own, I find myself saying this out loud with a piece of toast hanging out of my mouth whilst simultaneously trying to pull on a pair of black opaque tights. I'm trying my best not to get Marmite on them but it's almost inevitable that I will. The very concept of getting dressed and making oneself presentable to the outside world is slightly alien to many of us after over a year of Covid-19 lockdowns and social restrictions. Just a few weeks ago my fashion choices didn't extend far beyond daytime pyjamas or night-time ones, and personal grooming was completely side-lined while the nail bars and beauty salons were forced to close. I learned to pluck my own eyebrows after a few weeks, when I realised that they had joined forces to create a monobrow that Bert and Ernie would be very proud of. My healthy eating regime went out of the window fairly quickly, I spent far too many mornings trying to decide whether a 2015 Merlot was a good accompaniment to my morning coco pops, or if my breakfast grapefruit should be infused with a double gin. Everyday life as we knew it was turned on its head. Many of us, myself included, were furloughed from our jobs. My day job (when I'm not writing books), is as a technical trainer for a truck manufacturer. I train the technicians on new technologies and products, and how to fix the trucks to the highest standards, at our academy and headquarters in Buckinghamshire. The training was all delivered in a face-to-face format, and of course once lockdown was implemented, there was no more training. Suddenly, we found ourselves twiddling our thumbs at home and clapping for our amazing NHS on our doorsteps. It's been a long time since I felt as vulnerable and alone as I did while we were all forced to stay indoors to reduce the spread of the deadly disease, but I am thankful to have survived as so many were lost. I'm also thankful that my mental health although dented, remained largely intact. At the beginning of the pandemic, I lived in a house share with four others including the landlady, on a remote farm in Buckinghamshire. I had major surgery in early January 2020, so my lockdown started two months ahead of most people's. As I was recovering at home, I watched the events of the world unfold on the daily news with my housemates, going out only to get essential supplies and fight over toilet rolls in aisle 6 at Asda. Despite a mass vaccination administered by our incredible NHS of a kind not seen in our lifetime, we're still nowhere near what can be considered "normal life" just yet. I don't know if life will ever truly be the same again but at least we can travel and go about our business to some degree even if not quite as we did before.

Having narrowly avoided the almost certain Marmite on the tights disaster, I finish getting dressed. I've chosen a vintage style orange and black gingham top with a flattering square neckline and ruffled short sleeves. I've paired it with a black mid-length pencil skirt and smart black patent heels. I've always loved the vintage 1950's pin-up look, and although I wouldn't wear it daily, it is my go-to look for occasions where I want to make a good impression, or I'm just feeling particularly sassy. I don't usually wear much jewellery, and I don't own anything more valuable than the odd bit of Swarovski, so today I've gone for some simple silver hoop earrings and a nice set of fake pearls. My blonde hair is brushed and styled and I've put on fairly light makeup, opting only for a full red lipstick to emphasise my lips, which in current times, is kind of pointless as no-one will see my lips behind my leopard print face mask. Finally, after checking myself in the mirror seventeen times, I'm ready to leave the house. 'Car keys. Where are my bloody car keys?' If you are a woman reading this, I hope you will afford me some sisterly sympathy. If you are a man, you're probably rolling your eyes whilst thinking of all the times you've sat drumming your fingers on the steering wheel, waiting for a woman to find that illusive item in her bag. A woman's bag is the real-life equivalent of Doctor Who's Tardis. It may look small on the outside, but the interior is cavernous with a multitude of zipped compartments and hiding places. They must be in here somewhere.

Phone

Purse

Hairbrush

Phone charger

Lipstick

Perfume

Mascara

Chewing gum

Paracetamol

A pen

A 10mm spanner (don't ask)

A pair of pliers (also don't ask)

A receipt for motorcycle parts

A receipt for nail polish and lip liner

A spare facemask

Several panty liners, (one of which appears to be stuck to a half-eaten Twix).

GRRRR! I'm just about to tip the whole bag upside down on the bonnet of my car in frustration, when I check my jacket pockets and hey presto, there they are. I'm off.

I moved to a lovely little stone cottage in the Chiltern hills back in December 2020. Due to some pretty shocking lifestyle choices that I made in my twenties and thirties, I don't own my own home, and I'm still paying out good money every month for a lifetime of expensive overcompensating in the form of motorcycles (a lot of motorcycles). I'm just a lodger, but I have my own little annex in the cottage, it's close to work and it's a beautiful, peaceful place to live. The drive from my home in south Oxfordshire is around an hour and a half so I need to make good time. Actually, I need to defy the laws of physics as I'm already late. I'm heading to Daventry in Northamptonshire, to the Danetre hospital where I have an appointment with the gender identity clinic. It's just gone 8.30am and the rush hour traffic is the usual chaos, despite the fact that many people are still working from home. Using the national speed limit signs as a rough guide and driving in a manner that the Dukes of Hazzard would be proud of, I make it to Daventry with time to spare. This is surprising because my car isn't exactly a performance machine. It is slow, so slow that I get overtaken by litter. Honestly if I want to overtake someone it requires careful planning and at least a mile of clear straight road. I'm not a slow driver, and as a motorcyclist and self-confessed motorhead, I do like a bit of speed, but my beloved little car, my little Flossy the Fiat 500, just isn't built for it. Just last week I was overtaken on a dual carriageway by an elderly couple in a Skoda who were towing a caravan. I'm not sure who was more surprised, them or me. Despite its lack of performance credentials, I love that little car, it fits my personality and my love of all things vintage or retro just perfectly. Would I swap it for a Ferrari F8 Tributo? Yes, in a heartbeat, but that's not the point. I screech into the car park and aim my little Flossy at the nearest parking spot. I step out of the car as gracefully as I can manage with the lack of movement that a pencil skirt offers, closing the car door without looking at it and pressing my key fob over my shoulder to lock the doors. I strut across the car park with a smug grin and a sway in my hips towards the shiny glass double doors. I'm early, ten minutes early. I wish I could say that I planned it that way, but the truth is it was part luck and part due to "bending" some of the more important traffic laws.

'Take a seat Miss Carter.' I can't help smiling whenever I hear someone call me miss or madam or refer to me as a lady. The reason it has such a positive effect on me is because I'm a transgender woman. Believe me it isn't always this way. I get misgendered on a pretty regular basis, mostly by my mother, but it isn't intentional, she's just a little forgetful and had referred to me as her son, for forty-two years. Misgendering is when a person refers to you with the wrong pronoun. For example, a transgender woman identifies as female. She is dressed in female attire and is presenting herself as female. She walks into a coffee shop and orders her drink, but the barista refers to her as Sir when handing her the receipt, based only on his assumption of her gender. It's difficult to explain just how it feels in that moment, but when you have taken the decision to transition, to start your life over because it was that or death, this kind of comment is like a punch in the gut. All you want is to be accepted as the gender which feels correct to you, but people make assumptions and form opinions about what they perceive to be your gender despite what you wear or how you behave. Most of the time it isn't said with malice and it's just a simple mistake, but some people like to pick on those who stand out or are brave enough to be different, brave enough to be true to themselves. We live in a world of keyboard warriors who will happily attack others from the safety of their bedroom. The sad loss of Caroline Flack in the early part of 2020 is a stark reminder of how vile we can be to each other. The term for those who specifically target transgender or gender diverse people is "transphobic". Personally, I don't like the word because a phobia, by definition, implies fear. I'm afraid of spiders, but I don't call them hairy arsed 8-legged web wangers on Twitter (pent up issues). The kind of people who direct their venom toward transgender and gender diverse people are not in fear, they aren't scared, they are just bullies. Like most bullies, social media allows them to hide from their own insecurities while persecuting others, often behind the guise of religious beliefs or good old-fashioned family values.

For forty-two years of my life, I was a man. Not a very happy man, a down-right grumpy miserable angry-with-the-world kind of a man if I'm being really honest. I never really knew why, but relationships would be difficult for me. I didn't have many close friends. I couldn't talk to my parents or my sister. I definitely couldn't talk to my two brothers, who I would describe as old-fashioned at best and downright bigoted at worst. I always had to be busy, distracted with a project or a hobby. I loved organising things, tidying up, planning out how my project would go, what I needed to buy and what tools I would need. It helped me to feel in control of my mind and distracted me in a way that prevented me from searching my feelings too hard for answers I knew I really didn't want to hear. Being alone in my own headspace was bad for me. It was very bad, but not because I sat wondering why I wasn't born a girl, I just felt different. I felt like my feminine side was much stronger than it should be, and it made me feel as though something was wrong with my brain. I used to think I must be mad or have some kind of illness that made me feel so sad and lonely inside. Ironically those who knew my former self would say that I was always the joker, always the one to make you laugh. Hardly ever without a girlfriend and, to the unknowing eye, happy, confident and fulfilled. They would say I didn't take life too seriously and knew how to have fun. How wrong they were, but they're not to blame for that: I am. I worked tirelessly to fit in, be a man, be what's expected, show no weakness. I grew up in the seventies and eighties, a time when machoism was alive and well. Miami Vice was on the telly, all fast cars and shoulder pads. Rambo, the A-Team and Knight Rider were all role models for my impressionable teenage peers who wore their back-permed mullets with the pride of a lion. Films like Roman Holiday, Some Like It Hot and Grease were more my cup of tea, but I could never admit that to my friends. Thank you, Charles Ginsburg, for the invention of the video recorder!

As I grew from a boy into adulthood, I suppose it became normal to play the macho man character that I'd spent my teenage years creating, so that I could at least appear normal on the outside. When I say normal, I mean what I perceived that to be when I was a teenager who'd been raised with little understanding of gender or sexuality. Normal to me meant a man was a man and a woman was a woman. I was aware of what it meant to be gay, lesbian or bisexual, but that never came into my mind despite my parents' obvious distrust of anyone who was anything other than heterosexual. I suppose their generation grew up in a world where it was illegal for a man to have sex with another man: gay men were treated as criminals, chemically castrated or sent to prison. Alan Turing, the forefather of the modern computer, brilliant mathematician and World War Two code breaker, took his own life after being chemically castrated following a conviction for indecency. In contrast to my parents' rather old-fashioned views and my upbringing, I've always been a strong believer that love is love, no matter who you are attracted to or how you identify.

I learned to play my character day in, day out for years because I didn't have a choice - or at least I didn't think I had a choice. I was so used to pretending to be someone I wasn't, that in the end I didn't really know who I was anymore. This became my normality until my early forties, surviving on a diet of beer, whiskey, motorcycles, fast food and anti-depressants. I didn't know what I needed to do to fix the way I felt inside, so I just carried on until I finally snapped and I just couldn't do it anymore. I was exhausted, mentally and physically. I had no fight left in me and no will to survive. I was forty-two, living with a wonderful strong supportive partner and her ten-year-old son. I had a beautiful daughter from a previous relationship and a great job, but still I was spiralling out of control, losing my grip on everything, I couldn't concentrate at work and would zone out on my fifty-five-mile commute, almost crashing my car on several occasions. I couldn't face another year lying to myself and everybody else that I was OK. I was far from OK, I was broken.

Statistically, 48%, almost half of transgender and gender diverse people have attempted suicide and most have at least had suicidal thoughts. I'm one of those people, I too faced a decision: live with the pain, take my own life to take the pain away, or find the courage to get help. You see, that is the only real choice transgender people face. To go ahead with transition or live a lie for the rest of their lives.

Nobody chooses to be transgender. Forget the nonsense you've read in the tabloids. Forget the bile that is spilled out across internet chat groups in the name of religion or good old-fashioned family values. Nobody wakes up one day and thinks, 'I think I'll change my gender. I need a new hobby and Britain's Got Talent isn't on for another month.' Who, in their right mind, would choose to potentially lose everything? Job security, friends, family, a roof over their head. Who would choose to place themselves in danger and fear of verbal and physical attack - or even murder? Trust me, if I had been given a choice, my first choice would be to have been born a girl.

Failing that, my second would be to be OK with the body and gender to which I was born, to be OK with being a guy and live a happy life. Failing that, option number three is where I am right now, writing a book about how in the end, there was only one choice other than death - to transition, and accept that despite the male body I was born with, my mind is anything but that. Nobody chooses to be transgender; the only choice is how to deal with it. That's why I've travelled so far to be here in this waiting room at the Northamptonshire Gender Identity Clinic (GIC) in Daventry.

    I smile and turn away from the counter to walk across the polished floor, listening to the loud echo of my heels clicking in rhythm until I step onto the carpeted area of the waiting room. I always make an effort when I come here, it's like I have a point to prove. The doctors often comment on your appearance in their notes after each appointment. One that I can recall said, 'Amy was wearing jewellery and makeup and presented herself in a feminine manner.' I'm not sure why they feel the need to write stuff like this. If I turned up in dungarees and a hard hat, I wouldn't be any less of a woman. It harks back to the dark ages of gender gatekeeping by the NHS when you had to prove your femininity in order to be allowed access to treatment. Those gatekeepers would decide whether you had a successful chance of transitioning into the kind of woman who might slip under the radar and be seen completely as a natal female. This is known as "passing". I personally think that this ideology is very damaging and it puts huge pressure on individuals who already have enough to deal with. If the gatekeepers felt that these individuals had no chance of being identified as female by the wider public, they were often refused treatment. Thankfully, those days are behind us, to a point at least. Not all transgender women are Barbie dolls and not all transgender men are Action men. Our sense of gender is nothing to do with what we wear or how well we do our makeup or hair. It's so much more than that: it's who we are. It's what shapes our personalities, our loves and our passions.

      Looking around the waiting room at some of the other people sitting there, I'm happy with my choice of outfit. Smart but not overdressed and definitely not what could be described as something that might be worn by a "lady of the night". Growing up I never had the opportunity to get advice on makeup and clothes from my sister. Everything I know about clothes, what works, what doesn't, I've had to learn for myself by trial and error. Some transgender people, me included, can get it quite wrong, especially in early transition. Most transgender people, whether male or female, started out cross-dressing from an early age before realising that they were transgender later on. Without guidance you can have difficulty in separating ultra-feminine and sexually objectifying clothes such as what you might wear to a nightclub or your local theatre's rendition of the Rocky Horror Picture Show, from what you'd wear when handing over your cash to

Janet at Sainsbury's after doing the weekly shop. Fishnet stockings, black PVC miniskirts and animal print crop tops are not advised for everyday wear, especially if you're planning to go to a cake sale at the W.I.

The sound of my black patent heels is suddenly muted as I step onto the carpet, and in my head, it reminds me of my transition, my journey, the silencing of those inner voices. The voices that had nagged at me, chipping away at me all my life. Telling me that I'm not like my friends, not like my brothers. I felt different, a freak, just … different. No one ever knew I felt like this, and that is the reason I preferred to spend my time alone, better off away from people and although the life and soul of the party in one respect, behind closed doors, it was a very different story. As I've grown older, my understanding of why I feel different has become clearer and clearer. In 2015 I was diagnosed with gender dysphoria by this very clinic. There is no miracle cure or magic pill. The only way to relieve the dysphoria is to transition to the correct gender. In the case of non-binary people (who identify as neither male nor female), or gender fluid or bigender, (who feel that their sense of gender shifts depending on certain factors), their transition would typically be very different. Mostly, it would involve social transition, coming out to friends, family and colleagues, but not necessarily needing hormone replacement treatment or any surgeries to identify as the opposite sex. The term Transgender covers a wide variety of people, a spectrum, not just male to female and female to male. In contrast, if you are comfortable in your body and have never questioned your gender, then you are what is known as cisgender, although outside of the trans community no one really uses that term as it's only necessary in certain contexts.

In my case, I finally realised that I'm just a woman, trying to deal with the horrible truth that I was born with a body that I have never been able to love, understand or identify with. A woman who has always felt the need to be close to femininity for her own sanity yet too afraid to tell the world how she feels or who she really is. I lived a life dedicated to conforming to what is expected of a man, to be accepted, trying so hard to be liked. I tried hard to make people laugh, so that they would accept me even though I couldn't accept myself. After all those years, and all those tears, I could no longer hold her inside. I could no longer just cope with my situation, begging for crumbs of acceptance to make me feel worthy of life itself even though it was a false life. Almost six years ago, I opened Pandora's Box when I came out to the world and began my transition from male to female. There was no going back.

I take a seat, noticing that they've changed the carpet since my last visit. Gone was the regulation NHS blue weave that was showing its age, with frayed edges and faded patches where the sun from the windows had bleached the colour from it. It has been replaced with a carpet worthy of a Turkish bazaar. I find that I can't stare at it for too long as I can feel my eyes going slightly crossed so I look away. They've also installed a television to make the wait to be seen just a little more bearable. As usual I'm early for my appointment despite my best efforts to be late. I don't know why I always turn up early, it isn't like I'm going to get seen any sooner. Maybe it's the fear that they will turn me away or refuse to treat me if I anger them by being even a minute late. In truth, they are all wonderful people and I actually look forward to talking to them so I'm sure that would never happen. I'm late for pretty much everything else in my life: fashionably late is what I call it. My friends, my sister and my boss call it something else but I promised myself I'd keep swearing to a minimum in this book so I won't tell you what they call me when I eventually arrive, but it's quite rude and very uncalled for. I'm trying to absorb the programme on the TV, but the volume has been turned right down so I can barely hear it. It seems to involve an elderly couple with far too much money who have an overwhelming desire to move to Wales. They have a list of near impossible demands and the frustration in the host's voice mildly amuses me. I last less than five minutes before I lose interest. I struggle to comprehend that with all the possibilities that television brings to the modern world, people are actually entertained by this. Who actually enjoys watching two teams of overly enthusiastic people dressed in outfits that scream disappointment, as they trawl round a car boot sale looking for the kind of items that most sane individuals would happily take to the tip? Then, under the guidance of a so-called expert who just spent half their budget on an engraved bottle opener, they put them into an auction before celebrating a profit of a few quid like they've just won the lottery.

I find my eyes scanning round the room, taking in the changes since my last visit. There are some new posters on sexual health matters. Sexual health, ha! The chances of me catching a sexually transmitted disease are about as likely as me suddenly gaining the power of flight. It's been so long since I last had sex, that the price of condoms would probably shock me back into celibacy. I'm getting very bored now and resisting the urge to play games of mind-numbing inevitability on my phone. I examine the pattern on the new carpet. Gold and blue diamonds intertwined in a repetitive pattern that could potentially hypnotise you if you stare at it for too long. I'm trying to work out if the person who designed it is actually paid to create such bold and colourful designs, or perhaps they are part of some textile-based government science experiment. There must be a market for these psychedelic designs although I'm not quite sure what that market actually is.

The reception counter is huge. Metres of beech effect chipboard topped off with a security screen so that you can't strangle the receptionists. Holes are strategically drilled in the Perspex screen so that they can hear you, but you can't poke them with anything larger than a pencil. After a few more minutes the consultant pops his head around the corner and calls me in to his office for my appointment, my final appointment. This is the one where he'll discuss discharging me as a patient from the gender identity service, now that my transition is over. This journey has finally come to an end after five torturous, incredible, hateful, wonderful, hurtful years. So much has happened since all this started and I turned my life, and the lives of all those I held close to me, upside down.

  The doctor is the same one who saw me last time I was here when I was being referred for gender affirmation surgery. He has a kind nature, and a welcoming smile which I can't see today because of the need for both of us to wear a face mask, but I remember it fondly from previous appointments. His face is distinguished with worry lines and framed with a full head of salt and pepper coloured hair and eyes that exude knowledge, confidence and experience. We make the usual small talk about the weather and the traffic, but I can see from his face that he remembers the last appointment I had with him. There is a hint of nervousness, and I'm certain he remembers the emotional car crash of a trans woman blubbing in her seat as he tried desperately to stem the flow of tears by offering tissues. On that occasion, he quickly signed my referral paperwork, approving me for gender affirmation surgery, partly out of professionalism and partly to get the blubbering mess out of his office. Behind his facemask he makes more awkward small talk, and of course the subject of coronavirus and how the hospital had been affected comes up. Eventually we get back on topic and he seems more at ease. I too am feeling more comfortable and content as he asks me a series of quite probing questions about my recovery from the surgery, my hormone replacement therapy (HRT) and how my life is going now. My life, the one I never dreamed possible. This life, my life. I love my life and for the first time ever I love my body. Up until this point, I have been holding it together pretty well. Before the appointment I promised myself that I wasn't going to cry again despite my highly charged state of emotions. His final question would change all this though. The question is simple, and in any other context or situation it would present me with no problem at all, and I would answer with total confidence and determination. 'Amy, I have only one more question to ask. Are you happy for me to discharge you from the gender service so that you can get on with your new life?' All I have to do is smile and say yes, it's what I've wanted since I started my transition. It's the light at the end of the tunnel, the carrot at the end of the stick, but what I actually do, is get half-way through 'yes' before my voice cracks and I burst into tears. These are no ordinary tears, the kind that leak from my eyes when I'm chopping onions or watching injured animals being released back into the wild on BBC2. These are uncontrollable tears of relief, pent up frustration and anguish. Tears of a lifetime of living in a body I did not understand and had no care or respect for. The pain of losing friends and family, the hurtful comments from people who passed me in the street, the disapproving stares in the coffee shop. It all comes flooding back, and it feels so real in this moment. I know as I sit here crying in front of this poor man, who for the second time looks defenceless against the emotions of a transgender woman on the verge of emotional implosion, that I am writing my future, and that the end of my transition and the beginning of my life is finally here. I can bury the past, or at least put it in a box and label it with love. I can embrace my future and leave behind for good the broken shell of a man that I once was.

'Miss Carter, I'm happy to discharge you from the clinic, but sad that we won't be seeing you again'. He says this with what looks like a warm smile, from the creases it makes under his mask, and he seems to really mean it which takes me by surprise. If nothing else, my absence will save him a fortune in tissues and work-related stress. By now, fireworks are going off inside me and my heart is pounding in my chest. I'm so happy, I can't help the ridiculous grin that is now plastered across my semi-covered face, making a confusing contrast with the black eyeliner-coloured tears that have plotted a course down my cheeks, making them look like two alternative sat-nav routes. I have an overwhelming urge to kiss the man sitting opposite me, but this would be a bad move on several counts. It would also be preferable to avoid a restraining order, so I resist. I almost skip out of his office, walking through the waiting area, over the crazy mind-bending carpet, and past the reception desk. The two ladies behind the security screen are looking at me as if trying to work out whether I need sympathy or medication. Bursting through the doors into the car park, I'm practically dancing across the tarmac with its neatly painted parking bays to my little grey car. I'm still grinning like a Cheshire cat, I'm so happy, breathing in the fresh air of the Northamptonshire countryside and feeling the cool breeze on my face as it gently dries my tears. I suddenly feel the need to call my mum to tell her the news before I burst. My transition, the journey I started back in 2015 which has broken me at times and lifted me beyond what I ever dreamed possible at others, has officially come to an end, and my new life can finally begin. I have the world at my feet, and so many exciting possibilities, adventures, and choices ahead of me.

So, who am I?

Hello world, I'm Amy Kate…

Chapter Two
Where it all began

My childhood was fairly typical of a boy growing up on a council estate in the suburbs of Leicester. We didn't have much money, but we didn't want for much either. My parents did what they could to provide for us and I don't remember ever going hungry, or having nothing to wear for school. I have fond memories of my early childhood, especially the years before secondary school. Back then I didn't feel sad or depressed, I didn't have panic attacks or anxiety. I didn't spend my days wishing I was dead. I didn't stare at women with envy, feeling the knots form in my stomach as the daydream faded away and reality smacked me hard in the face. I was just a kid, a slightly troubled, shy, quiet kid.

My mum, June, began her life in a small Leicestershire mining village. She is a twin, which was quite the talk of the village back in the 1932 when they were born, even making a headline in the local newspaper. When she was just five years old, her mother died of cervical cancer. After my grandmother's death, my mum and her four siblings were distributed among various relatives while my grandfather dealt with the loss of his wife and made plans for the future. Sometime later he moved the family to Leicester, to an area close to the town centre so that he could find work. My grandfather, my mum, her twin sister Jean, sister Kay, and brothers Aubrey and William, spent the war years in a two-bedroom terraced house with a stone cellar. She recalls the hardship of rationing and the terrible air raids, like it happened only yesterday, running down to the cellar to avoid Hitler's bombs. My grandfather had found a housekeeper to look after the children while he worked: her name was Beatrice, but everyone who knew her called her Beattie. Mum describes Beattie as a nasty woman with no maternal instincts at all. She was also a heavy drinker and well known to the local constabulary. The stories that my mum has often recalled to my sister and me, would make you sick to your stomach, but they are not my stories to tell, instead, they are the painful memories of a lost childhood that my mum still carries with her today, in her eighty-ninth year on Earth. Eventually, my grandfather became tired of the excuses when he'd ask where the housekeeping money had gone, or the unexplained bruises on his children, and the many nights where the local police would bring home the violently drunk Beattie after last orders.

Beattie was eventually replaced by another housekeeper called Norah, again not maternal towards the children in any way but not quite the nightmare that her predecessor was. Mum spent most of her childhood afraid to speak or step out of line in fear of these housekeepers, and this has left lifelong scars, especially to her nerves. She can't stand fireworks or loud bangs, and any violence on the television has her cowering behind a cushion. Leaving school at fourteen, my mother became a seamstress after finding work at Corah's of Leicester.

She married at a young age and bore three children - two boys and a girl - all within a year of each other. But her husband worked away a lot, and Mum wasn't the easiest to live with due to ongoing bouts of severe depression and anxiety. Towards the end of the 1960s her husband left her, and she found herself a single mother to the children, now approaching their teens. Mum remained single for a number of years, raising the three children on her own and struggling like any single parent does. One night in 1971 she and some friends had been watching a singer in the local working men's club. The singer, a local man who called himself Jack despite his real name being John, was quite talented by all accounts and a good all-round entertainer. Mum describes his voice as being somewhere between bass and baritone. He also had the gift of the gab. He could charm the birds from the trees, sell ice to the Eskimos, and he definitely had an eye for the ladies. This is where all the trouble started.

After a fairly brief courtship, Jack and my mum married at Leicester registry office on Pocklington's walk. Jack moved into her home and the children seemed to accept him without too much fuss. My mum, at thirty-nine, was sure she had started the menopause, so contraception was tossed aside and caution thrown to the wind. Mum has always insisted that I was "planned", and as much as I'd love to believe this, the evidence suggests otherwise. From my sister's recollection, and my mum's somewhat sketchy version of events, the pregnancy, although quite a shock, went without drama until the second trimester when my mum almost miscarried. She had been decorating the house, as my biological father (let's just call him "the sperm donor" from now on) was pretty useless at anything other than singing and being a professional waste of oxygen. She had a bad bleed while half way up a ladder, and the doctor was promptly called. He prescribed bed rest and regular progesterone injections to strengthen the lining of her womb, and my mum reluctantly heeded the advice. After this drama, five months later, my poor mother braced herself to deliver her fourth child.

On a hot summer's afternoon in the closing days of June, 2pm to be precise, a beautiful brown-haired baby with a lazy left eye made an entrance into the world at the Leicester Royal Infirmary. At the time of my birth, Jack, the sperm donor, was in the pub celebrating my arrival with his friends and admirers. 'Congratulations, it's a boy', the doctor and midwife proclaimed to my somewhat exhausted mum. Of course, the sex of any child is determined at birth, if not during the tests in pregnancy, based only on what can be seen between the foetus's legs.

Only now in the twenty-first century are we starting to build up a picture of why some people are born with a brain gender that does not match their physical gender. Recent studies have indicated that the brain activity and even its physical structure, actually align with the person's inner sense of gender or subconscious gender, rather than with their physical sex, whether that be male or female. So, a man who feels that his subconscious gender is female, will have a brain that not only functions more like a female brain than a male one, but also has similar attributes such as physical size and neurological characteristics.

Of course, it isn't always that simple, the transgender umbrella is vastly diverse. Some transgender people do not feel that they belong to either the male or female binary. These people are known as non-binary. Some feel that their gender shifts, depending on how they feel or even what activity they are doing. These are known as gender queer, bi-gender or gender fluid. I could write a whole chapter on the variations of gender identities but this book is based on my own experience and as such it will focus mainly on transgender women or "trans women" as is the more widely used abbreviation.

Scientists and researchers are continually looking for the answers to why a child can be born with a brain sex that does not match their physical body, and the evidence is yet to be fully proven, but the belief is that hormonal imbalances - and even dietary influences during pregnancy - may be the cause of this phenomenon. There is no way to test for what is eventually diagnosed as gender dysphoria during pregnancy, or even early infancy at present, but science is rapidly making progress in this area and the answers are not far away. In my case I can only speculate, but Mum was carrying me around the time of her menopause. Her probable hormone imbalance and higher age increased the risk of abnormalities in the foetus. Mum has never smoked and is definitely not what you'd call a year-round drinker, except for binge-drinking snowballs, Cherry B and cheap cooking sherry at Christmas. All of this is mere speculation on my part, or maybe just a need for answers and a viable reason for the life I've led, and how I've always felt. After all, it's only human to wonder 'why me'. One thing I do know is that my mum blames herself to some degree, despite my best efforts to reassure her that there is no way she could have predicted my fate.

My mum and the donor picked the name Ian for me. To this day she doesn't know where they got it from. She recalls that the only criteria she was working to was giving me a name that didn't have initials that would get me bullied at school. My half siblings, James, Angela and Graham, were all in their teens by now and only James remained living at home. My sister Angela had a big part to play in my upbringing. My mum was back at work to make ends meet and had suffered a severe bout of post-natal depression a few weeks after I was born. The donor was spending more and more time working away or just not showing up for days at a time, so my sister would feed me and change me to help my mother out. I have always been very close to my sister, and I still am, and I truly believe that was strengthened by her part-time role of mother during my early childhood.

When I was around eighteen months old, my mum had had enough of the donor's irresponsible behaviour, running up debts and frequently disappearing, sometimes for several days. I don't think the donor put up much of a fight and I assume he went back to his philandering ways on the club circuit when they divorced. I suspect that my siblings only tolerated Jack, they didn't consider him any kind of replacement father and only kept the peace for my mum's sake, so they certainly didn't shed any tears when he finally packed his bags and left. Some months later my mum decided to join a friendship group. Today we would call it online dating, but back in 1975 you couldn't just swipe left or "super like" somebody. You either wrote to them or you sent a message to a telephone service and someone would forward that message to the recipient. After a string of disastrous dates including an overly enthusiastic man with wandering hands, a pig farmer with questionable personal hygiene and a projectionist from the local cinema with eyes that pointed in different directions, she had all but given up. One evening, out of the blue, she received a phone call from a man who had asked for her number from her friend. This led to a date over a cup of tea in the café of Littlewoods store in Leicester. In those days, Leicester had no Starbucks, Costa or Pret, but most of the big stores like Lewis's, Littlewoods and Woolworths had cafés which were popular meeting places. Over the next few weeks Robert and June became quite an item. He lived in Coventry and would come to Leicester most days to spend time with my mum before driving all the way home again.

After a while, Robert moved in with us, into our tiny box room at first. They didn't share a bedroom until they were married, which I think is very sweet although I suspect there was a little bit of late-night tip-toeing going on between rooms. This has been flatly denied by my mum who insists that she has only had "relations" four times, each resulting in a child. She also insists that "sex talk", which she categorises as any conversation relating to sex, should only be spoken about in the marriage bed (you can almost hear my eyes rolling). Robert found a job as a mechanic in a Leicestershire garage and everything was going really well for them both. So well, in fact, that on May 10th 1976 my mum and Robert were married at Leicester registry office, with yours truly being dispatched to perform the role of miniature page boy. Later that same year I was adopted by him so that I could have the same surname as my now-married mother. The sperm donor was thrilled by this news and happily signed the adoption papers, meaning he didn't have to pay any child support, which is ironic as he hadn't paid any up until that point anyway. According to my mum, during the adoption hearing, I wandered up to the judge and thanked him, before shouting very loudly, 'thanks judge, see you next year.' I avoided a charge of contempt of court on the grounds of adorability, and he suggested to my parents that they should buy me a special adoption day present, (result!). I remember it being a ball with a pair of zip wires going through the middle. The ball moved along the wires when the person at each end opened their arms, spreading the two lines apart. 1970s toys were primitive if not a little strange (Swingball anyone?). From the moment he met me and started dating my mum, he treated me as his own son. It takes more than just blood and DNA to make someone a father. He may not have been my biological father, but without question or complaint, he took on this young child, and he raised me as his own. This is my dad, Robert Carter, or Bob to those who knew him.

 My dad had been married once before and had four children, of whom only one was really close to him. The other three had moved away or lost touch with him after a very messy divorce, following his ex-wife's adultery. My dad's background is something I wish I'd quizzed him more about, but I do know that he trained as a mechanic and served nine years in the army, enlisting not long after the end of the Second World War. His army career is very sketchy, he didn't really talk about it and I doubt I'll ever know what he really did during that time, but I think it's safe to say he wasn't dodging bullets on the front line. For some of his army career he was actually attached to the 21st SAS Regiment. Not as a trained killer: he was a mechanic and a driver, driving anything from staff cars where he would ferry important officers between bases, to driving large trucks carrying centurion and chieftain tanks.

 The family home now consisted of my mum and dad, and little me. My brother James had moved in with his soon-to-be wife and I was upgraded to the big bedroom in our little council house. I don't really have many childhood memories from those days. I don't remember being so small. The only vague memories I have are of my brother Graham accidentally burning my leg with a welding torch while he was welding some new sills onto his Ford Anglia. I can remember the pain and the smell of burning flesh even to this day. Thankfully it was a minor burn and there's no scar. I also remember cutting my hand very badly when I fell off my bike at the age of about six. I was quite the daredevil on my little bike. I was balancing very carefully as I rode along a four-foot-high wall in the small residential car park where we lived. I lost my balance and fell onto the bonnet of a neighbour's car, a Humber Sceptre (showing my age). This car had an old-fashioned chrome bonnet ornament which went straight into my hand. I can still see the blood pouring from my palm as my mum washed it in the sink before wrapping it in a tea towel and taking me to hospital for three stitches and a tetanus jab. I still have the scar from that day, and despite the stupidity of what I did, I still think it was a pretty cool stunt, and in today's world, it would have gone viral on YouTube.

I may not have many solid memories of that time, being a young child with a new dad and a stable family home, but I do know for sure that at that age, I had no idea that I would end up feeling like there was something wrong with me. I place a lot of emphasis on childhood memories because I hear a lot of transgender people say that they knew from the age of three or four that something felt wrong, that they were not the gender to which they had been born. I don't dispute that for a second, we are all different, but in my case, I don't remember having any such thoughts. In fact, I didn't really think about gender at all back then. I was just a kid, who loved Tonka toys and hot wheels cars. I loved watching Rainbow, Button Moon and the Muppet Show. I loved playing in the sandpit my dad made for me in the back garden, and I had no desire to become Miss Piggy or Wonder Woman. Life was good as far as I remember. Like any kid, I'd push my parents' buttons once in a while, and my mum would lose her temper with me and I'd get a good hiding, but in the 1970s this wasn't that unusual. I also have to consider what my mum's childhood was like, and that this was what she had come to see as normal parenting. My dad on the other hand, never laid a finger on me, not once, but he had a way of letting me know that he was disappointed with me. A pair of bespectacled eyes would appear over the top of his well-thumbed newspaper, or from under the bonnet of a car he was working on. He wouldn't say anything, he'd just look at me, and no words would be needed. To all intents and purposes, my childhood at this stage was as normal as any other, at least by my recollection. As much as it would help to cement my case, I can't say I felt that I was a girl or had a feeling that I was trapped in the body of a boy at such a young age, but it really is an individual thing. Some people have felt since their earliest memories that their subconscious gender doesn't match their physical gender or sex, and some discovered the truth later in life. For me, it was a little later when I started to feel that things weren't quite right.

At around the age of seven I started to become curious about what was in the floral-patterned bag that my mum always left on the kitchen counter. I remember the bag smelling really nice, a smell I now know to be pressed face powder. My mum was no makeup artist and actually rarely wore any, other than a bit of lippy. She reserved anything more than this for weddings, funerals and jaunts to the pub, when she would wear a little powder and some blusher, but that was about it. My mum has always had a natural beauty and never really needed heavy makeup. I would often peek into the bag, gazing in wonder at its confusing and yet somehow enticing contents, but I never did anything else, always zipping it back up and wandering off to play with my toy cars. I also used to look in her jewellery box, a beautiful thing, faux marble with brown felt lined compartments and a clockwork ballerina that danced to the tune of the Nutcracker Suite. She had an oval pendant with a large amethyst stone (her birthstone) on a thin sterling silver chain. There were some other bits and bobs but nothing that would end up in an auction at Christie's. My mum didn't really wear jewellery. She has never even had her ears pierced, and even though my dad bought her several watches, she never wore any of them. My sister once got her ears pierced at the age of fifteen and my mum hit the roof. She said 'if God wanted you to have holes in your ears, he would have put them there Himself'. My sister made the fundamental mistake of pointing out that we actually already have holes in our ears or we wouldn't be able to hear, to which she received a good pasting. In my mum's wardrobe she kept her "best" shoes. Unlike me, with my somewhat unhealthy obsession with shoes, she has never worn a heel that would require any kind of altitude training, and most of them were either a mid-heel or flat. Quite reserved and respectable, some leather, some patent leather but all in fairly modest colours considering this was the late seventies when fashion was not exactly subtle. I remember putting them on and shuffling round her room. It didn't feel strange or bad in any way, and every once in a while, I would find myself back there trying on a different pair. If I had to describe my interest in feminine things back then, I'd say I was aware of them, curious even. I probably thought about them more than you would expect a boy of that age to, but I certainly didn't feel conflicted about who I was or what my gender should be at that point.

Many people say their school years are their best, but for me they were among my worst. I don't remember much of infant school other than pooing my pants in a painting lesson because the teacher didn't believe that I really needed the toilet (she never made that mistake again). I was a milk monitor until I was sacked for stealing an extra bottle from the crate every day when I fetched it from the caretaker (who says crime doesn't pay?). Primary school was much more fun, I liked my teachers, although I dare say they didn't like me all the time. I even liked the school dinners: fish fingers, chips and mushy peas on a Friday, pink custard on Wednesdays, and big copper water jugs on the tables. I began to work out that the way to feel good about myself was to make others like me. I became the class joker, putting this priority even above a good education. I was always in trouble at school - not for serious things like bullying, I never did that, it's just not in my nature, but I gained a reputation for misdemeanours and general mischievous behaviour. I was once dared by my class to pull a "moony" out of the class window during breaktime. Apparently, the assistant teacher on playground duty was deeply traumatised at the sight of my pasty white bum cheeks pressed up against the glass of the classroom window. She needed sweet tea and a chocolate digestive to recover. A letter was sent home to my parents for that one, and another pasting ensued. My form tutor, Mr Bull, was a great teacher, if a little old-fashioned in his approach. I still remember him fondly, with his wild curly auburn hair and reddish glow to his face, suggesting perhaps that his breaktime coffee was not only strong and black, but also topped up with something a little stiffer. He had a slipper in his desk drawer, which he affectionately called Fred. By the end of my four years in primary school, Fred and my backside were very well acquainted. Corporal punishment in schools was banned in 1986. Just my luck.

The worst part of primary school for me was games or P.E (physical education). I hated football and rugby and any sport which involved being cold or muddy. I just wasn't into the rough and tumble and I'd try to make excuses to get out of it. I fooled my mum into writing so many notes to excuse me from games, which I'm sure she saw through, but nevertheless I got away with it. Toothache, tonsilitis, growing pains… You name it, I used it to get out of P.E. I remember one term we had to move lessons to experience the wider curriculum, to prepare us for the move up to secondary school. I was put in the sewing class. I was one of two boys in a class of twenty girls. The other lad, Stuart, spent most of the lessons dropping his safety scissors so that he could look up the girls' skirts. I felt a strange sense of familiarity in this lesson, despite the fact that I couldn't sew, not even a button. I still can't. My sister just looks at me with despair, but I just don't possess the skills despite my best efforts to learn. I can strip and rebuild an engine with my eyes closed but needles and thread are totally alien to me. I tried really hard in that lesson because I really wanted to be there, and I wanted to be liked by the other girls too, but I couldn't work out why that was so important to me. On a subconscious level, I suppose I felt at ease, I felt safe in a way, which is ironic, as it's a miracle I didn't sew all my fingers together when we had the sewing machines out. Unsurprisingly, come the end of term the teacher suggested that I consider trying woodwork, or something 'more appropriate to my skills' as she so delicately put it.

    I didn't have many friends during my early childhood. Part of the reason for this was being an only child, in the sense that my three siblings had all left home. I grew up on an estate that was built in the late 1960s, and many of the families that moved there, including ours, already had older children, so there weren't many kids my age. My best friend, Elaine, lived at the top of my street. Even then, at the age of eight I found it so much easier to be friends with a girl. I never thought to question why, I just really liked spending time with her. We were in different classes at school but we played together at break times and she and I would walk to school together every day, and every afternoon we would walk home, often playing at her house before it was time for tea. Her father was a carpenter by trade. One Christmas, he gave her a beautiful doll's house which he had built for her. It was so big it had to be kept in their living room. We would often decide on the way home from school what we would play when we got home, and usually it would be me that suggested playing with the dolls and the doll's house. I didn't think about the fact that I was a boy playing with dolls, and the implications of that, or what it may have looked like to Elaine or her parents. I just enjoyed playing with them and it felt quite normal. I suppose, in a way, Elaine was my only link to femininity, and she enabled me to be feminine to a point, even though I didn't realise it at the time. The subconscious mind is an incredibly powerful thing.

      At home my toybox was filled with toy cars. I was obsessed with cars, trucks and motorbikes. I still am, and I can never imagine them not being an important part of my life. I had a fascination with them from a very young age. I think they represent a very gender-neutral toy. I never really played with soldiers or action men: they just didn't interest me. When I wasn't playing with my toy cars, I'd be out in the garage helping my dad to fix his car, or I'd go with him to my stepbrother's garage on a Saturday morning. I loved the smell of petrol and oil. I could spend hours there just wandering around looking at the wrecked cars that were kept round the back of the workshop. Looking back, I suppose it was quite dangerous and I'm lucky not to have chopped my fingers off or something worse, but the 1970s had a loose grip on health & safety at best.

Sometimes, my dad would take me to the local scrap yards in Leicester if we needed parts for his car, or for one of his friends' cars that he was helping them to fix. He had a long-term back injury so once we'd found the right model amongst the rows of scrap cars, often piled three high on top of each other, he would send me climbing up the pile with a socket wrench and spanners to remove the parts we needed. I was taking some front suspension arms off an old Volvo once, which was sitting on the roof of a Ford Cortina that had been badly mangled in a crash. I remember thinking this doesn't feel very safe but it is really cool. I must have good balance because I never fell off, but I lost count of the times I banged my head on those stacked up old wrecks. I loved every minute of that time I spent with my dad. I often think that the experiences we shared as father and son back then, bonding over our shared love of anything with wheels and an engine, was the closest I had ever been to being happy. While I was tuning an engine, cleaning out a carburettor or changing a set of spark plugs, I didn't think about anything other than the task in hand, and it felt great.

As my primary school years came to a close, Elaine was spending more time with other girls and making friendships which she would later take with her to secondary school. I was spending most of my time at home, away from my peers. I just couldn't connect with the other boys on the estate. I didn't know why, I just assumed it was because I didn't like playing sports or army or cowboys and Indians. If I wasn't hiding in my make-shift den at the park or playing with my toy cars, I'd be with my dad working on cars, watching old hot-rod movies together that we'd rented from our local video store, or going to motor racing events whenever he could afford it. I often think that if I could go back to any period of my life, it would be that. And if I could go back as a girl too, life would have been damn near perfect. My dad taught me so much about cars, engines, gearboxes and all manner of mechanical things without even breaking a sweat. At the age of ten I could strip a carburettor and explain how an internal combustion engine worked. Even at that age, I knew that I would one day be a mechanic just like him. There was no question to be asked and no choice to be made. There was just the certainty that one day, I'd be making my living with a spanner in my hand.

But before any of my dreams could become reality, there was the small matter of making it through secondary school in one piece.

Chapter Three
The high school years

With my eleventh birthday looming, I began to feel very anxious about going to "big school". There were only a couple of terms of primary school left and suddenly I found myself with a huge decision to make: which secondary school should I go to? The most difficult choice I'd had to make until then was chocolate or raspberry sauce on my ice cream. I'm not good with big decisions. I tend to over think them and over research them. Sometimes it works in my favour and I make a calculated and well-informed choice but sometimes I should learn to go with my gut. When I was a child, our local ice cream man would have testified to this. I remember him impatiently drumming his fingers on the counter of his van while my 99 flake slowly melted in his other hand, as he waited for me to make a decision. My parents told me that they had no preference over which school I went to, and the decision was mine. Instead of taking the pressure off me, it made me feel worse. If they had decided for me, at least I would've had someone to blame if I hated it. The choice was between City of Leicester boys' school, Spencefield secondary school or St. Paul's Catholic school. Elaine had chosen the Catholic school because she had some friends who were already there. I picked Spencefield because some of my friends on the estate were going there, and I saw it as the best of a bad situation. Little did I know that this would be the beginning of one of the worst periods of my life.

I started to spend more time out and about on the estate. It had lots of little parks which were quite hidden away, so there were plenty of places for me to build a den and hide from the world. Around that time, I began to daydream quite a lot. I would often dream that I'd been born a girl, but it never occurred to me to question why. More often than not though, I imagined my body as a robot, one so large that a crew of people would operate it from inside. In my imagination there would be two people in the head, and two in the body, operating the arms and legs. They talked to each other like the crew of a submarine or a spaceship. I was the commander, and the crew were always a mixture of men and women. Looking back, the inner speech that I developed was a coping mechanism for my anxieties, and maybe even my inner confusion over my gender. It allowed me to view my body as a genderless machine, rather than accept the reality that I'd been born a boy: a boy plagued by unexplained thoughts of femininity. Nowadays if I talk to myself, it's usually because it's the only way I can be assured of an intelligent conversation. This is to be expected when you work with a bunch of guys who are only interested in engines, beer and boobs. Back then, I found myself hiding out at the park for most of the summer holidays until it was time to face the music and prepare to go to my new school.

D-day, Disaster Day, had arrived. The day that I'd been dreading all summer. I walked to school with a couple of similarly apprehensive friends from the estate. We barely spoke to each other; such was the tension and worry among us. Like lambs to the slaughter, we walked through the school gates, none of us knowing what to expect, and only a few of us having the safety blanket of a bigger brother or sister at the school to look out for us. I had no-one looking out for me, and I knew it wouldn't be long before I had a target on my back because of it. As my parents were older than most at the school, they had an old-fashioned outlook on life. Because of this, I never had "the talk". Sex was rarely mentioned in our house and as such I was very naive about the subject. We weren't particularly religious either, despite my mum deciding to have me christened not long after I was born. The closest I got to religion was attending Sunday school for about three months. Before you congratulate me on my righteousness, I should confess that I only went for the free orange squash and chocolate fingers. The point is, I grew up thinking everyone was Christian and heterosexual because I had no experience of anything else. For most of the first year of secondary school, I was bullied by the boys for my lack of knowledge of a woman's anatomy. I learned the basics very quickly though, mostly to avoid beatings, and this was where my sexual education began, in the school playground, long before it was discussed by my teachers in the classroom.

The first year of secondary school was the worst of my entire school career. I felt alone, scared and nervous every single day. I was bullied because I was skinny, and as a family we didn't have much money, so my mum made some of my clothes. My clothes lacked designer labels and that was enough of an excuse to beat me up and spit on me. As if adjusting to a new school and being bullied on a daily basis wasn't bad enough, I turned twelve, and things were about to get even worse. I started to find new hairs on my chest and "down there". My voice started to crack every now and then, which was highly amusing to my family. While they were all cooing with pride at their little boy becoming a man, I was experiencing changes in my body and mind which I didn't understand and definitely didn't feel comfortable with. Puberty was the beginning of the troubles that have plagued me throughout my whole life. Before puberty, I was curious about feminine things, and maybe I thought about them more than I should, but puberty was about to change me in ways that would bring about the deepest of sadness and despair. The more masculine I became, the more detached I felt from who I was. The beginning of puberty made me aware of my maleness for the first time. Obviously, I was aware that I was a boy, but until puberty started to change me physically and emotionally, I didn't pay much attention to it. I began to dread looking in the mirror at the body hair that I was developing. It made me look far more masculine than the prepubescent smooth skin that I was used to. In contrast, all my friends were thrilled to have grown body hair, especially pubic hair. Some of the boys happily displayed their pubes, comparing them with their friends in the playground. Hairy chests were proudly exposed in the school locker room, and the stench of adolescent B.O was becoming very apparent from all of us. At school the talk of the playground was Sue Townsend's new book, "The secret diary of Adrian Mole aged 13 and ¾". The book is a humorous account of a boy going through puberty, and it quickly became the yardstick to which we all measured our own progress. As we walked to school on a Monday morning, the usual question would be, 'your knob got any bigger then?'. The idea that a penis would grow at such a rate that it could be measured over the course of a weekend seemed quite conceivable to us at the time. When it came to puberty, you couldn't win. You'd be bullied for not having grown enough body hair and you'd be bullied for having grown too much. You were either a "gaylord" for not having enough, or a "silverback" if you had more than your share.

    At thirteen years old my dad bought me my first razor because I complained every day about the moustache that was growing beneath my nose. My friends at school were all in competition with each other, trying desperately to grow a "Magnum", in homage to their hero Tom Selleck. I couldn't wait to get rid of my facial hair. Ironically, my dad thought I was being very grown up and manly because I was shaving at such a young age, but the reality was, I just couldn't stand the sight of it on my face. I was becoming very difficult to live with, even more so than the average moody teenager. My mum quickly grew tired of my mood swings, and I would often get home from school and go straight to my room without even speaking. I spent many nights just crying in my room or playing computer games alone, wishing I was someone else or that I'd never been born at all. Of course, all kids going through puberty are moody and tired. They're experiencing a vast array of emotions due to the hormonal changes in their body and brain. In my case, there was an extra layer, one that I wasn't fully aware of, but that was about to change.

In the summer of 1986, a new family moved into the house directly opposite us. I became friends with the youngest of the family, a boy around the same age as me. He had an older brother and a sister, and they all lived with their mum, a single parent. Their home was neither clean nor tidy, there were clothes distributed randomly around the house. Old pairs of tights sticking out from under the sofa, and leggings hanging over the banister that had been there for several weeks. If you weren't tripping over some discarded item on the floor, you were brushing dust and crumbs off the sofa before you sat down. One weekend, we were having a sleepover. We'd been playing pool most of the evening on the small pool table that the boys had in their bedroom. At around eleven o'clock, the boys got into their beds and I got into my sleeping bag. As we chatted, I noticed that right next to me was a pair of pink fishnet stockings, still attached to the matching pink suspender belt as if they'd been taken off in a hurry. I'd seen stockings and suspenders on television when I'd watched the Benny Hill show with my mum and dad, and I remember how they used to fascinate me, but this was the first time I'd seen them up close. I felt an overwhelming urge to put them on. A nervous knot formed in my stomach and I knew I wouldn't be able to sleep until I'd tried them on. Picture the scene, we were chatting away with the lights on, I was in my sleeping bag trying to put on a pair of stockings and suspenders without being noticed by the two boys. Of course, the correct way to put them on would be to roll the stocking between your thumbs and pull it up the leg, but I didn't know this at the time so I was trying to pull it up my leg like a pair of socks. Because they were fishnets, my progress was hampered further because my toes kept poking through the holes in the stocking. The boys must have suspected something was going on because it was painfully obvious that I was up to something, either that or I was having a minor seizure. After about half an hour of frustration as I wriggled around in my sleeping bag, I managed to get them on (backwards as it turned out when I was able to examine my handiwork). Despite this, the feeling that I got from wearing them was beyond what I'd imagined, it was an awakening. Sure, I'd tried my mum's shoes on a couple of times as a small child, but that had just been curiosity, hadn't it? This was the first realisation that these clothes, these taboo clothes of the opposite sex, just felt right on my body. There was nothing sexual about them, they didn't turn me on or make me feel all funny in my pants like the Whitney Houston poster on my bedroom wall; they felt like a warm hug from an old friend. I wore them all night, and in the morning I was reluctant to get out of my sleeping bag and go for breakfast, because I knew that once I took them off, the feelings that they evoked, and the experience, would be over.

    Clothes were an important part of our identity in the secondary school years. We were fortunate enough that we didn't have a school uniform, just a suggested dress code. I spent my first two years at secondary school dressed head to toe like Suggs from Madness. White grandad collar shirts, black tank tops and turned up trousers. The look was completed with neon green or pink socks, black brogues and black sunglasses (I wasn't brave enough to add the trilby hat). During our third year of secondary school, the breakdance craze had found its way to UK shores. I'm embarrassed to admit, but I was in a crew called "Breakforce". It took us all of a fifteen-minute school breaktime to come up with that incredible name. After school we would practise on a piece of lino that one of the lads had pinched from his dad's shed. Another had borrowed his mum's talcum powder to make it slippery enough, and the posh lad Matthew, brought his new Panasonic "Ghetto-blaster". With Herbie Hancock and Grandmaster Flash blasting out from Matthew's garage, we popped, locked, spun on our heads and did the windmill until the friction burns were too much to bear. In the mid-eighties, especially during the breakdance era, clothes were pretty wild and colourful: you could never describe them as conservative. We wore jeans called "baggies" mostly. They were elasticated at the ankle so that your high-top trainers could be seen and had zipped pockets in the thighs and an elasticated waist. Baggy tie-dye T-shirts and headbands completed the look. I remember watching the film "Breakdance". It was about a couple of guys called Turbo and Ozone, who were involved in the street dancing scene. There was also a female character called Kelly, who was from a contemporary dance background. Turbo and Ozone taught her to breakdance and they won a big competition at the end (spoiler alert). It was all very cheesy but hey it was the eighties. Apart from the paper-thin plot and fantastic soundtrack, what got my attention was Kelly, and what she was wearing. She danced in a Lycra leotard, leggings and leg warmers. I remember thinking she looked fantastic, but not in the wet dream inducing way that my friends looked at her. I was envious of her body and of what she was wearing. The shape of her thighs and bottom, her small perfectly formed breasts and smooth skin, all clad in Lycra which hugged every curve. What the hell? Was I going mad? A few weeks earlier I'd been wearing pink fishnet stockings and now, I was having these feelings again. I was constantly anxious at school, mostly due to the relentless bullying, but it became worse now that there was an extra problem to keep me awake at night and haunt my daydreams. At school I was falling behind in all my subjects. I started to revert back to playing the clown like I did in primary school, so that people would like me and not want to bully me. I was fourteen years old and beginning to fall apart. What the hell was wrong with me?

I decided to get a paper round to keep busy and earn a few quid. The shop keeper, Mr Patel, gave me two rounds: the Leicester Mercury, which was the daily newspaper and not too bulky, and the Sunday morning round. The after-school paper round was easy, thirty minutes and I was done, bag dropped off at the shop and home eating my tea. The Sunday paper round was the posh road near my school. Almost every house on my round had huge newspapers with more supplements than actual newspaper, which I'm sure they never had time to read. I'm surprised the weight of the bag didn't stunt my growth, as I dragged it up the steep hill on my aging BMX every weekend. The income I made from these endeavours paid for a few sweets and comics, but I was also saving a few quid each week for a rainy day. One day, I went to a local mini supermarket to buy a pair of tights. I'd been trying to pluck up the courage to buy them for weeks. I knew that a fourteen-year-old boy buying a pair of tights isn't something you see every day, so I had a back story all prepared. If the shopkeeper asked, my mum had sent me to buy them as she was going out and had laddered her only pair. After nervously grabbing a drink and some sweets, I headed to the rack where all the tights were on display. I was looking for the key word "15 Denier", because I'd seen it on my mum's tights when she'd brought new ones from the supermarket. I grabbed the tights and headed to the counter feeling slightly sick with panic. Standing at the counter, change in hand, "bleep" – a can of dandelion & burdock, "bleep" – a sherbet fountain, "bleep" - a pair of fifteen denier tights. To my surprise and relief there were no awkward looks and no questions asked. I got home with my brown paper bag under my arm and rushed to my bedroom. Drink, check. Sherbet fountain, check. Tights … Oh no! I had indeed purchased fifteen denier tights, but in my haste to get out of the shop and avoid any further anxiety and embarrassment, I had forgotten to check the little window at the bottom of the packet which reveals the colour of the tights. They were bright red. Once I'd got over the shock of the pillar box red hosiery, I put my purchases away where they wouldn't be discovered and went downstairs for tea. Later that evening, with my bedroom door locked, and my legs looking like they'd been dipped in ketchup, I sat on my bed wondering why this thing I was doing, that went against everything I'd been taught about being a boy, felt so natural and comfortable to me. I went to bed wearing the tights because I couldn't bear to take them off. This scenario played out over many nights to follow, and the feelings only got stronger as time went on.

      In primary school I only really had one close friend, and secondary school was no different. I got to know Wayne, who shared my love of Atari console games and eighties comedies like the Goonies and

Weird Science. It turned out that we only lived one street apart and we quickly became best friends. This friendship lasted into our mid-thirties until life and circumstances led to us drifting apart, but recently, those same circumstances brought us back together. Wayne shared his bedroom with his older brother Andy who was a proper Jack the lad. His other brother Steven was the polar opposite. Steven was always immaculately dressed in his "new romantic" style clothes and rarely went out, choosing to sit in his room and listen to records. Wayne's sister Tracy was a popular girl at school and being Wayne's friend meant that she and her friends would look out for us both. Wayne seemed to fly under the radar with the bullies, but I was bullied quite badly throughout the whole of my time at secondary school. I didn't see it at the time but my naivety, and my interest in female attire, especially what the girls were wearing each day, was reason enough for them to pick on me. My parents were regulars at the headmaster's office, complaining about my torn clothes or the bruises that appeared on my legs and arms. This was all to no avail though: the school didn't seem to care. Over the course of my time at secondary school I became friends with a few other guys, but only because they were essentially misfits like me. I didn't hang out with them much after school because only one of them, Colin, lived anywhere near me. During the summer holidays of 1986, Colin was killed crossing the road by a hit and run driver. He was just fourteen years old. This was the first time I'd experienced grief, and up until then I'd never been to a funeral or lost anyone close. I was devastated, and it affected me deeply. I've never forgotten him, and I still think about him to this day. Rest in peace Colin Edward Ronald Beech Jr.

In year four of secondary school, I did my mock exams. Throughout the year I had been dodging bullies with mixed success. With the thoughts and feelings that had been running through my mind relating to puberty, schoolwork and exam revision were the first things to suffer. I spent my evenings looking through the women's section of my mum's mail order catalogues, looking at all the beautiful dresses, shoes and lingerie, when I should have been studying for my exams. I used to select an outfit, starting with lingerie, then a dress, then shoes and jewellery and then I'd imagine that I was one of the beautiful models wearing it. When my mock exam results were handed to me, I wasn't even shocked by how bad they were. To be honest I didn't even care.

I'd known what I wanted to do when I left school since I was five or six. I wanted to be a mechanic like my dad. I didn't need much more than a pass in English, maths and a basic science to get on a youth training scheme (today's equivalent is a modern apprenticeship), so I did the bare minimum of school work to get where I needed to be. I chose to do work experience, opting to do three weeks in a truck workshop at a Leicester bakery. My job was to check all the trucks in the morning before they went out delivering to all the local shops. Oil, coolant, tyres, lights and fuel had to be checked. When they came back after lunch, I refilled the fuel tanks and cleaned the windscreens, mirrors and lights ready for the next morning. I loved that job, despite the fact that work experience was unpaid. I must have made a good impression too because when I left, the workshop manager had taken a collection for me and the other mechanics had raided the bakery, giving me a huge bag of cakes to take home.

Around the same time, my relationship with my dad became more and more difficult. None of it was his fault, I just found it harder to talk to him and to be close to him. I know a lot of teenage boys can find it harder to relate to their parents during puberty, and I'm not blaming gender issues specifically for this, but something was driving a wedge between us, causing a crack that would never fully heal.

At the age of fifteen I started to become more attracted to girls than I'd previously been. I know I was late to the party at fifteen, and many of my friends were either masturbating themselves into oblivion or were only a couple of bad choices away from fatherhood. I too had discovered masturbation, although I was never really sure what it was about women that turned me on, as I awkwardly fiddled with my "thingy" while turning the pages of the Razzle magazine I'd found in the park one day. The playground chat had moved away from discussing pubescent changes and had evolved into sex. Just sex (and occasionally what Bruce Lee films we'd seen). My friends were obsessed with porn, either magazines they'd pinched from Mr Patel's shop, or video tapes they'd secretly borrowed from their dad's "private" collection. Don't get me wrong, I'm not squeaky clean. I watched my fair share of porn at that age as well, but I didn't get excited by it like my friends seemed to. They couldn't wait for the women to take their clothes off and get stuck in, but I was quite happy for them to leave them on and just have a cuddle.

There was a girl in my form called Kara. She was very pretty, with shoulder length brown hair and a slim neck making her look like an angel. She was very pale in complexion and very slim. I remember at the time thinking about those attributes. If my mates had been asked to describe a girl that they fancied, it was usually along the lines of 'blonde, nice arse, good tits, talks too much'. I hadn't noticed any of those things; I was too busy picking out all the things that made her so feminine. Her cheekbones, her smooth jawline and rounded chin. Her cute little nose and beautiful almond shaped green eyes. I didn't know whether I fancied her or envied her, but I knew I had to ask her on a date. After registration one sunny morning, I plucked up the courage to ask her out. To my surprise she said yes. We agreed to go to the cinema to see "Big Trouble in Little China". That weekend, I walked to her house in my best chinos and a freshly ironed white shirt. She was wearing slim jeans and a blue top which made a beautiful contrast against her lily-white skin. On the bus ride into town we chatted away quite effortlessly. The date went well although we both agreed that the movie was awful. We held hands on the way home, chatting about the movie and trying to suck the contents of a McDonald's milkshake through the woefully inadequate straw. After the brain freeze from the milkshake had subsided, we arrived at her house. I kissed her on the cheek very awkwardly and said goodbye. Walking home I felt fantastic. I'd never experienced this before. I had a girlfriend! I thought to myself, 'this is brilliant, maybe I won't be bullied so much now'. In hindsight, that shouldn't have been my first thought after a date with a beautiful girl. Actually, it did indeed reduce the amount of bullying I received, as the rest of the term played out. Kara and I dated until mid-way through our final year of secondary school. In the end she dumped me. She said I wasn't passionate enough, and that she was ready to go further, and it was clear that I wasn't. I don't think she meant full sex, we were only fifteen, and even though that seemed to be a perfectly acceptable age to become a parent on my estate, she was a respectable girl from a respectable family. I was the problem; I was holding back. We hadn't even kissed properly, despite her attempts to pin me down. Now I knew how Adrian Mole felt, rejected by his beloved Pandora.

The final year of secondary school was hard. I was way behind with my schoolwork and my mock exam results had been a joke. I'd split up with Kara and to top it off there were problems at home. My mum has suffered with her mental health for most of her adult life. She has had bouts of serious clinical depression on and off, and some have resulted in her needing hospital care. She started to behave very strangely, sometimes making very little sense, and after some time my dad had to seek help because he couldn't cope. He contacted the local doctor who referred them to the psychiatric ward at the Leicester General Hospital. My mum was promptly taken there to get herself well. I remember her grabbing my dad's arm and saying, 'don't tell the kids I'm here'. She was referring to my older siblings who all lived away from home. My dad did what he thought was best and obeyed her wishes. Maybe that was wrong, but at the time his mental health wasn't too far behind my mum's, after having to hide the knives from the kitchen drawer and wander the estate looking for his wife on her frequent disappearances. My brothers found out that she was in the psychiatric ward through a friend of theirs who was a nurse. This was the start of a chain of events which tore the family apart. Wayne and I were standing at the bus stop waiting to go into town one Saturday morning, when there was a screech of tyres and a car pulled up alongside us. My brother Graham appeared from the passenger seat. 'Get in' he snarled, as we were bundled into the car. Wayne and I found ourselves being driven at high speed to his house, where both my brothers interrogated me about why I, a fifteen-year-old boy, had not informed them about the situation with my mum. After an hour of this I'd had enough, I lost my temper and stormed out, with tears streaming down my face, followed by a very confused looking Wayne.

A few weeks later my mum was released from hospital and came home looking and sounding a whole lot better. I was relieved to have her back but still a little wary of her, and I found myself constantly watching out for any signs of a relapse. On the Sunday after she got home, we had a visit from my brothers. They'd come to confront my dad over why he hadn't informed them that my mum was in hospital. Raised voices quickly became intense shouting, but the voices were only those of my brothers. My dad said nothing, maybe because he was outnumbered, maybe because he had no defence against their argument. I sat at the top of the stairs crying and listening to the commotion below. They eventually left after saying their piece, but my brother James left with these parting words, 'While he is alive, I will never set foot in this house again'. This is a promise my brother kept, and it was the last time I would see him for over fifteen years.

While all this was going on, cross-dressing and daydreaming over the outfits in the Littlewoods catalogue had stopped completely. My own mental health was pretty poor at the time and as my GCSE exams approached, it became even worse. I got through my exams, having made as much effort as I could under the circumstances. My results were as awful as I'd resigned myself to expect. Grade D for English, F for maths and E for science. The rest aren't even worth a mention.

My career teacher had arranged an interview for me with a local Vauxhall dealership called

Errington's. If I was successful, I would start work in July and college in September. It was only a short walk to the garage, so on the day of my interview, smartly dressed in all new clobber, topped off with a paisley tie which was very fashionable during the late eighties, I walked the mile or so to the garage to meet with the service manager. After a short interview, in which my knowledge of engines gifted to me by my dad seemed to impress him, he offered me a position as an apprentice mechanic. I walked home full of pride, smiling from ear to ear as I told my parents about my new job and future career. The end of school was a bit of a non-event, especially as we didn't have proms back then. We collected our exam results, our final classes finished at the end of term and people just seemed to fade away. With my college place secured and a full-time job as an apprentice mechanic sorted, I took the time to relax and hang out with my best friend Wayne after what had been a disaster of a year.

When I wasn't hanging out with Wayne, I spent a lot of time alone. I didn't see it coming but I was starting to spiral into what would be the first of many periods of deep depression throughout my life. I had completely shut out all thoughts of femininity that had dominated my mind while I was dragged through puberty kicking and screaming. I'd created a mental shield to all things related to the desire to be a woman, to dress like a woman and to feel like a woman. I'd locked all that up in a box and hidden it in some deep corner of my mind. I began to create a persona, a teenage guy with a bit of attitude and a carefree outlook. This fake personality that I displayed every day evolved as I aged but ultimately remained anchored in masculinity, overcompensation and male bullshit. It was what I thought I needed to do to appear normal, whatever that means. I never even considered talking to my parents about how I felt. I knew it would be a bad idea but at the same time I needed help. I was lost and full of self-hatred and despair. I started shaving my armpits and pubic hair because I just couldn't stand the sight of it. The chest hair came next, but this proved to be more difficult because puberty had given me chest hair that a small family of badgers could have set up home in. My self-loathing continued, and I began to despise my testicles for their role in my puberty and the creation of all the things I hated about myself. The deeper voice, the body hair, the Adam's apple and so much more. This hatred has been etched into my mind throughout my whole life, only being resolved at the end of my transition, when a kind surgeon dealt with the problem once and for all.

    Eventually, I plucked up the courage to speak to mum about my sadness, but nothing else. I lied about my reasons and hoped that she wouldn't see through it. A visit to the doctor was booked and due to my lack of any credible reason for my depression, he suggested I take some little blue pills (Lorazepam) and get some fresh air. Up until this point the only pills that I'd ever taken were the Sanatogen chewable vitamin C that mum gave me every morning. Mum was both relieved and worried in equal measure. Relieved that there appeared to be no real reason why I'd been so withdrawn and obviously struggling with everyday life, but worried that her fifteen-year-old son needed to take anti-depressants when he seemed to have so much going for him with a new job and a place at college. She also worried that her own mental health issues had somehow been passed on to me and that perhaps it was hereditary. Little did she know: the worst was yet to come.

Chapter Four
The big wide world

September 5th 1988, my first day in the big wide world of work. I should have been feeling nervous and excited, but the little blue pills had left me feeling numb emotionally. I felt no love, no hate, no shame, no guilt, and certainly no pleasure. It took a fairly momentous occasion like going to work for the first time in my life to even raise my excitement levels above mediocre. I knew that how I came across on my first day would have an impact on how the guys in the workshop would treat me from that day forth, so I was desperate to make a good impression. Garage workshops are a bit like men's locker rooms: full of testosterone and bullshit. There are very few female mechanics working in the motor industry so it is very much a testosterone pit, and guys can be very cruel to the young apprentices. Thankfully, common sense and health & safety laws have all but seen the end of these pranks and misogynistic behaviours now, but in the late eighties, being bullied as an apprentice was seen as a rite of passage, the making of the man.

On my first day at work, I was pointed in the direction of my new mentor, a mechanic named Chris. He looked like he'd been on the wrong end of one too many rugby scrums, with his messy unkempt hair and big bushy moustache that underlined his crumpled, damaged nose. At first, we got on well, then after a week or so he started playing pranks on me. I like a laugh, but when it's relentless and just plain nasty, it becomes a problem very quickly. My mental health wasn't exactly tip-top either, so being bullied in the workplace, just like I had been at school, was about as welcome as a dose of the shits. Most of the jokes and pranks were harmless, sending me to the local ironmonger in the village for sky hooks or a long stand, or asking me to fetch a bucket of steam from the parts department. I had been forewarned about these things by my dad, who had prepared me well for the world of work, and as such I knew how to play them at their own game. The first thing I did was get the local ironmonger on my side, letting him in on my cunning plan. Then, one day, when Chris sent me for a can of tartan wheel paint and a long weight, I played him at his own game. He sent me off with a big stupid grin on his face, and as I walked toward the ironmonger's shop in the village, I hatched my plan. I asked him to write a note saying that the tartan wheel paint was out of stock, but the long weight (wait) would take about an hour. I thanked him, and with a giggle and a wink, he waved as I left the shop. I went to the Fish & Chip shop next door to get a big bag of chips with extra salt and vinegar. I walked over to the park across the road and sat on the swings for exactly one hour, eating my tasty treat. I returned to a very angry looking Chris. He knew exactly what I'd done but he clearly wasn't used to being played at his own game. 'Where the hell have you been?' I was trying my hardest not to laugh, despite the fact that several of the other mechanics had come over to see what all the fuss was about and were now in hysterics which wasn't helping. I handed him the note, picked up my spanners, and carried on fitting the brake pads that I'd been working on before I left.

The more I played them at their own game, the more intense the bullying became. Once, I was cable tied to a milk float, driven by a milkman who was a friend of one of the mechanics. If you're unsure what a cable tie is then you haven't seen Fifty Shades of Grey (just saying). They had arranged for him to drive me round the local area for about an hour as I sat on the back, tied up and surrounded by empty milk crates, before he delivered me back to the workshop to six chuckling mechanics. I made the stupid mistake of confiding in one of the mechanics about the little blue pills one day after he asked why I often looked so sad and he rarely saw me smile. From then on, all the mechanics called me doctor death. On many occasions I was thrown in the skip with the rubbish. Not for any particular reason, just because they could. In hindsight, if I'd just taken it on the chin, I'd have probably had an easier ride, but school had hardened me to some degree and I'm not someone you should mess with unless you're prepared to see it through. People who have been bullied for a long period of time will do one of two things: curl up in a ball or learn to fight. I learned to fight. Not physically, I was never an aggressive man, but I would give as good as I got.

Most of the guys at Errington's were great. I got on really well with them, but Chris and I were like chalk and cheese. I played my part in a lot of the pranks too. Most of the time they were harmless. I remember two occasions where things didn't go exactly according to plan though. We used to have a pint or two on a Friday lunchtime at the Cedars pub across the road from the garage. You'd never get away with drinking on the job nowadays but hey it was the eighties. We got Shaun the valeter really drunk. When we went back to work, he locked himself inside a customer's car and fell asleep with the keys in the ignition. We were afraid he would throw up in the car and we couldn't wake him up. The customer was due to collect his car, so we had to break into it and drag him out. He was fine afterwards but he must have had the mother of all hangovers. The second incident involved the police. We had a really cocky apprentice called Austin. We were really sick of him, so we got him drunk and stripped him to his boxer shorts and put him in a wheelie bin. We wheeled it to the end of the drive and left him there asleep slumped over the bin while all the traffic through the village passed him by. A passer-by must have called the police because about an hour later we saw two officers pushing a wheelie bin up the drive towards the workshop with a very drunken Austin still inside. 'This yours? Mind where you leave your bins' they said before walking away laughing their heads off.

About a month after starting work, I started college, studying Motor Vehicle Technology. I was in a class with a friend I went to school with called Andy. We weren't close friends back in our school days, mostly because I used to avoid other kids from the estate, choosing to hide in my den at the park or stay at home instead. Andy lived a few streets away from me which meant we'd take the same bus to college every Thursday. College was dramatically different to secondary school. I enjoyed every minute of it, and I did really well too. Instead of dropping out of every subject with no qualifications, I regularly got distinctions and merits for my work. My college tutors were kind and patient with us. Even Mr Bacon, who spent most of our chassis technology lessons talking about World War two tanks. I got on well with all of them and I couldn't soak up the knowledge fast enough. I had left school disillusioned, with not a single GCSE over a grade D, but here I felt motivated and encouraged. I was finally in a place where there were no bullies, and my results were far better than I'd imagined. Thanks to my college tutors and my dad, my passion for automotive technology, for cars, bikes, trucks and anything with an engine and wheels, is as strong today as it was all those years ago.

     I haven't mentioned many people in this book by their full name, purely to protect their identity, but I will tell you about one man. His name is Gary Sleath. Gary was my college tutor from 1989 to 1991. He had the patience of a saint. He must have been in his late twenties at that time, which makes his tolerance of our teenage antics even more impressive. Throughout my career I've had the pleasure of working with Gary as a colleague, as well as my first experience of him when he was my tutor. Gary and I worked together for many years, and last worked together at Volkswagen Group UK. He worked with the VW apprenticeship team and I was a technical trainer for Audi. After seven years in the job, I left to work for DAF trucks, and I hadn't spoken to him for quite a while other than the odd catch up on Facebook. I was lying in my hospital bed, recovering from gender affirmation surgery on Tuesday 21st January 2020, when I received a text message from a friend. He told me that Gary had passed away in his sleep due to heart failure. He was just fifty-nine years old and one of the most physically fit men I knew. I was devastated, crying for hours. I must have looked a state because the nurses kept coming into my room to comfort me and sit with me. Gary was a great man and there was very little he didn't know about cars. He was also a true gentleman and a trans ally, fighting my corner when I came out as trans at Volkswagen. I'm writing this with tears streaming down my face. I will miss him forever. Rest in peace Gary my old friend.

With college going brilliantly and work going well despite the bullies, I started to get hold of my depression. Although mum had her concerns, I stopped taking the little blue pills and flushed them down the toilet. I was too busy at work to think about being depressed, and too happy at college to let it infiltrate my thoughts. At home it was another story. I had time to think, time to let those nagging thoughts get under my skin. Why did I feel so sad? Why couldn't I just be happy? I had no clue, I drove myself crazy looking for the answers when really, they were there all along. I had locked them away so securely in the back of my mind, that they couldn't possibly be the problem, could they? My relationship with my mum was starting to get very frayed just as it had during my early puberty. She was so proud of me when I went off to work, telling me that my first week's wages were my own, all £29.50 of it. After that she expected me to pay £10 board each week. I kept my promise, paid my board each week and things were mostly fine, but I was finding it harder and harder to talk to her. We used to get into fierce arguments, and I'd end up storming off because I could feel my temper getting out of control and I needed to be alone. My dad was very much a spectator in all this, and I found his neutrality equally hard to deal with, because it felt like he wasn't interested in why I was so unhappy. Eventually, even work, college and my friends couldn't save me from the black dog of depression, and I had a nervous breakdown at the age of sixteen. I was forced to take two weeks off work and the little blue pills were reintroduced into my daily routine. When they were first prescribed, I'd stopped taking them after a few months because I hated the way they made me feel, but the doctor was adamant that this was the way forward, and the magic pills would fix the problem. Once again, I resigned myself to living with numbness and complete indifference.

      Two weeks later, upon my return to work, my boss suggested that I transfer to the other site, at

Great Glen in Leicestershire. It wasn't much further away, and I would be able to take driving lessons soon so the logistics would only be a short-term problem. The Great Glen site was smaller than the Evington main site, with only four mechanics including me. I felt at home there, the guys were kinder to me and I was treated much more as an equal, even though I was still an apprentice. The foreman, Gary, was like the cool kid at school, everyone looked up to him. I didn't see it at the time, but he was very good looking. He was tall with curly blonde hair cut short and neat, and piercing blue eyes and a great physique.

I on the other hand did not have a great physique. I weighed around eight stone (50 kg) when I left school. I was so skinny I had to run around in the shower to get wet. One day after watching me trying to undo some particularly overtight wheel nuts on a Bedford van, (and once he'd finished laughing) he suggested I try lifting weights. Gary had some weights and a bench at home, and he invited me round to have a go. I'd never lifted weights before but after the session, I felt great. I felt strangely masculine which I'd never really felt before. I continued to train with him for the next few months and I became quite obsessed with it. After a while, I bought my own weights and started working out in my bedroom. I started reading bodybuilding magazines and watching Arnold Schwarzenegger movies. I was taking protein supplements and eating a diet designed to gain muscle. This became more than a means to get stronger; it became an obsession, a way to avoid any thoughts of femininity. Without even realising it, I had begun the process of overcompensating, something I did for the rest of my life as a man.

In August 1989, I had my first proper driving lesson. I say proper driving lesson because my dad had taught me how to drive when I was fourteen years old in car parks and quiet country back roads. A local man by the name of Bill was recommended by my colleagues at work. I booked my first lesson and waited nervously for the day to come. Bill turned up in his little red Vauxhall Nova. He greeted me with a cigarette hanging out of his mouth and a voice that suggested that he'd been a heavy smoker for most of his life. He seemed nice, if maybe a little old fashioned, which made me feel quite at ease. His car smelled like an ashtray, the smoke still lingering from the cigarette he was smoking when he arrived. I tried to put this out of my head and concentrate on the road, but I ended up asking if he minded me opening my window, which seemed to put him out a little. I had twelve lessons with Bill, one a week until I took my driving test. Despite my nerves, my dad and Bill had taught me well, and I passed first time.

Like the bodybuilding, driving provided another distraction. I'd saved up a few hundred pounds to buy my first car, a little blue Vauxhall Chevette. I drove it to college, staying after hours to fix it in the workshop. I loved that car, and now that I was earning a little more money, getting out and about was becoming quite a regular thing. If I wasn't out driving with my best friend Wayne, I'd be at the pub with him or my workmates. One summer evening I was sitting in the garden of the Rose & Crown nursing a pint of shandy, when Kara walked in with her friend who she introduced as Tracey. I hadn't seen Kara since leaving school, but we had at least parted on good terms. I remember my first impression of Tracey like it was yesterday. She was beautiful: she still is. Tracey is a natural brunette with beautiful skin and a figure that most women would kill for. Over the course of the evening, I found myself being more and more drawn to this captivating girl. We exchanged numbers and became friends, but I knew I wanted her to be my girlfriend. It took me weeks to pluck up the courage to ask her out, but when I finally did, she said yes, and later that evening we had our first kiss. This was the first time I'd kissed a girl properly. I held back with Kara, but it felt right with Tracey. I can still remember that night, kissing under the streetlight outside her parent's home (oh god - do you think they saw us?).

Tracey and I started to spend a lot of time together. We lived about two miles apart, so it was easy for me to drive to her or walk if I was low on petrol or cash. At the age of 17, neither of us had lost our virginity, and as we spent more time together, it felt as if things were naturally going in a direction that would soon change that. One night, after a very embarrassing visit to the local chemist for "supplies", we held hands while watching a movie and, well, you know, things happened. I remember it being very awkward. I hadn't a clue if I'd done it right and I'm not sure if Tracey did either, but we held each other afterwards and felt safe in the comfort of each other's arms.

      Tracey and I turned eighteen within a month of each other. We were very happy, and things were really moving forward for us. Her Nursery nursing career was going really well, and I was almost at the end of my apprenticeship. As our sexual confidence grew, we started to experiment in the bedroom. I bought Tracey some white stockings and suspenders, with matching bra and panties. For safety reasons, namely her mum and dad finding out, she decided it was better if she left them at my house, so I put them away at the bottom of a drawer in my bedroom. We were very naive, and like many teenagers, we were trying out things to see what we liked and what we didn't. All I could think about when I was alone in my bedroom was that bloody white underwear in the drawer. I resisted the temptation for weeks until one night, I just had to try them on. Just like the first time, the feeling of the stockings was wonderful. Not sexual or kinky, just soft, feminine and delicate. It had been around three years since I last cross-dressed, and I had buried those feelings deep in my mind. I knew deep down that it was the real reason for my depression and anxiety, but I wasn't aware of just how much. Feeling very guilty about the situation, I decided to tell Tracey, even though I knew that she would probably dump me and call me a pervert. To my surprise, she was very understanding and even encouraged me to put them on while she was there. It felt so good to have someone that I loved tell me that it was OK to wear these things, to express myself in a way I'd never openly been able to before. In hindsight, I think that Tracey thought it was just a turn on for me. A kink, rather than an inner desire to explore my femininity. For whatever reason, she was okay with it, and every once in a while, she would suggest I put them on.

    One downside to both of our career choices was that neither of them paid very well. We were always broke, and as such we couldn't save much money. As we saw our friends start to go on holidays abroad, put down deposits on houses and plan their futures, it started to cause friction between us. We began to argue a lot, and after some time we decided to split. I missed her terribly, so much so that after a few weeks we decided to get back together. I think Tracey had her doubts about us getting back together, but we did genuinely love each other, and although my cross-dressing had become a far bigger issue than either of us had envisaged, she gave us a second chance. At this point I had a collection of clothing stashed under my bed. Shoes, skirts and hosiery mostly. One night, Tracey had given me the green light to wear some feminine things while we watched TV together. From out of nowhere, I asked her to call me Emma. After I'd said it, we both felt very awkward, and it was clear that I'd overstepped the mark. Back then, I had no idea that I was transgender.

I didn't even know that the word transgender or transsexual existed. I had no idea that one day I would be sitting here, a confident and happy woman, telling my story. In my mind, I was just a troubled guy with a feminine side that seemed far stronger than the masculine, despite my best attempts to suppress it. It was a dark secret that I wished would go away so that I could be like my friends and get on with my life.

Andy had been lucky enough to get a job at a local motor racing team in Leicester. He regularly got tickets for me to go racing with him and I'd hang around the paddock helping out with the race cars, setting tyre pressures, checking wheel nuts and filling the fuel tanks. This turned into paid casual work when they were short-handed, leading to many weekends away running Formula Ford, Formula 3 and Formula 3000 race cars for them and other teams. It also meant trips to Europe to race at tracks like Zandvoort in the Netherlands and Spa Francorchamps in Belgium. I'm sure this all sounds great but working as a race mechanic isn't as glamorous as it looks on TV. More often than not you are up at ridiculous o'clock when most sane individuals are still sleeping. Then, after consuming yet another Little Chef breakfast with your eyes half shut, you drive to the racetrack. The glitz and glamour of the pit garages is saved for the likes of Formula 1 or British Touring Cars at most events, so when you arrive, you find a spot in the paddock and build your workshop before you even think about working on the race car. The truck is turned into a mobile workshop with awnings and special flooring. Then the cars are unloaded and placed in their respective make-shift garages. Toolboxes, tyres, parts and equipment are unloaded and set up, and then there is the hospitality area to set up as well. I loved the work and I love the sport. I have some great memories, like meeting Jensen Button and Kimi Räikkönen when they raced at Haywood racing during the early part of their careers, or doing a flying lap of Spa Francorchamps in a Ford Galaxy during an off day at the European Formula Ford festival. At twenty years old, if I wasn't at work, I was at a racetrack. Tracey and I were drifting further and further apart because of that and other issues that we just couldn't see eye to eye over. Eventually, for the second time, we split. This time, we actively avoided each other because we both knew that we needed to be apart, and seeing each other would be difficult. It was very difficult. I was spiralling out of control again, depression hitting me hard as I locked myself away and withdrew from everything and everyone.

After a couple of months of this my friends were getting fed up with me. Andy and Wayne knew each other pretty well by now as we spent a lot of time in the Rose & Crown. Wayne suggested we go on a lads' holiday. I'd never been on an airplane before. I had been on ferries with the race trucks, but I'd never flown anywhere. I'd also never been on a holiday without my parents. As I write this, I am laughing to myself at how silly that sounds. There I was at twenty-one years old, looking at my friends who were practically jumping up and down at the idea, with my stomach doing somersaults and my brain freaking out with anxiety. After I'd calmed down, we decided to go into town to look at some brochures, and we ended up booking a holiday to Magaluf in Majorca. I was excited and scared in equal measure as the days counted down to our trip. It was June, and the weather was great. The flight was fairly uneventful, apart from experiencing turbulence for the first time and thinking we were going to die in a ball of fire and twisted metal. We eventually arrived at our hotel around midnight, getting into our third-floor room with a decent view of Magaluf town. Andy and Wayne decided they wanted to jump into the pool. Not from the diving board like a normal person would, from the balcony of our third-floor room. Despite my protests, and with reckless abandon, they both jumped at the same time, making a huge splash into the pool below. There were my two friends, bobbing up and down in the pool, laughing their heads off like school children as I watched with my head in my hands from the balcony above. After a few minutes they started complaining about the cold water and the effect it was having on their gentleman parts, and we all finally went to bed.

The next day we had lager and a full English for breakfast (cultured). We found a spot on the beach and proceeded to damage our skin with factor zero cooking oil. I wish I could say I was exaggerating but back in the nineties, factor two was considered to be expert level tanning oil. As a lily-white sun virgin on day one of your holiday, you'd be lathering on a factor fifteen before going all in with the factor two after a few days. These days, when it's sunny, I won't leave the house without factor fifty sunblock on.

That evening, we decided to check out the local nightlife. We found a great club called Bananas, right underneath our hotel. Behind the optics at the bar there was a long glass window which at first glance looked like a huge fish tank. On closer inspection, I saw that it was in fact a swimming pool. My mind made some quick calculations, working out our exact geographical position before it hit me, and I spat my drink out with uncontrollable laughter. With lager shooting out of both nostrils and tears filling my eyes, I laughed hysterically as Wayne and Andy looked at me like I'd lost my mind. Once I'd recovered my composure, I casually drew their attention to the long glass window, explaining that it was actually our swimming pool. The swimming pool that they had jumped into last night around this time when the club would have been filled with punters. Punters who undoubtedly saw them both with their shrivelled genitals bobbing up and down below the surface, covered only by a pair of ill-fitting boxer shorts. I have never seen two grown men look so embarrassed. They gulped down their lager while looking at their imaginary watches, quickly suggesting it was time we moved on to another bar.

A few days later we got chatting to a group of girls from the north-east who were on a hen weekend.

Andy wasn't with us because he'd been drinking McDonald's coke with ice in it despite our warnings and had ended up with a bad dose of the shits. We went to a few bars and clubs with the girls, eventually ending up in an open-air bar drinking with them until the sun came up and the delivery trucks were arriving with fresh fruit and bread for the local shops. It had been such a good night just chatting about where we were from, what we liked and didn't like and what life was like in our respective parts of the country. I felt so at home with this group of girls, we had such a laugh and I didn't want it to end. Being around groups of women has always felt very comfortable for me. I just feel like I fit in better with women than with men. Even now, I have some fantastic male friends but most of my close relationships are with females.

When we eventually rolled into our apartment around 8am, Andy was fast asleep having spent most of the night on the porcelain potty. The place smelled like a sewage farm, so we pushed Andy's bed, with him still sleeping in it, onto the balcony of the apartment, closing the patio doors behind him. We left him there for hours while he slept off the effects of the bacteria-infused Spanish tap water. He did eventually see the funny side of it, and the rest of the holiday went really well. The days consisted mostly of getting up at lunchtime, eating too much, drinking too much and then finding a spot on the beach before going out at night for more drinks and finally a club. I'm glad I went on that holiday: it taught me a lot about myself and it helped me to build up my confidence. It also helped me to move on from Tracey and push away any thoughts of femininity. Stereotypical lads' holiday or not, at the end of the day, we did have a good laugh.

We never repeated that trip, but we did start to hit Leicester's nightclubs pretty hard when we got home. We did the clubbing scene to death. For around two years or so, Wayne, Andy and I would be out clubbing on Friday and Saturday night every week without fail. On Thursdays we would go to student nights for the cheap drinks, and on Sundays we would go to the pub. In my early twenties, my liver took one hell of a beating. All this clubbing meant that I met and dated quite a few women. I wasn't a player and I never did one-night stands, but I did have more girlfriends than the average guy. I'm not proud of that, and it was never about notches on the bedstead. I would date these women for a while, loving being with them and getting to know them, then, a few months later I'd start to make excuses to avoid sex. I didn't know why; I just didn't want to have sex. It wasn't because they were unattractive, far from it. It was me; it was all in my head. There was something about having sex that felt wrong to me. I tried hard to work out what it was. Was I gay? I didn't look at guys in that way, but I had to admit to myself that I was at least curious about what it would be like to be with a man. At the gym I would often stare at men with impressive muscular physiques, but that was envy not attraction, wasn't it? I quickly dispelled those ideas as total rubbish and tried to carry on but this confusion and indifference towards sex continued for many years.

In 1996, I decided that I'd had enough of Errington's. I wasn't earning much money and I knew I could do better elsewhere. I was working on cars, vans and trucks and for less money than the other mechanics who only worked on cars. I got a job at a Land Rover dealer in Leicester. I was finally earning sensible money and I got on well with most of the mechanics. I became friends with a guy in the parts department called Shaun. He used to get picked on for being quiet and I didn't like that so I'd stick up for him. Shaun and I became great friends over the years that I worked there, and even though I don't see him now because he moved away, I know that if I needed a friend, I could pick up the phone and he would be there. The other mechanics were nice enough fellas but there was still that laddish culture. Taking the piss out of each other was mandatory and relentless. I just didn't get the conversations. Sexism, racism and misogyny doesn't even begin to cover it. I felt ashamed of being a man because of the views and opinions I heard from them. I was starting to feel more and more out of touch with my male friends and colleagues and once again I began to isolate myself. At the same time, I was rejecting everything that was feminine as the familiar confusion filled my mind. My collection of clothes and shoes were bagged and sent to a charity shop. I started Thai boxing classes and began lifting weights again, something I'd stopped doing after Tracey and I had split. I was in full overcompensation mode. It turned out that I was quite good at Thai boxing or Muay Thai to give it its proper name. I became quite well respected in the club and fought in several inter-club competitions. I even spent some time in Bangkok, training alongside professional fighters. I love Muay Thai and I still practice this martial art today, although these days I just shadow box for my own fitness rather than fighting for a club.

The over-compensating got worse and worse as the year went on. One day we were all sitting around at tea break and someone said, 'Let's do a parachute jump'. He had read that you could do the jump for free if you got enough sponsors for Cancer Research. Eight people agreed to jump out of a perfectly good aircraft that day, but by the time the jump training day had arrived, it was down to just three. The excuses we heard were pathetic. These macho men with all their bravado and bullshit suddenly exposed for what they really were: cowards. Myself and the other two had collected a lot of sponsors, and we arrived at the airfield to do our training. The jump was to be the next day, so we had an evening meal in a local pub then settled down for the night in their freezing cold World War Two accommodation block. The training day had been pretty easy and I really enjoyed it but now the nerves were kicking in. This was a static line jump. This means a cord is attached to the aircraft and then hooked to your parachute so that when you jump from the plane, it opens automatically. Or at least that's what's supposed to happen.

After a light breakfast and a few silent prayers, we headed out to the equipment room to get our parachutes. Taking them out to the airfield we were greeted by the instructor who was wearing a T shirt with the slogan "Have you hugged your reserve today?" (hilarious). I did indeed hug my reserve parachute as I turned to my friends whose faces were ashen grey. I decided to hang back a bit and let the other five people get on the plane first (the plane with no door that looked like it'd come runner up on scrapheap challenge). My genius plan to get in last was a big mistake. As the instructor ushered us inside and attached our lines to the aircraft, his comment sent a chill down my spine. 'Last in, first out; you're brave son.' I hadn't thought this through at all. As we taxied down the runway, with my legs dangling in the wind from the open doorway of the aging plane, I had never been so scared. We took off, circling the airfield a couple of times before a red light came on in the doorway. The instructor shouted, 'when the light goes green, push yourself as far from the aircraft as you can'. In what felt like a second the light went green and without even thinking, I pushed myself out of the doorway, leaving the relative safety of that rickety old aircraft. I fell for what seemed like ages but was actually just a few seconds before I felt a tug and looking up, I saw that my parachute was open - kind of. The lines had become twisted so the parachute wasn't fully open. I was falling faster than I should have been and I had no way of steering. We had been trained in what to do in these circumstances and we also had radio earpieces, so with the guidance of a nice lady on the ground with binoculars, I kicked and kicked until finally I spun round in the air and the lines untwisted. The canopy opened fully and the steering lines became free. From this point on I gently floated to earth, landing with the precision of a Ukrainian gymnast. My two colleagues also made safe landings although one was perilously close to a group of cows in the next field. Feeling very proud of ourselves, we strutted into work like proud peacocks on Monday morning, revelling in the attention and telling our stories of bravery to all who would listen.

A while after moving to Land Rover, I met a wonderful Asian girl called Sharon. We dated for a while before moving into a little flat in Leicester where we were very happy. Wayne had found himself a girlfriend and had moved in with her, and Andy was living with a girl in a small village in north Leicestershire. A year or so later, Wayne decided to propose to his future wife. I was very honoured to have been given the job of best man; I organised a stag weekend in Blackpool, carried out my duties on the big day and gave a speech which to my surprise went down very well. Despite all this manly responsibility, the thoughts and feelings I had tried so hard to supress had started to creep back into my mind, occupying my thoughts and making me feel once again like a freak. I confided in Sharon after the wedding and like Tracey before her, she was very understanding. Here I was, a mechanic, bodybuilder and martial artist, trying my hardest to be a man and yet becoming more and more absorbed by thoughts of femininity with each passing day.

I began to feel that working as a mechanic wasn't right for me anymore. I loved working on cars and trucks but the environment just didn't make me happy. I felt alienated from my colleagues, I came home every night stinking of axle and transmission oil and my nails were permanently black despite the scrubbing. I was twenty-eight, and it was time for a change of direction. I saw a job advert for an automotive teaching position. It was at the college where I'd done my apprenticeship in Leicester. It was very surreal being interviewed for a job by the very people who had taught me some ten years earlier. Much to my surprise I got the job. I handed in my notice at Land Rover and prepared myself for a whole new career.

As I learned the ropes of the new job, sitting in with other trainers to learn how to deliver the courses, I quickly realised that this was definitely for me, even though it was scary at first. It's amazing how big that room seems when you're standing at the front. After around a week or so of sit-ins, I was asked if I would assist one of the trainers, a man called Ted. Ted got a few minutes into explaining the finer points of fuel injection before turning to me and saying that he needed to make a quick phone call and could I take over for a few minutes. That's the last I saw of Ted for the rest of the day. Talk about baptism of fire. I worked in that department for eighteen months, learning my craft and becoming more and more confident in the classroom. I applied for an internal transfer to the MG Rover training programme. It was better money and came with a company car. I passed the interview successfully and settled in quickly. My career was thriving, but still something was missing. Everything I did was about trying to fit in. I was Thai boxing, drinking with my mates, lifting weights, and watching motor racing with my dad at weekends. My overcompensating was off the charts. It's not that I don't like doing those things, I didn't do them under duress. It's just that I felt like I should do them because it was what was expected of me. I hadn't cross-dressed in a while and Sharon had respected my decision when I told her that I hated feeling this way and I needed to stop. Like so many times before, I'd bagged up what clothes and shoes I had and took them to a charity shop. As I dropped the bags in the charity shop doorway, I knew that it was only a matter of time before this fragile existence, all based on a lie, would come crashing down around my ears and those old familiar feelings would come back to haunt me.

Chapter Five
Transformation

With every scrap of female clothing that I owned banished from the flat and deposited at the local RSPCA shop, I tried hard to move on with my life and be a man. Not just for myself, but for Sharon too. She had been so understanding of my situation, but she deserved better than this, and so did I. I threw myself into bodybuilding, working out at the gym five or six times a week. I was getting through about a hundred pounds worth of protein powder and supplements per month and I increased my Muay Thai boxing classes to three times a week. Friends and colleagues started to notice my increase in muscle and size, but they also made another observation, one that I wasn't expecting. Many of my friends commented on how I often looked like I wanted to kill someone, like I was full of hatred. People even started to avoid me if I looked like I was in a bad mood. I always felt angry with the world, but I didn't realise that I was showing my feelings outwardly. Despite my best efforts to hide how I felt, body language is very autonomous and rarely does it lie. My colleagues at work started to ask if I was okay. 'yeah, why wouldn't I be?', I'd snap back in response. The same thing was happening when I went home to visit my parents, by now in their seventies. I was often moody and would hardly speak, making it awkward for everyone. My dad was deaf in one ear and I had no patience with him when he asked me to repeat most of what I said to him. I was beginning to lose my grip again, but I was so intent on beating the femininity out of my mind and my body, that I didn't care who I hurt. If they didn't like it, they could just get out of my way. I regret those times so much because it caused irreparable damage to my relationship with my dad, and he deserved so much better than that.

My job with MG Rover involved teaching apprentices aged sixteen to nineteen. The majority of my time was spent in the classroom or the workshop, teaching the young apprentices and assessing their skills. It was equally important to visit them in their respective workplaces, to check on their progress and deal with any issues like bullying or helping them with their coursework. There was government paperwork to fill in so that funding could be claimed, and as a qualified assessor, it was my job to observe them doing certain jobs to a competent standard in the workplace. These observation visits took me all over Great Britain, from Glasgow to Portsmouth to Machynlleth in deepest mid-Wales. Most of my patch was around Birmingham, and I could squeeze three visits into one day if traffic was on my side and the apprentice was all set up when I arrived. On one run, I used to stop at the dealership in Aston before moving on to the next dealership in West Bromwich and then finally Telford before heading to Shrewsbury for an overnight stay in a hotel. The next morning, I would do my Shrewsbury visit then head to Machynlleth for the next one. One of my favourite shortcuts across Birmingham took me through an area called Handsworth. One day I was crawling in slow traffic (as is often the case in Birmingham), when I noticed a shop. The name of the shop was Transformation. The internet was quite new-fangled back then, or at least it was to me, but when I got home after my two days of visits, I did a bit of research. I learned that it was a chain of three shops owned by a woman called Stephanie Anne Lloyd. It specialised in selling garments, shapewear and all manner of things to the cross-dressing community. I found myself intrigued by this website and I must have spent at least an hour looking through all the things for sale. I eventually snapped out of it, switched off my computer and tried to forget about it, but I couldn't help wondering what went on behind those closed doors and heavy dark coloured curtains in the windows.

    Every month, I'd have to do that same run through Birmingham, and every time I passed the shop I would stop outside and think about what went on in that Aladdin's cave of femininity. In my head it was something like the dressing up shop that Mr Benn visited in the children's TV show I watched as a kid. Bugger, now I've got the theme tune stuck in my head, and if you're old enough to remember the show, so have you (sorry not sorry). Why was I tormenting myself? Those old familiar thoughts and feelings were creeping back into my head despite all the overtly masculine things I was doing to feel like a man. What did I have to do to get rid of them? I couldn't be any more manly than I was already being. I found myself longing to visit the shop despite my better judgement. I suppose I'd say my heart said yes and my head said no. This went on for several weeks, and the obsession with the Transformation shop made me begin to lose focus on my relationships with Sharon, my family and also my friends and work colleagues. Sharon and I were arguing all the time and my relationship with my dad was at a point where we barely spoke. I tried to mend things with my mum, but it would almost always end up in an argument and I would storm out of the house and drive home angry.

One rainy Saturday morning, when Sharon was in Coventry visiting her parents, I decided that enough was enough. I had to know what went on in that shop. I made the journey to Handsworth from our little flat in Leicester. I must have sat outside the shop for an hour, afraid to get out of the car. I eventually plucked up the courage, and after realising that the shop doors were locked, I nervously rang the doorbell. After a few moments I was greeted by a nice friendly looking woman in her mid-fifties. She introduced herself as Sandra and asked me if I was a member of the cross-dressing community because they had to be careful who they let in. I gave her a brief explanation of my situation (leaving out as much detail as I could), and she welcomed me into the store. I wanted so desperately to experience the makeover service. This involved choosing an outfit, undergarments and shapewear and then makeup and a hairstyle from a printed menu. Then, you were escorted into a studio to be fitted for the clothes and underwear, before your makeup and hair was done by one of the ladies in the shop. When they had finished, you could either choose to sit around in the shop, read a book, browse through their stock, or you could go out for a while and then come back later to be returned to your everyday look. I could feel the excitement building inside me as Sandra explained how the service worked, but it wasn't cheap. A hundred pounds got you four hours of being who you wanted to be. I didn't have that kind of money with me, so I browsed around the shop, looking at all the clothes, shoes, shapewear, underwear, wigs and makeup. I spotted some boxes above the till. I asked Sandra what they were. 'Oh, they're boobs my dear', she said with a wry smile. Looking very confused, I was about to ask her to explain what she meant as she reached for one of the boxes and opened it. There in the box was a very pert pair of silicone breast forms. 'You'll need a pair of these if you want to fill out the corsets that we sell.' She handed one to me, it felt cold, and a bit like raw chicken but without the sliminess. My mind was in overdrive, imagining my body with breasts and feeling more feminine than I'd ever felt before. I thanked her for showing me and continued browsing before settling on a black skirt that to be honest I could have got for a fraction of the price in any high street store. Leaving the shop, I could feel my heart racing. I looked around to see if anyone had noticed me leaving, then ran around the corner to my car before heading for home. It would be two more weeks before my work schedule took me past the store again, and despite my best efforts to fight it, I could barely think of anything else.

The day of my Birmingham visits came around again, but this time I'd arranged to take half the day off work. I planned to do my two Birmingham visits, then have the full afternoon off before heading to the hotel in Shrewsbury that evening. I hated deceiving Sharon, but I felt like I had no choice. In my head I justified my actions by convincing myself that at least I wasn't having an affair. I'd got the money together without too much fuss because I rarely spent any money on myself other than the bodybuilding supplements and Thai boxing classes. I shaved my face and underarms as well as I could before leaving the flat. I felt so guilty, I could barely look Sharon in the eye. I got through the two observations with the apprentices, quickly scrawling up my notes and rushing off as soon as I was done.

No small talk with the other mechanics, no banter or jokes. I was on a mission. I arrived outside the shop just before lunchtime. I ate my sandwiches as quickly as I could despite feeling so nervous, and I tried to forget that they'd made me feel quite sick.

It was Sandra who greeted me at the door, and once again welcomed me into the shop. After some small talk about the traffic and the weather she asked me if there was anything in particular that she could help me with. I nervously asked her if I could see the makeover menu, at which point her eyes lit up. 'Ooh we are going to have such fun my dear', she said trying to put me at ease but at the same time looking like an excited child at a birthday party. I picked out a classic office style look, with mid-length fitted black skirt and white blouse, with black heels. I was ushered into a changing room, and the shapewear was thrust through the curtains by Sandra's enthusiastic hand for me to put on. There was a box containing latex breast forms. They felt similar in weight to "real" breasts, but they were very cold to the touch. I was given knickers that had special pads in them to enhance my buttocks and hips, and a matching black bra. I pulled on the knickers and tucked away my bits and bobs and then put the bra on. Now for the breast forms. I dropped them into the ample bra one at a time and oh my god they were cold! It was like putting a bag of frozen peas on each nipple. The bra sat heavy on my chest with the D cup breasts in place. Next, Sandra tied me into a black corset, lacing it so tight I that thought I was going to suffocate. I soon relaxed and got used to the tightness of the corset, and I finished dressing. Black stockings, black skirt, black heels and white blouse. I felt incredible. Not sexual in any way, it didn't turn me on to be wearing these clothes, it made me feel alive, it made me feel happy. I will never forget the way I felt that day as I looked in the mirror at my body, with the hourglass curves of a woman staring back at me.

      Sandra sat me in a chair in front of a large mirror with a row of bulbs either side. She expertly applied a heavy foundation to cover my beard shadow, which by mid-afternoon was beginning to show. She effortlessly applied powder, blush, eyeliner and eye shadow to create a feminine makeup look. I don't have many features that I'm proud of as a woman, but I love my long thick eye lashes. Sandra almost squealed in delight when she saw them and couldn't wait to apply two thick coats of mascara, making them look like false lashes. A generous coating of red lipstick and red nail polish was applied before she began fitting the wig, styling it with both hands while chatting away with a comb between her teeth. When she had finished, she pointed to the full-length mirror at the other end of the studio. 'Before you go to the mirror, what's your name sweetheart?' asked Sandra. I wasn't expecting this question, I panicked. I said with my voice quivering, 'I, er, erm, Ian?' 'No, not him, what's *your* name my dear?', she asked, as she looked me up and down admiring her handiwork. I quickly racked my brains for a name. From out of nowhere I blurted out 'Elise'. Since the "Emma" incident with Tracey had gone so badly wrong, I hadn't considered a female name before that moment, at least not consciously, but as the name passed over my full red lips, it felt like it really was my name. 'Elise, is that French? It really suits you' said Sandra. From that moment on, for the rest of my visit to the little shop that had such a huge impact on me, my name was Elise, and Ian had faded away as if some distant memory.

    I stood up, expertly balancing on my high heels (I'd had years of practice). I walked over to the mirror and took in the sight before me. I was a woman. Not only that, I looked in proportion. I had long slender legs and curves in all the right places. My long curly brunette hair was piled high on my head, with a few curly tresses cascading down each side of my face, framing it perfectly. I felt attractive, I felt feminine and for the first time ever, I felt at peace with myself. I was smiling uncontrollably, it seemed like it was the first time I'd ever smiled. I love the bewilderment on a baby's face when it learns to smile for the first time. That was how it seemed in that moment, as if smiling was a new concept that I'd only just become aware of. A tear formed in the corner of my eye and before I could blink it away Sandra was dabbing at my eye to prevent me from undoing her handiwork. 'Well, we don't get tears very often. This is more than just dressing up for you, isn't it? This is who you are. I can see it in your eyes.' She said this while placing her hand gently on my heart and looking deep into my eyes. I couldn't speak, half of me wanted to run out of the shop and drive as far away as possible, and the other half was rooted to the spot, trying to make sense of the words that were still being replayed over and over in my head. She didn't know me. This was just an experiment, exploring my feminine side, nothing more. I'm not a woman, how could I be? I was born a boy and now I'm a man. I'm just curious, this is just dressing up… Isn't it?

I sat in the shop reading magazines while trying my hardest to cross my legs in a feminine way, which wasn't easy with my over developed thigh muscles. All I could think about were Sandra's words. 'This is who you are. I can see it in your eyes.' They went round and round in my head, tormenting me, almost mocking me. Over the few hours I sat reading a book and drinking coffee, taking great care not to spill it on the white blouse, a few more people entered the shop. They browsed for clothes, shoes or shapewear then on seeing me they would smile politely before making their purchases and leaving. When the time came to remove the makeup, hair and clothes I felt a deep sadness come over me, but at the same time a confusing sense of relief. I walked out of the changing room as my old self. Holding back tears, I hugged Sandra and thanked her for the experience. She handed me a polaroid picture that she had taken while I was standing in front of the mirror, and on the back, she had written "Elise". 'Take care my darling. I hope to see you again soon.' She said, as I smiled and left the shop. On the drive to the hotel, I couldn't work out what the hell was going on in my mind. I'd had the most wonderful experience, seeing myself as a woman just the way I'd pictured myself in my dreams and most secret thoughts, but I felt guilty, deeply guilty for letting go of my masculinity. I felt like I'd let everyone down by not being the man they expected me to be, even though no one knew I was even there. I cried myself to sleep that night in my lonely hotel room. The worst part was that I wasn't sure why I was crying. Was it because I'd let my guard down and allowed my masculinity to be overcome by my inner femininity? Or because I felt that I'd experienced true happiness that day, as I stared at my female self in the mirror for the first time? The guilty feelings stayed with me for weeks after, and I never visited the shop again.

A few months later as winter started to set in, I was wading through endless piles of marking and assessment paperwork one evening when Sharon walked into the flat with a big grin on her face. 'You'll never guess what I found' she proclaimed. She showed me an advert for a local cross-dressing group that she had seen advertised in the local paper. It was only about a mile from our flat and they held a coffee evening on the first Saturday of the month. That was this Saturday, three days away. I told her I was done with all that, biting my lip hard with the guilt of my recent trip to Transformation still gnawing away at me. She said she knew I'd said I was done with it, but she also knew that I wasn't happy. There was no pulling the wool over her eyes. Sharon is a very clever woman, both academically and intuitively. I agreed to go along with her to have a look, but only if I could go in my normal male clothes. Since the last purge of all my feminine things there was only a skirt and a pair of tights in the box under the bed anyway. We didn't mention it again until Saturday came around. I think Sharon felt that if she brought it up, I'd change my mind and find some excuse not to go. On Saturday evening, we took the five-minute drive to the dimly lit car park of the local community centre. In the large grounds there were trees and hedge rows that gave it privacy from the terraced streets surrounding it. We walked up the stairs where we were greeted by a person dressed in a long white dress and wedge heeled sandals. She introduced herself as Jackie before explaining the rules of the group and looking me up and down as if to question why I'd come dressed in male clothing. Jackie asked me why I'd come to the group but before I could answer she explained to me that she identified as a male and that cross-dressing gave her comfort and relief from the pressures of her job. I swerved her question, and we went into the room to mingle with the others. Sharon and I got into conversation with a few members of the group. They were very friendly genuine people. What I couldn't get over was how relaxed they all seemed, casually sitting around chatting while wearing women's clothes, some of them in front of their wives who had also come along. We stayed about an hour before making our excuses to leave. There was something comforting in that experience, but also something that didn't sit right, and I couldn't put my finger on what it was. It was also obvious that Sharon wasn't comfortable at all, and although she didn't say anything on the way home, I could tell that it hadn't been at all what she'd expected.

When the next meeting came around, I found myself asking Sharon if she wanted to go. She looked at me as if I'd asked her to walk over hot coals. 'I thought you'd got it out of your system', she said, as she scowled at me with her piercing green eyes. I didn't feel totally comfortable there, but I did at least feel like I was with like-minded people. She told me she was going to Coventry to see her parents for the weekend and if I wanted to go then I should, but she didn't want to hear about it afterwards. Her words stung me, sending new waves of guilt through my body like a tsunami. Sharon went to Coventry on the train that Friday night, and I went shopping, buying a cheap dress from Dotty P's and some other bits and bobs in town. On Saturday afternoon, I got myself ready in the flat, with minimal makeup I borrowed from Sharon's extensive array of products, and the new dress and flat shoes. I had a cheap brunette wig that I got from a party shop in town, which completed the look. I caught a glimpse of myself in the hall mirror on my way out. I looked ridiculous, the absolute opposite of Sandra's incredible work when she effortlessly transformed me into a decent-looking woman just a few months earlier. With my bulging muscles and hairy arms stretching the flimsy material of the light green frock, it was almost enough to stop me leaving the flat. But I had come this far, I was determined to see it through. I ran to my car as fast as I could to avoid being spotted by the neighbours, driving to the meeting with sunglasses on, hoping to avoid detection. Once in the privacy of the car park I started to relax. The second meeting was much the same affair as the first. No one seemed interested in the fact that I'd plucked up the courage to present myself in female clothing, and I was glad about that: I was blending in. As the evening ended and we all said our goodbyes, I found myself wondering about what had made me feel uneasy the first time. It felt like none of the people in the group had any desire to be women. They were happy to describe themselves as men who liked to wear women's clothes. Well, to all intents and purposes, that was exactly what I was, so why did this feel so wrong to me? Why did I feel like I didn't connect or identify in the same way as these people? I couldn't find the answer despite how much I thought about it over the next few weeks. I was glad I had gone that evening, but it raised more questions than it gave me answers. That second meeting would be the last time I went to the group.

    Another family Christmas came and went. Sharon was away with her parents and I was at my sister's, playing the clown and making my family laugh. Sharon is from a Sikh family who are very traditional. She wouldn't let me meet her parents because she knew that they wouldn't accept me. This was just another elephant in the room for us and one of the most common causes of our ever-frequent arguments. Sex had become pretty much non-existent and I was making all sorts of excuses to avoid it. Over the course of spring, we grew further and further apart, barely speaking for days on end. Sharon went to Coventry almost every weekend and it was becoming more and more difficult to be civil to each other. We called a truce for my thirtieth birthday. We'd arranged a meal for family and friends in a local Chinese restaurant. The evening was a disaster, I got completely drunk, so much so that I fell out of my brother's car when he dropped us back at the flat. I was sick in the kitchen sink and Sharon made me sleep on the sofa with a bucket before going to bed in disgust. The next day I told her that I wanted to split up. She didn't take it well. She punched me on the jaw and slammed the front door in my face. A few days later I collected my things when she was out at work and left the key on the kitchen table. I had been given my old room back at home with my parents. It wasn't ideal, recently turning thirty and celebrating with a three-day hangover, being punched by my now ex-girlfriend and moving back home with my parents.

My mum was glad to have me back as it turned out. I became quite close to her again after moving back in, and we formed an alliance which we both needed. She was dealing with my Dad's ill health and constant pain which made him irritable, and just having someone else in the house made it a little more bearable. My mental health was once again at a low point and she was trying to cope as best she could, so we became an emotional crutch for each other. I had once again purged all my feminine things by bagging them up and taking them to yet another charity shop. I felt like I had to be the man, strong and capable. I stopped Thai boxing and lifting weights at the gym. I needed a new distraction; I felt an overwhelming urge towards hyper-masculinity, and it needed to be even more manly than the bodybuilding and martial arts.

I decided to get a tattoo. I found a local tattoo studio, run by a guy called Kurt. My first tattoo was a small tribal design on my lower back just above my bum. As the weeks went on Kurt and I became good friends and I spent most Saturdays at the shop helping out and taking bookings in exchange for free tattoos. I would also fix his car in exchange for tattoos and after a while I became pretty heavily inked. My legs are covered in tribal tattoos to just above the knee, I have two Chinese dragons, one on each hip, one green and one red. My shoulders are covered in gravestones and skulls and ghostly figures, and my back has an angel holding herself in sorrow with the words "the devil within" below. The majority of my tattoos relate in some way to my internal struggle between femininity and masculinity. I wasn't all that conscious of that until it was pointed out to me some years later. At the time I didn't even consider what I was doing. I had no respect for my body and permanently marking it with ink didn't seem to matter. It never really felt like my body. I know that might sound silly, but I never felt comfortable with it, I didn't understand it or identify with it. I hated it. I'd worked hard to change it, making it even more masculine by lifting weights, but all that did was make me even more disconnected from it in the end.

  My Saturday mornings were now occupied with the tattoo shop, and Kurt was gradually colouring me in. I still felt like something was missing. I had been single for about six months but that in itself didn't bother me. I have never had a problem with being alone, it has often been good for my mental health to back away from family and friends for a while. This was different, I still had those familiar feelings. I still woke up having had dreams of being a woman or having been turned into a woman in some bizarre outlandish story that had played out in my head during the course of my often-broken sleep. One day while teaching my third-year group who were all in their late teens or early twenties, the subject of motorcycles came up. A few of the lads had 125cc bikes and one of the older lads had just bought a Suzuki GSX-R 600. I've always liked bikes and watching bike racing with my dad, but I'd only ever ridden a few. The first was a Honda C90 moped which I bought when I was fifteen for two pounds. I got it running properly and sold it for twenty pounds. The next was a 50cc scrambler that one of the mechanics at Errington's had brought to work to take across the fields at the back of the garage. The third was a Yamaha RD350 LC which I rode to the end of the road and back (which might have bent one or two traffic laws). I decided that I'd get a motorcycle and learn to ride. I booked a three-day intensive course which had a pre-booked test at the end. I took to it really well and found the lessons quite easy. I instantly got the bug for motorcycles and it has never left me. By day two I was doing emergency stops, turning round in the road (which sounds easy but requires good balance at such slow speed), and I was riding to a good standard according to my instructor. I passed my test first time despite the heavy rain on the day. I was so happy, and it brought back memories of passing my car test as a seventeen-year-old. A week later, I headed to a motorcycle shop in Peterborough to buy my first ever bike, A Kawasaki Ninja 600. It was used and had seen its best days, but it was mechanically sound and that was all I needed for my first bike. That first ride home from Peterborough to Leicester was such a thrill, I was hooked. Motorcycles have been a huge part of my life since 2001 when I took my test. I can't imagine not being able to just throw on a helmet and some leathers and go out for a ride to clear my head. Of all the things I've done to escape my feelings and thoughts of femininity, riding my motorcycle was the one thing where total concentration on the road meant I forgot about everything else.

Riding bikes and working on them in the garage at home had become my only real pastime when I wasn't at work. I spent most of my evenings in the garage. I had a motorcycle lift, my big red Snap-on toolbox, a workbench, a comfy swivel chair, a radio and even a small fridge. I lined the walls with pictures of bikes, some with half naked women draped over them that I'd taken from magazines. I used to sit there with a beer in my hand looking at those beautiful women straddling the motorcycles. Instead of being turned on, which I assume was the whole point of the shot in the first place, I just felt jealous of them. All I could think about was what it must be like to wake up every day with that body, that hair, those feminine features. It may have been just a single garage at the back of a council house, but it was cosy, to me at least, and had everything I needed to escape the outside world. Sometimes, while working on the bike, I'd wear a pair of high heeled black suede ankle boots that I kept in the bottom drawer of the toolbox. The rest of my clothes would all be male, jeans, T shirts or hoodies. Pottering around the garage in my heels listening to the radio and working on my bikes made me feel in control of my inner feelings. It didn't fix anything but at least it was a place to hide. I had built myself a fortress of solitude. For the next three years I bought bike after bike after bike. I'd buy a brand new one, ride it for a few months, get bored then need a new distraction, so I'd trade it in, at a loss against the cost of the next one. This behaviour cost me thousands of pounds in the end, and I'm still repaying those debts to this day.

In December 2003, my dad had fallen in the snow breaking his hip. He eventually recovered but he wasn't well. He had to give up driving because pressing the pedals caused him so much pain. He spent most of his time in his chair in front of the television or doing crossword puzzles. I was still finding it hard to talk to him and living under the same roof just made things worse between us. I started treating him with contempt, almost seeing him as a burden to me and my mum. We had a pretty crappy Christmas with dad being in constant pain and my mum dealing with her own pain as she waited to have her worn out knees replaced. I made no effort, hiding away from everyone, and I think we all just wanted it to be over so we could pack up the tree and get back to ignoring each other without the forced smiles and empty celebrations.

When January came around, I got a phone call from Wayne. I had barely seen him since he got married and settled down. He had two children by now and had moved to a bigger home. We were still friends and we chatted on the phone, but we didn't spend any time together like we had in the past. His sister-in-law and her friend had set up a charity specialising in still birth and neonatal death to support bereaved parents. They had arranged a launch party and Wayne wanted to know if I'd go, just to make up the numbers. I had nothing better to do so why not I thought. Little did I know that this decision would change the course of my life forever. We arrived at the church hall where we were greeted by the usual banners and balloons and I picked out a few faces that I knew from days gone by. As the evening went on, I noticed a woman with stunning eyes and a great smile looking at me from time to time. I couldn't take my eyes off her either. This was like a scene from a cheesy movie, but it was really happening. She approached Wayne, asking him who I was and if I was single. I approached Wayne's wife and asked her the same. With a bit of matchmaking, I was introduced to Louise, who happened to be one of the co-founders of the charity. We instantly had a connection, and over the next few weeks things developed really fast between us, but neither of us seemed to mind.

Things were going so well that around four months into our relationship, we decided to have a baby together. I was approaching thirty-one and Louise was a little older with a daughter who was two and a half. It just seemed like the next natural progression for us. We were all but living together and I rarely spent any time at home. Within a month of "trying", Louise excitedly produced a plastic wand with a very clear blue stripe in the little window. I was so excited, telling all my family and friends. At the same time, I decided that after fifteen years I couldn't really remember why I was angry with my brother James anymore. We hadn't seen each other or spoken for all that time. This had put pressure on my family at Christmas and parties or events where they would have to choose which one of us to invite. With a baby on the way, it seemed like the perfect time to mend some bridges. I called him up, and after a few tears we decided to meet. There were lots of hugs and apologies and it felt really good to have finally fixed things. The only fly in the ointment was that being as stubborn as a mule, he was still adamant that he wouldn't set foot in our house while my dad was still alive. I had no choice but to accept this and I tried to put the needs of the whole family before my own and my dad's. I tried to spend as much time as I could with James, his wife and their children, who were now in their early teens. There was an awful lot of catching up to do and I invested a lot of time in making sure we did just that.

While things were going well with my brother, things were gradually getting worse between Louise and me. We had started arguing over the stupidest things. It almost felt like the arguments were engineered as a means to an end. I don't know to this day if that was just my own paranoia or the truth, but shortly before we were due to have our first baby scan at twelve weeks, Louise dropped a bombshell on me, she wanted to end our relationship. I was devastated. I hadn't been easy to live with, that's for sure, and I knew that my mental health had been a bit sketchy over the last few months, but this really did come out of the blue for me. Looking back, I don't blame her, she is very protective of her own space and her family and she saw something in me that rubbed against that. I was angry, this was not how I had imagined being a father. I didn't want to be the kind of dad that picked up their child and took them for a McDonald's happy meal once a week. We got through the twelve-week scan barely able to be civil to each other. The twenty-week scan was even worse but again somehow, we got through it. Things went quiet for a while between us but as the due date got nearer, there were things that needed to be discussed, one of which was baby names.

    Louise insisted that she didn't want to know the sex of the baby and I was fine with that (one of the few things we did agree on). However, this meant that we had to come up with a boy's name and a girl's name. Louise was the first to strike with the name Martha. I am deeply sorry to anyone named Martha, but at the time, with the pressure of the situation I was in, I hated it. She said Martha, I heard Eastern European shot-putt champion. I counter-acted with Verity, thinking it was a sweet and ever so slightly posh sounding name. I retracted it a few days later when I was leaving a multi-storey car park in Leicester town centre. A man wearing a very flammable looking shell suit with a cigarette dangling from his mouth was trying to load his considerable array of children into the family car. As I was about to get into my car, I heard the man shout at the top of his voice in a thick Leicester accent, 'Veriteh, get in the fucking car'. Aaaaand Verity was off the table. A few weeks passed and much internet research was done before we both agreed on Zach for a boy, and Jodie for a girl.

As summer came to an end and the nights started drawing in, I felt like the whole world was against me. I was finding it hard to keep my head above water. My dad's health was deteriorating fast, and my mum had finally been given a date for her knee replacement surgery. I was unable to see Louise because things were just too strained between us. I longed to feel my child kick in her tummy and do all the silly things parents do, like singing to the bump and reading stories to it. In my darkest hours when I really wasn't sure if I could go on, I sometimes felt envy towards Louise. 'What the hell was that about?' I'd think to myself, snapping myself out of it as quickly as the thoughts had entered my head. They did enter my head though; I was jealous of Louise for being able to carry a baby and give birth. This was all getting too much; I could feel myself spiralling out of control at a point in my life when I needed to be strong for my unborn child.

Chapter Six
The emotional rollercoaster

As autumn proceeded to turn the trees and hedgerows into a beautiful array of reds, golds and browns, day-to-day life was becoming harder and harder. At work, I was teaching on autopilot, not caring about the quality of the training I was delivering. I have no idea how I managed to stand there for six hours a day, teaching the finer points of transmissions, electronics and fuel injection to teenagers who were barely listening at the best of times. In a few months' time I was due to become a father, which should have filled me with joy, but instead, my mind was filled with anger and apprehension, due to the situation between Louise and me. I spent most of my time alone. I would either be in the garage working on my bike, where I'd often lose my temper, throwing spanners at the wall in frustration, or I would be out riding it like I'd stolen it. I didn't care if I made it round the next bend, nothing seemed to matter much. My parents had enough problems of their own with their ill health and all I was doing was adding to their misery with my short temper and foul moods. While I was out riding at very stupid speeds, I rationalised my behaviour by convincing myself that everyone would be better off if I left this world in a ball of flame and twisted metal. As I rode down twisty country lanes at speeds well in excess of the safe limits, I'd often imagine the kind of accident it would take to ensure I didn't survive. If I wasn't out contemplating the very point of my existence on my bike, I'd be at my friend Kurt's flat getting hammered. He was a good friend, but his life was equally as destructive as mine, so we weren't exactly a tonic for one another.

My mum finally received a date for the first of her knee replacement operations. She'd experienced major surgery in the past, having had a hysterectomy in her mid-forties when I was around six years old, but this didn't seem to ease her nerves at all. I often wondered if the experiences of the psychiatric wards she had been admitted to in the past had left some emotional scars, if not physical ones. My dad's health was deteriorating fast. He was in constant pain and he was losing weight, which was unlikely to be down to healthy eating, considering his opinion that Chinese takeaways were healthy. His argument that they 'use a lot of beansprouts' wasn't fooling anyone. The day before my mum was due to go into hospital for her knee surgery, my dad collapsed at home. He was taken to hospital by ambulance. I was at work in Nottingham and with all the fuss, my mum didn't have the time to call me to let me know. I came home to a note on the kitchen table saying "*Dad in Glenfield hospital, don't worry. Mum xx*". My dad and I were barely speaking and I knew I was being a terrible son, ignoring him and almost despising him for being a burden to my mum. Despite this, I jumped in the car, raced across town and ran through the hospital like a madman. When I came to the ward my mum was by his bedside, he was hooked up to all sorts of drips, wires and tubes, with monitors bleeping and screens displaying a multitude of information about his failing health. I couldn't take it in at first. I'd never seen my dad vulnerable like this, so frail and weak. I had to hide around the corner until I regained my composure. He was awake, chatting with my mum and looking quite cheerful, which was a surprise to me. 'Just a precaution lad', he said to me as his eyes caught sight of me behind my mum. She said the same and told me not to worry but I could see that there was more to it than they were letting on. He grew tired due in part to the medication they had given him and also the difficult day he'd had, so we left him to sleep and I took my mum home.

     The next day I dropped my mum at the General Hospital which was only a mile or so from our house. Leicester has three hospitals and now I had a parent in two of them. For the next five days I went to work in Nottingham as usual, and on the drive home I'd stop at the first hospital to see my dad then go to the second to see my mum, who had got through her surgery with no issues. By the time I got home it was after nine o'clock and I was exhausted. On the sixth day, the day before my mum was due to be released from hospital, I went to see my dad after work as I had done every night. He looked very weak and his skin had gone slightly yellow. I asked him if he needed anything. He asked for some refresher sweets because they helped when his mouth was dry. I went to the vending machine to get them and when I came back, he was closing his eyes, looking very tired. Despite the state of our relationship at that time, something in my mind made me hold his hand as I was about to leave, squeezing it gently and looking into his half-closed eyes. I wanted so desperately to say I love you dad, but I couldn't get the words out. As I looked into his half-closed eyes, I could feel the love between us, a love that I'd neglected and betrayed because of my own anger and hatred of the world. With his eyes now closed, he held my hand, giving it a squeeze as if to acknowledge my thoughts. There seemed to be an almost telepathic connection between us, each of us saying I love you without a single word leaving our mouths. I gently responded by squeezing his hand, and as he relaxed his grip, I left him to sleep.

Mum came home from hospital on a bright but chilly Thursday. I was at work in Nottingham, so my brother Graham collected her and settled her in at home. When I got back the neighbours had come round and had made her some tea. I'd been to see my dad on the way home. He was asleep when I arrived, so I got him two packs of refreshers, left them on his bedside table, and left for home. I was so happy to see my mum back home and looking well if not a little tired. We chatted about the day she'd had, and she asked me how dad was. Before I could answer her, the house phone rang: it was my dad. His voice sounded weak and he couldn't hear me very well but I passed the phone to my mum, and they chatted for a few minutes, catching up on how she was doing and how glad she was to be home. From what I could overhear, (both of them had poor hearing so they were shouting every single word) he seemed relieved to know that his wife was finally home and on the mend. After telling him that she would visit him tomorrow with me, she hung up the phone. My mum was home and seemed happy, and my dad was fading away in a hospital across town. As I listened to them talking (shouting) on the phone, the reality of how difficult the last few weeks had been for all of us began to sink in. I needed to be alone for a while, so I headed to the garage to work on my bike. It was long past midnight when my head hit the pillow.

      4.30am, on Friday November 26th 2004, a time that will be forever stamped into my brain. My mobile phone rang. I jumped up in bed, startled by the noise. As my eyes adjusted to the darkness, I answered the phone. 'Mr Carter?' 'Yes', I replied while rubbing the sleep from my eyes and trying to think who the hell would contact me at such a ridiculous hour. A nurse from the Glenfield hospital gave me her name but my confusion and tiredness made me instantly forget it. 'Mr Carter, I'm afraid I have some bad news. Your father passed away a few minutes ago in his sleep. He did not suffer or feel any pain'. I should have had questions, tears, anger, pain and god knows what emotions flying around in my head but all I could say was, 'OK, thank you', before hanging up the phone. I went into my mum's room, and asked if she was awake, which of course woke her up. I told her what the nurse had said, and she said she was expecting it. I gave her a hug and went to bed. No tears, nothing. Looking back on that night, and the days that led up to it, my dad was dying, he knew he was dying, but he held on until he knew that his wife was safely out of hospital and back home, passing away just hours after talking to her. For the last seventeen years, I have lived with the guilt of how I treated my dad in his final years, often ignoring him, or being short tempered with him because he couldn't hear me. I even wished he was dead from time to time when things were bad between us, or my mum was struggling to cope with looking after him. I was so angry back then, often taking it out on him and my mum. As the old saying goes, "you always hurt the ones you love". Transition may have silenced my inner demons regarding my gender, but I will never forgive myself for the way I treated my dad, the man who raised me as his own son.

      In the morning, my sister came over to help us get organised. We went to the hospital to get my dad's personal effects and talk to the nurses. I asked the nurse if there was anything that they could have done for him, but she explained that he and my mum had requested that a DNR (do not resuscitate) note was made in his records. I'd seen the sign above his bed and dismissed it thinking it was some doctor's code for his medication or some tests they needed to do. I was so preoccupied with my own problems that I didn't even acknowledge it. That day when I had rushed across town and ran through the hospital, walking in on them both as they were talking, he had asked her to let him go peacefully, and she had agreed. Multiple organ failure was the cause of death.

It was recorded as natural causes due in part to his age (seventy-six) and a life of heavy smoking. When we got home my sister started bagging up his clothes and going through the things in his wardrobe. I wanted to tell her to leave his things alone but she was only trying to help. He didn't leave a will because he didn't really have anything to leave but I kept his gold cufflinks, a glass engraved with the name "Bob", and a few photos. In the garage were some of his old tools, all well used and past their best, but I kept them because they were the tools we used when we worked on the car together. We shared those tools many times and holding them in my hands made me feel close to him.

In the week between his death and the funeral, I locked myself away, mostly in the garage, thinking about my relationship with him and remembering the good times we had when I was younger. I finally began to grieve, sometimes crying for hours at a time. Some of my dad's family made the trip from Coventry to pay their respects at his funeral, and a few of our neighbours came along to say their goodbyes. My dad wasn't particularly religious, but his family had links with the Salvation Army, so I arranged for one of their ministers to deliver the service. I stood at the front of the chapel at the crematorium, holding my mum's hand, trying my hardest to hold it together. I made it through most of the service, but as the final hymn ended, I couldn't hold my composure any longer. I broke down, crying uncontrollably in front of my mum and my whole family. The last thing I remember of the service was watching my dad's coffin slowly disappear behind the curtains as the music played, and the family and well-wishers all started to leave. I stayed until the chapel was empty and the coffin had disappeared from sight. As I sat there in the chapel, I felt the guilt and the hurt of letting him die without telling him how much I loved him, burn a permanent scar into my brain. A scar which is as fresh today as it was on that day. We arranged for his ashes to be scattered in the garden of remembrance the following day, but neither my mum nor I could bear to be there when they did it, so we left it in the hands of the undertakers.

We held a wake at a local pub straight after the service, where everyone shared stories of how they knew my dad and told funny tales of the times they'd shared with him over the years. My uncle Bill was stealing sandwiches and hiding them in his jacket pockets. He had form for this and did it at every family event, thinking nobody knew when actually, everybody did. My mum was trying to keep up with all the "I'm so sorry for your loss" sherries that were being bought for her, and I was being patted on the back, or given strong alpha-male handshakes followed by 'You did well today son. He'd have been proud of you'. Kind words of course but in my head all I could think was, 'I'm not your son, my dad is dead and what makes you think I did anything to deserve his pride?'.

As you can imagine, Christmas was no barrel of laughs. My mum and I (the widow and the grieving son) were invited to my sister's for Christmas dinner. We did our best to have fun and my mum seemed to be in quite good spirits which was good to see. Nobody in my family remarked on how quiet I was despite them knowing that usually I was the joker, with the whoopee cushions and the cans of silly string. I just didn't have it in me - I felt broken and exhausted. New Year's Eve was another "just get through it" event, and neither my mum nor I stayed up after ten o'clock. I'd drunk the best part of a bottle of whiskey by then and my mum had been on the sherry. I lay in bed, the room slightly spinning, staring at the ceiling and contemplating my New Year resolutions. Jesus Christ, where would I even start? The one thing that dominated my thoughts as I faded into alcohol-fuelled unconsciousness, was that my only job now was to be the best father I could be to my unborn child. I owed it to my dad and to my child, to be a better father than I was a son. That night, I made a pact with myself. I had responsibilities now, I'd already let down the man who raised me. I couldn't afford any more mistakes. My secret, my femininity, my longing to live my life as a woman, must remain a secret that I would take to the grave.

January 28th 2005. I arrived at the Leicester Royal Infirmary after stopping at the newsagent to buy a copy of the Times as a keepsake. I met with Louise and her sister Jane. We made small talk while we waited for the consultant to arrive to talk us through what was about to happen. Louise had been scheduled for a caesarean section due to complications in her previous pregnancies. Louise left with the theatre nurse to prepare, and I paced up and down the waiting room like an expectant father from a time before they weren't allowed to be in the delivery room, let alone film the birth on a GoPro. At 9.46am, my beautiful baby daughter was born, weighing a healthy eight pounds and one ounce. I was ushered into a small room where my daughter was being cleaned and wrapped in a warm blanket. She had a hospital identity tag on her wrist with her name on it and a tiny nappy had been put on her by the midwife. She smiled at me and said 'would you like to hold your daughter?' With tears in my eyes, I smiled as she handed her to me. As I looked into her sparkly eyes, full of bewilderment at this new world she was seeing for the first time, I knew that I would never love anyone or anything more than I love my darling little girl.

In the following weeks, Louise and I tried to repair our relationship for our daughter's sake. It lasted less than a week before the arguments ensued, so we decided that it would be best to concentrate on being parents, and that was that. I saw as much of my daughter as I possibly could during her first weeks, and my family got to spend time with her too. Outwardly, I was the strong father to a new-born baby girl, but inwardly, I was barely holding it together due to the sheer array of emotions I was going through. With my father's death and the birth of my daughter being just eight weeks apart, I don't know how I got through that time, but somehow, I found a way.

A few months later, the relationship between Louise and me had improved greatly. We were in a good routine as co-parents and I was spending plenty of quality time with my little girl. I wouldn't say I was in a good place, far from it, but I was at least beginning to function as a human being again. At work, I'd become very attracted to a beautiful woman called Claire. We'd often chatted at the photocopier or on work nights out, and I found myself captivated by her eyes and beautiful smile. I decided to ask her out on a date. The date went really well and was followed by many more. We dated for quite a while, and I was very much in love with her. Claire has a kind heart and a warm loving nature, and I loved spending time with her, but despite this, for one reason or another it didn't work out. Looking back, I think I was just too emotionally broken at the time, and no matter how much I loved her, I wasn't in the right place to share my life with anyone. Claire and I have since reconnected through social media and become close friends. She understands me so well, and we've had long talks about the past. Because of the pact that I made with myself after my dad's funeral, I never confided in Claire about how I felt, but I think that if I had, she would have understood, just as she has now.

My daughter's early years were magical for me. I loved watching her learn to walk and talk. I loved taking care of her when she was poorly, teaching her to use the potty and later to ride a bike without stabilisers. We did everything together, like baking cakes (which usually ended up with more cake mixture on her face than in the bowl), going to the farm to feed the animals and ride the ponies, trips to the seaside - all the things a father should do with his little girl. I know in my heart that I did my best for her and always put her first but I will always wish that it could have been different, that I could have made things work with Louise and been there for her every day. During those years my gender issues seemed to ease a little. They were still there but they were manageable. I still felt that my feminine side was much stronger than my masculine, but I'd learned to hide it so well that no one would ever know unless I told them.

By the time my daughter turned five, I was working for Mercedes-Benz as a trainer and spending a lot of time in the peak district with a good friend called Lynn. Lynn is a body piercer from Derbyshire. We became friends when she was piercing a friend of mine and the conversation turned to cars. I fixed a few problems on her car for her and we just hit it off. She had a caravan in a remote village where we would often go on a Friday night to get drunk and watch old movies on her little television set. On Saturday morning we'd have a fry-up in the local greasy spoon and then go shopping in Bakewell or take a walk up to Monsal Head to take in the views. I'd head home to Leicester on Saturday evening to be ready to see my daughter early on Sunday and she would head back home when the mood took her.

Lynn and I both love motorcycles. She went to all the big biker rallies. She always camped, meeting lots of new and interesting people. I never did the rally scene. I think I was too shy or maybe just too scared that spiritually conscious people would be able to see right through me. She did however manage to persuade me to go to the MCN (Motorcycle News) live bash at Butlin's in Skegness. It was a fantastic event with stunt shows, ride outs and a marketplace where you could buy bike parts, clothing or just hot food and a brew. Set across a full three days from Friday to Sunday, there was something to do or see on every day. In the evenings, bands played in the different clubs within the complex. On Saturday night, it was fancy-dress night. Lynn had picked an American police outfit with sexy skirt and stockings. I'd left it to the last minute as I was kind of hoping I wouldn't have to dress up. Lynn persuaded me that I would be the odd one out if I didn't so I'd better sort something quick. The day before we left for Skegness, I raided my wardrobe. I racked my brains for some inspiration. All I needed was something simple that would pass for an outfit that I could later ditch when everyone was so drunk, that they wouldn't notice or care. It came to me in a flash of inspiration. I pulled out a box from under my bed. This wouldn't work, surely? It had to, there was no time for anything else. As I packed my bag ready to leave for the weekend with jeans, t shirts and a few pairs of trainers, I also packed a long black skirt which covered my ankles and rested on my feet, a pair of black flats, and a black roll neck sweater that I had in my wardrobe. I stopped at the party shop in town for the rest of the outfit: a large crucifix on a chain and a nun's habit. This was just going to have to do.

When we got to the event, we were in bike heaven. There were custom bike shows, a wall of death, and stunt riders performing all sorts of tricks for the excited crowds. When Saturday evening came around, Lynn went into her room in the chalet to get ready, and I did the same. She hadn't asked me what outfit I'd chosen, so her jaw nearly hit the floor when sister Mary Hinge came waltzing into the lounge. 'Will this do?' I asked as she tried to regain her composure. Once she'd finished laughing hysterically, we left the safety of our chalet to head to the club. I felt very vulnerable and exposed. I hadn't cross-dressed in front of anyone since the group I went to in Leicester some years earlier. Within a few metres of walking towards the club, my fear began to turn to excitement. I felt good, really good. I felt free. That's all, just free. Not sexy, not horny, not naughty, just free. I loosened up very quickly as the evening went on, helped by a few cold beers and the odd whiskey chaser. I blessed a couple of barmaids with holy water from the ice bucket, and in the men's toilet, I couldn't help having some fun with the burly tattooed bikers who were staring at me. 'What, you've never seen a nun take a piss standing up before?' I said, while hitching my skirt up round my waist and blessing everyone who came into the toilets with my free hand. I'll always remember that night, not just for the laughs and the bands and the beer, but because for the first time ever, I was dressed as a woman in public. It was so good to walk among other people who didn't seem to mind or care what I was wearing (except for a few nervous looking Hells Angels in the men's toilet). We did the event the following year, but I thought Lynn might suspect something if sister Mary Hinge made another appearance, so with a bit of imagination, Dr Randy B'stard was created. I bought a white lab coat, a child's toy stethoscope, and some thick-rimmed joke glasses. I topped it off with a sew-on patch, with the nickname of my favourite MotoGP rider, Valentino Rossi. His nickname is "The Doctor" (see what I did there?). My mum sewed the patch on to my lab coat and I laminated a name tag, clipping it onto the pocket. Job done. While it was fun being Dr Randy B'stard for the evening, I longed for the emotions I'd felt while dressed as sister Mary. We never went again after that year, partly due to how busy we were, and partly because the event started to become a bit stale.

Life had been fairly steady for quite some time. My daughter was growing up so fast and I loved every second of the time we shared together. I rode my bikes, worked hard during the week and spent my weekend split between my daughter and getting drunk with my friends. I almost felt normal. If I wasn't spending time with Lynn, I'd be at Kurt's flat or I'd just get drunk on my own in the garage while polishing my bike. After a while I decided that another level of overcompensating was needed, so I took up golf. A few of the guys at Mercedes-Benz played and so did my friend Tristan. He and I spent a few Saturday mornings on the course in Leicester. He'd lose the will to live while trying to teach me how to hit a ball in a straight line, or any direction really. Through perseverance and sheer pig-headedness, I eventually achieved a level of competence that would get me by, and I started to play with the guys at work. One evening, we decided to get eighteen holes in at a course near Derby. The weather had been changeable all week but we weren't prepared for what came next. On hole number one, bright, warm sunshine and clear skies. By hole number five there were dark clouds and showers. By hole number ten it was raining hard. By the sixteenth hole it was getting dark and it started snowing. After eighteen holes of what we now refer to as "snow golf", I sat in the clubhouse shivering, clutching a hot chocolate, dripping wet and looking like I'd just been rescued from a stricken ship in the North Sea. I vowed never to pick up a golf club again, unless it was to beat to death anyone who suggested a round of golf.

A few months later I was made redundant from Mercedes-Benz, and I started working for Mazda as a technical trainer, teaching adults instead of apprentices. I cut back on the drinking to try to be a more sociable person. I decided that a curry club would be a good idea. I hadn't seen much of my best friend Wayne, Shaun from Land Rover or Andy and

Tristan since we were all so busy with work. The curry night became an instant hit and the five of us met up once a month, despite our busy lives. It was nice to catch up with each other over our favourite food, and it brought us closer together as friends.

I didn't have a lot of friends, just a few close ones. There was Kurt, my drinking buddy and the guy who was responsible for colouring me in. There was Lynn, who I spent time with in the peak district chatting about bikes or just putting the world to rights, and there was Wayne, Andy, Tristan and Shaun, the guys I went motorcycle racing with and who shared my love of Indian food. I ended up being best man for Wayne, Andy, Tristan and Kurt over the years because I could write funny speeches and I was great at organising things. I'd been a best man four times. Four times! All I wanted to be was a bloody bridesmaid. There's no justice in the world. With Lynn, Kurt and my daughter taking up my weekends and the five of us guys meeting once a month for curry night, this was just about all the social interaction I could handle, and I still felt the need to be alone to recharge after spending time with my friends.

The Mazda job lasted two years before I moved to Vauxhall as a young apprentice training manager. It was a hybrid role, meaning I was in charge of the training program but I still did some teaching. It was based in Luton at Vauxhall headquarters, so my commute became even longer, which meant more time alone with my thoughts. A few months into the job I was summoned to Germany for a conference. Raytheon, the company that was contracted to deliver training for Vauxhall, is a huge American company with their fingers in many pies, one of which is defence. The European conference was a yearly chance to meet with people from all over Raytheon's very diverse business portfolio, people that you wouldn't normally come into contact with. I'd been to Germany once before for training with Mazda at their headquarters in Cologne. That trip hadn't gone so well, I got food poisoning from some dodgy chicken in the staff canteen. This time, I'd be travelling to Russelsheim near Frankfurt, with my boss and two other colleagues.

I was discussing the trip with a colleague one day when he gave me some advice. He said, 'the Germans love it when you appreciate their hospitality. Compliment them on the food, they'll love it.' This seemed like a very good plan, and I asked how I'd go about this, as I knew about three words in German, all related to ordering a beer. He said, 'if you are enjoying the food, simply say mmm, das Essen macht mich geil.' I asked him what it meant, and he said, 'das Essen macht mich geil means the food is lovely'. I had no reason to doubt the man standing opposite me, after all, he had no sense of humour that we were aware of, so I memorised my phrase ready for the appropriate moment. We arrived at the conference in our smartest suits. After a few minutes we all filtered into a large boardroom with an enormous oval table made of polished mahogany. The obligatory introductions began, going around the table one by one. I could see that I'd be next, after a very good-looking black guy in a suit that definitely wasn't off the peg in Topman. 'Hi, my name is Clarence, I'm from Ohio but I currently live in Berlin where I head up the Patriot missile programme', he said through his whiter than white perfect teeth. Patriot bloody missiles! How the sodding hell do you top that? 'Hi, my name is Ian, I'm from England and I am the Vauxhall young apprentice training manager', I said in a very shallow voice. I had no love for my testicles back then but even I felt like they shrank just a little bit during those introductions.

Next came lunch. Time to unleash my cunning plan. This would redeem me from being in the shadow of the irritatingly good-looking Clarence and his Patriot penises, or so I thought. I was seated opposite a lovely German woman called Frauke, the operations manager for Raytheon Europe. We were chatting away as the lunch dish arrived, a lovely Pork schnitzel with potatoes and sauerkraut. I took a few bites and it really was tasty. This was it, there was relative quiet around the table, so I seized the moment. 'Mmm. Das Essen macht mich geil!' I said confidently, and with slightly more volume than was needed to reach its intended target of Frauke. There was a short pause before Frauke spat her food out, bursting into uncontrollable laughter. Then, the laughter spread around the table very quickly. Within a few seconds, the entire room was laughing hysterically, at me! After the hysterics died down, I asked Frauke, 'What did I just say?' With tears in her eyes she said, 'you just told me that the food makes you horny!'

The "horny schnitzel" incident was on day one of a three-day conference. Imagine how much mileage my colleagues got out of that little nugget. Bastard!

Despite the humiliation I placed upon myself in Russelsheim, I was doing a pretty good job of managing my small team in the UK and balancing that with teaching my own groups as well. After a while though, the job became a lot more stressful, and I felt that it was time to look for a new challenge. I had an interview at Volkswagen Group UK and was offered the position of Audi Technical trainer. It involved a fifty-five-mile commute from Leicester to Milton Keynes every day, and this meant yet more alone time with my thoughts. I'd think about my dad, my spiralling motorcycle debt, what type of beer to pick up on the way home, and more often than not, why no matter how hard I tried to overcompensate and come across as ultra-masculine, I still couldn't hide from my feelings. What else could I do? I'd jumped out of a plane, I rode a motorcycle, I was covered in tattoos, I'd learned martial arts, built a muscular physique with years of bodybuilding, worked as a race mechanic, and I could fix pretty much anything with wheels and an engine. I was running out of ways to prove my masculinity. The problem was that deep down, I knew that the person I was trying to prove it to the most, was me.

Writing this, I'm trying to remember my fortieth birthday, and I can't. The last time anyone threw a party for me was when I turned eighteen, and that was an awfully long time ago. I hadn't planned to do anything anyway, just let it quietly slip by and hope no one noticed. I probably got drunk alone in the garage and I probably had a curry with my mates at some point but there were no fireworks or group of friends enthusiastically jumping out of the darkness to surprise me. I'm not much of a party person anyway and being the centre of attention is not where I'm at my most comfortable, despite how I make my living. At that point in my life, I had a bright, happy, eight-year-old daughter, a good job, and I found myself in another period in my life where I seemed to have everything under control, sort of. I'd gathered together a little collection of shoes, tights and skirts which sat in a box under my bed. I never wore them, they just sat there. That box was my comfort blanket, my teddy bear. It helped me enormously to just own a few feminine things, it kept me sane, like that pack of cigarettes that smokers trying to quit keep in the kitchen drawer just in case.

Life was going so well that it felt like the right time to start dating again. I had been single for about a year so I decided to try my luck with online dating. I built my profile, added a recent picture of myself that wouldn't look out of place on Crimewatch, and then forgot all about it. A few weeks went by and I hadn't even checked for messages, and then one day I looked in the inbox to find a new message. As I read it a warm feeling came over me, and memories of the past came flooding back. 'Hi, it's Tracey, I'm not sure if you remember me.' Tracey, my first love, the one who took my virginity, (it has since grown back due to a distinct lack of sex) and the woman who was my whole world back when we were teenagers. Of course, I remembered her: it had been twenty years but I'd never forgotten her. I had tried to find her over the years but without success. We did briefly bump into each other in a pub once but I was too shy to say anything other than hi, and I kicked myself for days afterwards for not talking to her properly or giving her my number.

I messaged her back, telling her that I'd never forgotten her, and it would be lovely to meet up even if just for a coffee and a chat. We arranged to go for a drink a few days later and see where it took us. When I walked into the pub garden, there she was, sitting at a table, looking every bit as beautiful as she did when we were in our youth. Our birthdays were just one month apart so I knew she had recently turned forty too, but she barely looked thirty. We hugged and talked for hours before heading back to her house for coffee. As I kissed her cheek on her doorstep, I felt the familiar warmth of her skin and the smell of her perfume, and in that moment, we were eighteen again. I drove home with a mile-wide smile, recalling all the good times we shared in our youth and wondering what the future might hold for us.

Tracey and I spent a lot of time together as the months went by. I sold my motorcycle to try to get a grip on my debt, and I spent less time with Kurt and Lynn (mostly for the good of my liver). Wayne was absent without leave on most curry nights due to his shift patterns, but I still met up with Andy, Shaun and Tristan each month. My job was going well, I'd rekindled my love for Tracey, and our children were getting on well too. The little box of femininity sat under my bed undisturbed, untouched, but never far from my thoughts. One evening when Tracey and I were watching TV with a glass of wine, she asked me if I still wore women's clothing. I had no reason to lie to her so I told her about the box, and that I hadn't touched it in months. She seemed relieved that I'd been completely honest with her and we didn't really talk about it again for quite some time.

After about nine months of dating, Tracey and I decided to move in together. We found a lovely place to rent on the west side of Leicester near the motorway. It was a three-bedroom semi in a nice area with a reasonable rent. Our children would have their own bedrooms and there was a nice back garden for them to play in. I was apprehensive about leaving my mum alone in the house, but I knew I couldn't stay there forever. We made the place look lovely, with a huge trampoline in the garden for the kids, nice new furniture, and pictures on the walls. I painted her son's bedroom blue and my daughter's pink, colours which they chose themselves. We discovered our local pub which was a short walk from the house, met some of the neighbours, and started to get our bearings in our new area.

For a couple of years, our life was fantastic,
but it wasn't long before the cracks started to appear.

Chapter Seven
Pandora's Box

The first couple of years in our lovely house were fantastic. We were happy, settled, and life was good. I can't put my finger on the exact turning point, but I can say with certainty that I was the primary cause because of my moods, my lack of interest in sex, and my avoidance of long-term commitment. Something was stopping me from taking our relationship to the next level. It wasn't Tracey: she's gorgeous, fun to be with and she has a kind heart. Sure, she has her faults but who doesn't? It was me, all me, but I was so blinded by my own problems and insecurities at the time that I couldn't see the damage I was doing to our relationship.

I proposed to Tracey about a year after we got back together, truly believing that she and I would be together forever. The pact that I had previously made with myself to keep my cross-dressing and my inner gender conflict a secret was still relatively intact, and besides, I had been totally honest with Tracey about it. She knew that I had some feminine things stored under the bed, and I had explained to her that it was never going to be anything more than that, I had it under control. Like anyone who has been on the receiving end of a marriage proposal, she expected the next steps to start happening, like planning the wedding, maybe even buying a house instead of renting. I danced around these as much as I could, scared stiff of marriage and being tied into the role of husband and father. It wasn't the commitment to Tracey that bothered me, it was the commitment to living the rest of my life as a man that I couldn't bear, even though at that point in my life, I was unaware that there was even a choice. After a while, arguments started to become more and more frequent, and the atmosphere in the house was becoming harder to live with. Our children were caught up in all this too, and I hated them hearing us taking cheap shots at each other and arguing over the most stupid things. My daughter's mum and I split before she was born, but despite this I have always tried to spend as much time with my daughter as possible. She has always had her own bedroom wherever I lived and growing up she spent most weekends with me. After a while, she started to make excuses not to come at weekends. This got worse over time and eventually it ended in a massive argument with her mum and me. Before long, she wasn't coming to stay at all and didn't want to see me. I was devastated, I didn't know why she couldn't bear to be with her own father. I'd always tried to be the best dad that I could be. What more could I do to make her happy? Children are incredibly perceptive. My daughter is nobody's fool and neither is Tracey's son. Despite our best efforts not to argue in front of them both, they could see that there was tension between us, and they must have heard the late-night arguments long after they'd gone to bed. He would go out into the garden and bounce on the trampoline, or kick a ball around to get away from the atmosphere, but my daughter, I suppose, felt like she couldn't: she just felt uncomfortable, and it was ultimately my fault. Being unable to contact her or spend time with her (on her wishes) broke me, and I fell into a deep depression. I just couldn't see the point in anything.

At work my concentration wasn't the best. I struggled to show any enthusiasm for the subjects I was teaching, and although no one said anything, I'm sure most of my colleagues could see how bad things were. I started to spend time googling things like, "am I a girl" and "male to female" after work or at lunch breaks. I watched countless videos on YouTube of transgender people explaining how they had always known they were trans. Trans? Transgender? I'd never heard of the word. I knew what a cross-dresser was, I begrudgingly identified as one myself, but transgender? Changing your gender so that your body matches the way you feel in your head and your heart? At first, I dismissed it. I thought that I was only feeling this way because I missed my daughter, but the more of these videos I watched, the more I felt like I understood these stories, and I could relate to many of their experiences. I heard the words of Sandra, the lovely lady that had helped me at the Transformation shop, 'This is more than just dressing up for you, isn't it? This is who you are. I can see it in your eyes.' Her words tormented me as I watched video after video, absorbing the information, feeling their pain, and celebrating their euphoria as they emerged from transition. I could see the difference that transition had made to them, not just the obvious physical change, but their smile, the way they communicated, their energy and zest for life. It was clear that transition had been the right choice for them.

During my research I came upon a video that had been posted by a transgender woman called Sona Avedian. It was inevitable really, as I'd watched just about every video related to the subject of transition and transgenderism by this point. Like many of the others, she had created a timeline of her life in pictures, with subtitled narration and some uplifting music from Avril Lavigne in the background (the greatest hits of Slipknot might have given the video a different tone). As the video played, I found myself becoming completely immersed in it, much more than the others. Sona and I had lived similar lives, overcompensating to extremes, trying so desperately to prove our masculinity, not just to our family, friends and colleagues but ultimately to ourselves. She was a self-confessed petrolhead like me and played the joker so that people would like her, just as I had done from a very early age. The only difference in our stories was that she had served as a U.S Marine as a young man. The closest I ever got to military service was playing with my Action Man when I was a kid. By the mid-point of the video, she explained that she'd got married and had a daughter, and lots of photos of a proud father with his little girl were shown one after another. At this point I broke down. I was shaking, I started crying, partly in sympathy for her story, partly for how much I missed my own daughter. The more I watched through my tears, the more I was beginning to piece together my life, seeing it laid out in my mind like a jigsaw puzzle. Toward the end of the video, Sona showed herself in early transition, looking so happy, despite still looking somewhat masculine at such an early stage. It ended with pictures of her after transition, looking slim, beautifully feminine and radiantly happy. By this point, I was a total mess. I felt a complete connection with this woman's life, and yet still my instinct was to deny it. I drove home in shock, not knowing what to think or what to do. I couldn't be transgender, could I?

    I barely spoke to Tracey that night. I went to bed and laid awake all-night thinking about what I'd seen. Although I didn't know it at the time, that incredible woman, Sona Avedian, saved my life. She made me understand what being transgender meant, and showed me that transition was possible, even for an angry looking bald guy covered in tattoos. I don't know how many lives she saved as a U.S Marine, but she sure as hell saved mine.

    In the days and weeks that followed, I grew more and more depressed. The absence of my daughter from my life was killing me, and my after-work personal research had uncovered truths that I wasn't ready to accept. I had opened Pandora's box, and whether I liked it or not, there was no way to close it, and no way to deny how I felt. I've been in some desperately dark places before, but until that point, I had never actually considered planning my suicide. The thought of ending my life became almost an obsession, although I never told anyone. Part of my journey home from my workplace in Milton Keynes took me along a stretch of the A5 near Rugby in Leicestershire. It's an arrow straight mile or so from the industrial estates of Daventry, before climbing uphill toward the village of Watford, near Watford Gap services. I found myself thinking about ending my life almost daily, and how easy it would be to crash my car, leaving this world almost instantly if I got it right. With clinical precision, I drove along that stretch of road each day, working out how fast I'd need to go to ensure I didn't survive, and where the best place would be to crash. This wasn't a cry for help, I never told anyone. I just wanted to die, to end my pain and the pain I was causing my daughter, my partner and her son.

I don't remember exactly what day it was; the days had begun to blur into each other, but I decided that on that day, I was going to die. I didn't write a note, I didn't put my affairs in order, I just left the house, went to work and did my job like any other day, void of any emotion and dead inside. Driving home, I didn't cry, I didn't think of anything, other than that straight piece of road, which was always busy with trucks. All I needed to do was reach around seventy miles an hour before turning my wheels into the path of an oncoming truck. I came off the last roundabout and started to accelerate. Truck after truck passed me as they headed towards the warehouses of the industrial estates or the M1 motorway. Just as I reached the speed I had so callously calculated, I started to cry. The tears just kept flowing; I couldn't stop them. I was coming to my senses, and in doing so I realised the selfishness of my plan, potentially killing or injuring an innocent truck driver, or at least leaving them with mental scars that would last a lifetime. I pulled the car over and sat there crying for at least an hour. I was broken, I had no will to live, no hope, and no plan for the future. I felt lost and completely alone.

I never told Tracey about that day. When I got home, I made some weak excuse about having hay fever to cover the fact that my eyes were red and swollen, and my white shirt was wet with fresh tears. The arguments at home began to get worse. I was withdrawn and quiet, and Tracey saw this as indifference towards her. Our lives had become dull and boring. We went to the pub most Fridays and would make it our mission to get drunk. I usually visited my mum on Saturday morning while Tracey exercised at home. On Sunday, we did the food shopping. One Sunday, after doing the weekly shop, we were unpacking the bags in the kitchen. Tracey had been quite frosty on the car ride home, but this wasn't all that unusual, so I thought nothing of it. As we put the groceries away in the cupboards and the fridge, I could hear her behind me slamming cupboard doors and huffing and puffing. I turned round to ask her what the matter was. 'You know exactly what the matter is' she said, with venom in her eyes and anger in her voice. I had absolutely no idea what the matter was, so I asked again, 'what do you mean?'. She said that she was sick of seeing me eying up women every time we went to the supermarket. It made her feel ugly and unattractive and I was a bastard for making her feel that way. She said it was obvious that I didn't find her attractive anymore if I could look at other women but couldn't bring myself to sleep with her. 'You might as well go and fuck them, because you don't seem to want to fuck me', she cried, with pain in her voice and tears rolling down her cheeks. My heart sank. She was right, I did eye up women, but not for the reasons that she had concluded. I was envious of them, what they wore, how they walked, the way they wore their hair. I longed to be like them, to feel what it is to be a woman, to live my life as a woman, the way I felt inside, the way I'd always felt. I slammed a packet of chocolate Hob-Nobs down on the counter, and without turning to look at her, or even considering the consequences of the words that were about to leave my mouth, I blurted out, 'I don't want to fuck those women, I want to *be* them'.

The silence that followed was deafening. I started crying, deep sobs that I had no control over. I went into the lounge and stood at the window. Tracey came up behind me, putting her arms around my waist, and with softness and compassion in her voice, she asked why I hadn't told her this before. I didn't know what to say, I told her about the research I had done and how I felt that I wasn't just a cross-dresser, and that I had realised that it was much more than that. After forty-two years on this god forsaken planet, I had finally worked out that I am, and always have been, a woman.

In the days that followed Tracey and I barely spoke. When we did it was to argue over the most trivial things. I was angry with myself and moody all the time. One day, a work colleague stopped me as I was walking into the office and said, 'I don't know what's troubling you, but you look dead behind your eyes. Where has Ian gone?' She was right, I was emotionless, or what little emotion I did have was just sadness and despair. I felt so alone, I didn't feel that I could talk to Tracey, I'd put her through enough already. I couldn't talk to my family or friends because none of them knew anything about how I felt, how I'd always felt, because I'd hidden it so well for most of my life. I had no one to talk or share my thoughts and feelings with.

At my lowest point, I decided to write a journal to try and make sense of what was happening to me. I didn't write every day, only when I had something I wanted to say, or there was a specific date or event that I needed to record. I wanted to be able to look back on it as a measure of my progress in the future, although at the time I wasn't even sure I had a future. I would like to share that journal with you. It isn't terribly well written, just the ramblings of a person struggling to cope with the realisation that something was very wrong with their whole existence. These are my thoughts and experiences from that time, before transition began, and before I'd even decided that transition was right for me.

Let's start at the beginning, at the point where I had decided it would be better for everyone if I did nothing about my recent self-discovery. At that point, I was still adamant that I would stick to my plan, keeping my secret and taking it to the grave. No one except Tracey could ever know that I believed in my heart that I was a woman. Sona may have opened my eyes to who I was inside, but I still felt that my responsibilities as a man outweighed that, and I owed it to my daughter, to Tracey, and to everyone to carry on, however hard it had become.

Journal foreword:

This journal is solely for the purpose of documenting what I now believe to be gender dysphoria, and how it manifests itself within me on a daily basis. I have decided to write down my thoughts and feelings in the hope that I can make sense of it all and make the right decisions. Life is short, and we all deserve to be happy and live our lives according to what feels correct within us. After forty-two years, I am finally ready to say it, I am transgender, I am a woman.

The question is, what to do about it…

Just writing the words "I am transgender, I am a woman" gave me so much relief. Even if no other living soul would ever read them. The foreword of my own private journal became a self-declaration, an admittance that I'd previously denied myself. In order to move forward with my life, I had to be honest with myself about how I felt, and who I was. I had taken my first step. As the weeks went on, my resolve to do nothing about my feelings became too much to bear. I knew that something needed to change sooner or later. I'd either take my own life, or I'd face my demons and seek the help I needed to transition. I was so confused, consumed and conflicted. My heart just wanted to be free. I wanted to be able to live my life and express my femininity, but it meant hurting everyone I held close, and potentially losing everything.

Friday February 20th, 2015

Having come out to my partner around three months ago, things at home are understandably tense. She has been supportive, but at the same time feels vulnerable and uncertain about our future. She is also going through some health issues of her own which have affected her hormone balance and as such she can be angry much of the time.

I have done as much research into what it means to be transgender as I possibly can, and every fibre of my being wants to transition, but this is not an easy decision to make because I feel like I'm letting everybody down. They all know Ian, and I assume they like him. My problem is that the Ian they know is just a lie, an act or a front that I put on every day to try to fit in as a male. This isn't new, it's how it's always been. I have told my partner that I will definitely not transition, and I am trying my hardest to keep my word on that despite my strong urges to be the woman I truly feel that I am. Life is not always fair and if I have to remain in this empty male shell then I will have to find a way to be at peace with it, but I cannot make any guarantee to anyone that I will be able to do that. I have seriously considered suicide and I know I should value my life, even if it is based on a lie, but I've had overwhelming thoughts of how much easier it would be for everyone if I were dead.

I hate feeling like this, and I wish for a day not filled with thoughts of despair and longing to be a woman. It's as if in coming out and finally admitting I am transgender; I have somehow slammed a door behind me in my mind and I can't go back. In some ways this has offered relief, but in others it has replaced denial, suppression and overcompensation, with despair and even more self-loathing. I hope for better times ahead, starting with seeing my doctor next week. I will document the outcomes after my appointment.

The decision to seek help from my doctor was made during a conversation with Tracey. She could see that I was barely coping, and something was about to give way. She was the one who suggested that I speak to someone, although neither of us knew what I should say or even what good it would do. At least it offered hope, hope that he would see what I see, and wave some magic NHS wand which would turn me into a fairy princess (still deluded). On Monday, I called the surgery and made an appointment for the following Friday. It felt like the longest week of my life, filled with excitement, worry, nervousness and fear. I had no idea what I would say to this man or woman. All I knew was that

I had to say something, because I couldn't take much more.

Friday February 27th, 2015

The last week has been the hardest yet, with constant arguments at home and overwhelming thoughts of ending my life during the time I have to sit and think at work. At the lowest point, I lost my temper during an argument with Tracey and put my fist through our living room door. I hate the fact that I lost my temper but, in a way, it has led to a better understanding from her of what I'm going through. I wish I could help her to come to terms with it as I'm having to, but as yet I don't know how. I'm hoping that my doctor will refer me to a gender clinic, and when I get to see the gender therapist, he or she will have some ideas of how to help her deal with this, how to help both of us. The doctor's appointment is this afternoon after work and I have spent the whole day feeling scared and nervous, not knowing what to say when I get in the room. Tracey has agreed to come in with me so hopefully that will help.

Post appointment…

The appointment went well, better than expected. The doctor looked quite young and I hoped that this would mean he would have an open mind to my problems. He seemed completely unshaken by the fact that I just told him that I thought I was transgender. I answered his questions about why I felt this way, and he asked some questions about my sexuality, I'm not sure why. Anyway, the outcome was very positive. He has agreed to refer me to the gender clinic in Daventry at the Danetre hospital. They have around a twelve-week waiting list so I'm hoping I can use that time to start to gather my thoughts ready for the therapist's questions.

I feel very relieved that the visit to the doctor is over with, I was dreading it, but it was nowhere near as bad as I thought it would be. Since then, I am feeling a lot better about my dysphoria and thoughts of doing something stupid have begun to leave my head. I don't know what the future holds, but at least I'm now going to get the help I need, because burying my head in the sand clearly isn't working.

The young doctor was seemingly unshaken by my revelations, but like many doctors he had little training in gender matters, so he was unsure of what to do. Thankfully, I had researched the process thoroughly. I handed him a piece of paper with the details of the gender clinic and asked him to refer me to them. Back in 2015, the gender clinic at Daventry was a newly opened unit, and as such their waiting list was very short. Currently, the average waiting time to be seen by a gender clinic for a first referral appointment is around three to four years. Not weeks, not months - years. There are less than a dozen gender clinics in the UK at the time of writing, with around 14,000 trans and gender diverse people waiting to be seen. It doesn't take a skilled mathematician to work out that this is woefully inadequate. The suicide rate for transgender people in the UK is around 48%, almost half. Many of those suicide attempts, successful or not, occur while the individual is waiting to be seen by a gender identity clinic.

Thursday March 12th, 2015

I called the gender clinic yesterday to ask if they had received my referral letter from the surgery, they had not. This upset me a little as it feels like I am not making any progress now that I have decided to take this massive step to seek help and maybe even to begin transition. It feels like I'm in limbo, stuck in this body with no means of doing anything to fix it until the letter from the gender clinic drops through the door with that magical appointment date. Instead of being miserable, I took matters into my own hands, (as any self-respecting girl would) and called the surgery to remind them of the procedure for referral and where to send the letter. The receptionist had the letter, which had been dictated by the doctor but not sent. After two weeks! Really? The receptionist told me that the letter will be posted today so next week around this time I will call the gender clinic to ensure it has arrived.

Friday March 20th, 2015

Today I called the clinic to ask if they have received my referral, which they have, so now the waiting starts. I guess this is my twelve-week countdown timer. The last week or so I have kind of been in guy mode. By that I mean I felt like I needed to display very male behaviour, trying hard to be one of the lads. These patches never last long though and soon enough I'm back with those old familiar feminine thoughts and feelings. I was playing old songs from the "Grease" movie soundtrack this morning on the way to work, with tears rolling down my cheeks. Last week it was Iron Maiden at maximum volume. Only a trans person can understand the cruelty that gender dysphoria places on you. No matter how badly you feel about your gender, and the body you are stuck with, once in a while you go into such deep denial that you start to question if you are actually trans at all, then a few days later, the realisation and the pain returns. I just hope that someday soon I can begin to be my true self. I can't go on living like this, it's tearing me apart.

Tuesday April 14th, 2015

Things at home with my partner are going from bad to worse. I am constantly angry and moody and cannot give a definitive reason why. We haven't had sex in a couple of months and that is becoming a real problem for her, but I just have no sex drive. In the two and a half years we have been together we haven't had much sex anyway, but it is getting worse. Looking back over my past relationships, that has always been the case. I guess at the beginning I want sex when it's all new and exciting, but after a while I start to make excuses to avoid it. I have told her that when we have sex it somehow doesn't feel right for me, I feel wrong or uncomfortable in the male role during sex. She thinks that it shouldn't matter, and that trans or not there is no reason why I can't enjoy sex. I wish I knew how to tell her what it feels like to hate your body and physical gender so much, that you can't face using that body to give and receive pleasure.

    Looking back over my life with this fresh perspective, I have had a lot of relationships, something I'm not proud of. They were never trophies or bragging rights to my friends, just failures on my part. I never really committed to anyone, and if I'm honest I used those women to be close to femininity. Subconsciously, I felt the need to be close to a female because I couldn't be a female. I treated all my ex-partners more like friends than lovers, and now I'm starting to see why. What worries me is that this fact, coupled with some recent dreams I've had where I have a boyfriend who takes me out on dates, could suggest that my sexuality may not be as straightforward as I thought. One thing I do know completely, is that I am not a gay man. I may be a straight or pansexual woman, but I am certainly not a gay man. I suppose only time and HRT (hormone replacement therapy) will make things clearer for me but for now, I'm focussed only on my gender dysphoria and the process that will follow to resolve that.

Wednesday May 6th, 2015

I've just been away to Germany on a work event, and although it was a busy four days, the thoughts in my head were just as bad if not worse. Being away from all my feminine things felt alien to me, even if they mostly sit in a box under the bed. They're like a comfort blanket, and knowing they are there is helpful. The train of thought that led to my discovery that I have gender dysphoria has opened my eyes and made me look back at my life, at all the choices I made, either with girls or jobs or money. I spent so much time and money creating distractions in an attempt to be normal like my friends. Only now can I see clearly how unhappy and alone I really was. The person my friends and colleagues all know is a fake, a character I play every day to get by, to appear "normal". I don't want to act this way, I certainly don't want to look this way, everything about me is fake. I can't even stand hearing my own name or being referred to with male pronouns.

It seems at home that my partner thinks that because I've been trying to act more male for her, that things are getting back on track, but they are not. I hate my role in this relationship and long to be seen as the female that I am, or at least feel that I am. Only the clinic can help me now. I feel very sad and very alone. I'm not sure how much longer I can do this. I am not a man, that much is clear to me, and having to behave as one when you feel the opposite, is cruel and painful.

Reading through these journal entries, I can see how the decision to take my secret to the grave and seek help to live with my feelings evolved into a desperate longing to begin transition. Throughout March, April and May, life was a mix of hope, despair and loneliness. Hope that the clinic could help, despair because I felt like I was close to breaking point, and loneliness, because I still didn't have a single soul to talk to about how I felt. Every day at work all I could think about was getting home to see if there was a letter in the post from the gender clinic. The day couldn't come soon enough. After what seemed like an eternity, the postman delivered the letter that would change my life forever.

Friday May 29th, 2015

The letter has finally arrived with my first appointment, July 3rd at 10.30am. I'm excited but scared in equal measure, so to distract myself, I have begun work on my coming out letter. I am not going to rush it as it will be the most important and probably the hardest letter I've ever written. I want it to explain what gender dysphoria is, how it has affected me and what I intend to do about it. I know it will mean losing people from my life, but while this makes me sad, I also think that if I knew they were transphobic or had such closed views on the subject, then perhaps I wouldn't have chosen them as friends in the first place. So yes, there will be collateral damage, and life will be tough, but I know in my heart that it is all worth it, and that I will be a better person for it. I just hope that one day my daughter will want to see me again, and accept me for who I am.

Friday July 3rd, 2015

Today was my first appointment at the gender clinic. I wore a grey skater dress I got from new look, and some patent brogue style shoes with a heel. Tracey helped me to put on some makeup and she came with me for moral support. I saw a man called Dr Stevens who was absolutely lovely. What a nice funny and understanding man. I was so nervous before I went in, but he made me feel at ease and we even laughed a few times along the way. He asked about my family and where I sit in the grand scheme of things, how many siblings I have, their ages etc. He asked about my daughter and my mother too. We talked at length about my partner Tracey and how this has affected our relationship. He also asked how I felt, and when the realisation hit me that I am transgender. That was an easy one to answer, and by the end of the appointment I kind of got the impression that I certainly hadn't told him anything he hadn't heard before.

The next steps are to wait for an appointment with a clinical psychologist. In order to be diagnosed with gender dysphoria, a diagnosis must be made by two experts separately, hence the second appointment. I think it is fair to say that the ball is well and truly rolling now. Next week I will finalise my coming out letter, but I'm not sending it out until I'm ready. I know it's early days, but I am already feeling better. I just have the hurdle of convincing Tracey that this is the right thing to do now.

It's been five years since I last read these journal entries. I wish I'd handled the situation with Tracey better, she deserved better, but I never meant to hurt her. She's a wonderful woman and if I could wind back the clock and find a way to have got to this point without causing her any pain then I'd have taken it in a heartbeat. In hindsight, our relationship would have probably ended at some point in the future anyway, because we just didn't make each other happy. She wanted commitment and to feel safe and secure, and to know where the future was going; who wouldn't? I wanted to bury my head in the sand and avoid any commitment that I couldn't easily back out of, subconsciously hoping that one day I could be who I wanted to be perhaps. Similarly, losing my daughter for those years hurt so much that I felt like there was no point living. Any fight I had in me to keep up appearances and soldier on with the father, brother, son routine had long since left. To this day, my daughter and I have never really spoken about that time, and we probably never will.

So here we are. The beginning and the end. The beginning of a new adventure, as I began to learn more about my true self, and the woman that I had finally realised it was possible to become, and the end, of a life I so desperately longed to leave behind. I began to say goodbye to my old self. I was never happy as a man, nor even as a boy when I was young, so saying goodbye to the empty shell that I had become over the years was cathartic. It was a strange and confusing time, filled with wonder and fear for the unknown, but also with arguments, bitterness and resentment. The decision to transition, and the beginning of that process, was in many ways, the hardest time of my life. I had such a huge task ahead of me, a mountain to climb and no clue how to do it. I didn't know any other trans people and I still had no one to confide in or ask for help. As the process I had embarked upon began to take shape, my biggest fear was people's reaction when I came out to them. Only time would tell how that would go.

Chapter Eight
Was it something I said?

The conflict that was raging in my head over the absolute need to transition, versus doing what was best for my partner, my family, friends and career, began to fade almost into insignificance as time marched on. It was as if I had accepted my fate. I knew that even if I decided not to transition and once again bury my feelings in male bullshit and overcompensation, that it would eventually lead me back to the same place. Thoughts of suicide had filled my head for long enough: there had to be a solution, a way to be happy while making sure that everyone else was too. I didn't want to lose everything, but I knew that something big had to change if I had any hope of living a life where I could be comfortable with who I am.

It wasn't because I didn't care what everyone thought, or that I had no interest in anyone else's feelings but my own, it was just that I couldn't be the person they wanted me to be any longer. I was exhausted. I stopped caring if anyone saw through me or not and my behaviour was becoming defiant of the role of the man that I'd played for so many years. I began to let my guard down, showing my true colours. People were starting to notice the cracks in my armour, manifesting as a perpetual sadness and indifference towards things that I once had such great enthusiasm for. My daughter was still refusing to see me, and I couldn't see an end to that situation, despite the hope that one day she would change her mind. My relationship with my partner was broken, in fact it was pretty much irreparable at this point. We had reached a point where we wanted entirely different things from our lives. She didn't sign up for the situation she found herself in, and I hated myself for putting her and her son in it, despite the fact that I never intended things to end up where they had. She is a straight woman, and the prospect of a lesbian relationship with a trans woman was understandably not on her radar. It was only a matter of time before the inevitable end of our relationship would come about.

My focus shifted away from managing the situation at home, treading on eggshells and avoiding arguments, to planning my future. I had no clear goals at that time, just hopes and dreams. I knew I wasn't ready for transition; it is a massive undertaking, but I had to do something to regain a sense of control over my life.

I started by choosing a name. If you are a parent, then you will know how difficult it is to choose a name for your new-born child. Choosing a new name for yourself is equally problematic, and a concept that not many people have to undertake. In my usual way, I researched and researched until I'd come up with a shortlist. Baby name websites are great for this task. At this point I would like to add a note of caution to any trans people who are reading this, and are about to choose a new name for themselves. Consider the consequences of your choice. Lavender Chlamydia Tinkerton sounds lovely as it rolls off your tongue in your YouTube makeup vlogs. It would be a wonderful name for your pet guinea pig too, but when it's flashing across a giant LED screen at the doctor's surgery or blasting out of the speaker system in Asda, 'Lavender Tinkerton to customer services please,' it doesn't sound quite so cute.

"What's in a name? That which we call a rose, by any other name would smell as sweet."

William Shakespeare

Over the course of a few months, I went through dozens of names. I tried using them to describe myself on my journey home from work. The first choice was Lola. I love the name, but for a few different reasons, it just didn't fit. Firstly, it sounded too young for a woman in her forties. That is important. Is your chosen name age appropriate? Secondly, while driving home from work one day, the Kinks began to play on local radio. The song "Lola" is about a guy who meets a cross-dresser in a soho club. It isn't exactly respectful to the trans community, and I doubt you will find it on many trans women's Spotify playlists if you know what I mean, so that one was dropped pretty quickly.

Next up was Charlotte, or Charlie for short. I liked this a lot and it ended up being a close-run thing with my chosen name. Something just didn't feel right with it in the end. It may have been down to the fact that at the time I was chatting quite a bit with a trans woman called Charlie Martin, who has gone on to become a successful female racing driver, and a wonderful advocate for trans people in sport.

This toing and froing with names went on for some time. I went through names like Laura, Julia, Hannah, Imogen and several more I can't even remember now. One day I was driving home in my little bubble of thought as usual, when "Back to Black" by Amy Winehouse came on the radio. I have loved Amy's music since the first time I heard it many years ago, and I've been a fan ever since. Her tragic passing back in 2011 left me feeling physically sick and heartbroken. As was often the case, a tear fell from my cheek as the song played, and this got me thinking, Amy, short, only two syllables like Ian. This would be easier for people who knew me, and would have to get used to addressing me with a different name in the future. I looked it up to see how age appropriate it was, and sure enough it was the fifth most popular baby name for girls in the year I was born. I also looked up the meaning. Its origins are French, and it means "beloved" although the French spelling Aimee has way too many vowels in it for my liking.

For a few weeks I kept using the name to myself in the car or when no one was around, and it just felt right. It fitted, I liked hearing it and it didn't make me cringe in any scenario I could imagine it being used to address me. Choosing a middle name was easy. My middle name is Kate, just like my grandmother's. Her name was Dorothy Kate; she died of cancer when my mum was just five years old. I never met my grandmother, so Kate is a tribute to her memory, something that my mum absolutely adores. The final job was to decide on a surname. Some trans people want to move away from the life they once knew, starting a whole new life and identity in a new town or city, and in some cases even a new country. Most don't take such drastic steps, remaining in their old town, old job, and old circle of friends. The decision to change your surname is a very personal one. In my case, I could have chosen to take my mother's maiden name, as she was now a widow, but that didn't feel right to me at all. As I have explained in previous chapters, my dad adopted me when I was three, so that I could have the same surname as my mum and dad after they married. He raised me as his own child and never once complained about that responsibility. How could I disrespect the effort and love that he put into raising me, by discarding our family name? In the end, it became a simple choice: Amy Kate Carter. I love how it sounds, and I love that I can use Amy Kate or just Amy. Some of my close friends call me aims, which annoyed me at first, but I'm fine with it now as it was pointed out to me that people often shorten your name not out of laziness, but because of the familiarity and comfort of their relationship with you.

It felt really good to have taken some positive steps towards my eventual goal of transition. I was beginning to get my shit together and for the first time, I felt like there was hope. I still didn't know what the hell I was doing, and I guess I was learning as I went along, but with each passing day came a step forward. I decided that it was time to take the plunge and come out to people. By this point I knew that my future would involve transition, so there was no point in hiding anymore. My plan was to tread softly, choosing to come out to my boss and work colleagues first, then my friends and family, and finally my daughter.

August 27th, 2015

My second appointment came through yesterday, so I thought I'd write down my thoughts. I have an appointment to see the clinical psychiatrist on November 2nd. My partner Tracey understandably feels that things are moving too fast, and I can understand where she is coming from. She doesn't want me to transition, despite the support she has given me, so if I start now, or in three years' time, it will always be too soon for her. In other news, I came out to my boss Terry after work today. He was naturally shocked, but acted very professionally. He is going to support me and help me to come out to everyone at work when the time is right.

I remember the day I came out to my boss Terry, as if it were yesterday. I'd worked at Volkswagen Group UK for six years by this point, so I was a well-established senior trainer and pretty much everyone who worked there knew me. I asked him if he could spare half an hour at the end of the day, and I arranged to meet him in my classroom. I think he expected me to hand in my notice, having found another job, but he definitely didn't expect what was about to happen. I'd been really nervous all day, sitting alone at lunch and avoiding the usual chatter over coffee breaks. He came into the room characteristically on time, and with notepad in hand, he sat at the desk, looking at me expectantly. By now I felt sick, my nerves were getting the better of me and I knew I needed to get this done before I lost my nerve, so I just blurted it out. 'Terry, there's no easy way to say this, I'm transgender.' After he picked his jaw up from the desk, he nervously asked me how it would affect my work, and what my long-term plan was. After a lengthy explanation, and some awkward questions, we shook hands, and he was gone. I sat at my desk for at least an hour, just taking in the gravity of what I'd just done. It was out there now; Tracey and a handful of medical professionals were no longer the only people who knew I was trans. Considering the fact that Terry had never met a trans person before me, and was fairly new to the role of manager at the time, he handled the situation brilliantly.

September 1st, 2015

My boss Terry has told the senior managers here at Volkswagen about my situation. They have been fine about it and have also offered their support. I'm hoping that when I come out properly to everyone, that this reaction is typical of most people. So, the next big hurdle is coming out to friends, family and colleagues. I plan to do it all in the same week if possible. The only exception will be my daughter, as I am not currently seeing her, for reasons I'd rather leave out of this journal. I'm hoping that the situation will sort itself in time, but for now there is no point in further fuelling the flames by dropping this bombshell on her.

September 11th, 2015

My boss Terry has scheduled a meeting for 3.30pm next Friday, so that I can come out to the Audi team. I guess I need to finish my coming out letter pretty quickly. I have been working on it on and off for a few months now, so there are no excuses. I'm really nervous about coming out to my team, but at the same time, I can't wait to tell them. It's the first step to coming out to everyone in my life, which I really want to do now. I will write again next Friday after the meeting, to record how it went.

Coming out is never easy for anyone - gay, lesbian, transgender, Marmite enthusiast, whatever. Telling the people that you hold dearest that you aren't what they thought you are is hard, and there are no rules on how to do it. Some sit down with their family and friends for a chat over a meal, some write a letter or an email, some throw a party, coming out to the world in a shower of glitter, balloons and gluten free cupcakes. I chose to write a letter. I felt that this was the only way that I could get my thoughts and feelings across without missing important information which could make the situation even more challenging for everyone.

When I had finally chosen a name, I had all the elements I needed to finish the letter. The letter was emailed to all my colleagues at Volkswagen Group UK, some two hundred people. It was planned to coincide with the meeting with my Audi team mates, a team which I'd been a part of since 2011. I made several photocopies for my close friends, my siblings, my mum and my daughter. This is the letter that signified the beginning of my transition. Once I had told everyone what I needed to do and why, there was no way to unpick it, and hell would freeze over before I would want to.

To my friends, family and colleagues,

I have taken great care in writing this letter, because what I want from the outset, is to pre-emptively explain the things you may wish to know, and to answer the questions you will most likely want to ask. Regardless of my wishes and best intentions, there will remain things that you do not know, and there will remain questions that need asking. All I can say is that I will try as hard as I can to explain everything fully.

The reason I am taking so much care, putting so much effort into making sure that what I say is what I really and truthfully want to say, is because I am writing to you all to tell you that I am transgender. If you saw this coming, that's great! To be honest in the last few months I haven't tried so hard to hide it. If you didn't, please read on so that I can explain to you all what this means.

All my life, I have felt that something was wrong. I have always felt wrong in my own body, like I didn't fit in, as though the world I live in seemed somehow alien to me, and did not fit at all with what was happening around me and happening to me. This condition is called gender dysphoria. It is both biological and chemical, caused during foetal formation by what scientists believe to be hormonal irregularities. My brain has physically developed as a woman's, but it's in the body of a man, and it has been this way for the entirety of my existence, regardless of how I've been raised, or how my life experiences have influenced me.

Imagine for a second what that would be like. Imagine yourself, in the opposite body, and unable to do anything about it. You see the world as a man or woman, but have to live as a woman or a man, trying to meet the expectations of society, having to behave and fit in with the gender that you outwardly portray. Everything about your existence is laced with lies, and there's nothing that you can do about it. This is how it is for me, how it's always been for me. If you've always seen me as a 'blokey' bloke with the motorbikes, tattoos, martial arts etc. then I guess it means I'm a good faker. I'm sorry if this makes you feel betrayed, or wronged, that was never my intention.

For years, I felt that there was nothing I could do about how I felt, and so for years I didn't intend to do anything about it. Unsurprisingly, this didn't work. Being transgender, as I have found, is not a habit you can break, a mind-set you can force your way out of, or something you can treat with psychotherapy or drugs. It is a genetic condition, that will never ever change.

I haven't always known it was possible to transition. In fact, until recently, I had never even heard of the word "transgender". Believe me, it was quite a shock to finally discover why I'd always felt so sad, alone and disconnected from the world. So, the time has come to do something about it. I am transitioning from male to female. It's the only cure for my condition, and despite being scared to death, I am strong enough to take it on. It means that at some point in the future, I will no longer be living as or identifying as a male. It means that I will be undergoing hormone replacement therapy to cancel out my body's male hormones, replacing them with female ones. It means that I will be physically developing as a female. In short, it means that I will be, a female.

It also means that I will be undergoing a long process to change my official documentation, in order to reflect my female identity, which will include a change of name. Soon enough, my name will be legally changed to Amy. After many hours agonising over what name to pick, Amy just feels right to me. My middle name will be Kate, after my late grandmother, and so I can go by Amy or Amy Kate.

Above all the rest, this is the part I want people to understand the most. This is the part where

I'm going to pour my heart out, and where I'm probably going to cry a lot. I want to make it clear that this is not a choice. I am not deciding to become a girl. This is me allowing myself to be who I already am, but openly and outwardly. It is the only route that I can take, because I am tired of lying about who I am. In transitioning from male to female, I am going to become a second-class citizen in the eyes of many people. I am going to be opening myself up to discrimination and hate. I am going to jeopardize my job security. I am opening myself up to abandonment and rejection by my partner, our children, my family and my friends, which is not something that I would choose to do unless I felt that there was no choice.

Coming to terms with this has been the hardest thing I've ever done, and it has constantly sent me into periods of depression and loneliness. Nearly every personal problem that I've had over the course of my life, can be traced back almost certainly, to supressed gender identity issues. Coming to this realisation, and finding acceptance within myself, has taken years, and even after that, the fear and uncertainty of what to do about it made me desperately unhappy.

Coming out and actually telling someone 'I'm transgender' was a prospect far too scary to even consider. Instead, I withdrew inside myself, jealous of people braver than me, full of self-pity, and all because I was too scared to just tell someone that there was something wrong with me. It took being completely at rock bottom and beaten, for me to finally tell my partner Tracey, who has been far more supportive than I deserve. I've put her through hell this last year or so, and for that I'm truly sorry. Despite how scary it was, and despite how scary it still is, it will get easier, and that's why now I'm able to close my eyes, hold my breath, and send this to all of you; something that I wasn't sure I'd ever be able to do.

I'm writing this letter to everyone in my life, so that you can all know what I'm going through, because I feel like it would be unfair for you not to know. I know you didn't ask for me to spill my heart out like this, and I know it may be shocking to even hear it. I don't expect you to write back with encouragement, give me three cheers or be my personal support group. I just don't want to give people the wrong impression of me anymore, and this letter is my first step in showing you who I really am. If this means you don't want to talk to me, or be around me anymore, that's okay. I really do understand. I can't ask for acceptance from everyone. I don't even expect it. I just want everyone to know who I am and why.

For the near future, know that my transition is underway. Things will be changing about my dress, my mannerisms, my voice, and my looks, but keep in mind that underneath it all I'm still the same person. Same likes, same dislikes, same jokes (sorry, not sorry), same tastes. I know it's going to be strange and different, and I know most of you have never had to go through this before. It's okay, neither have I. I know there will be awkward situations. I know I'll be accidentally called Ian and referred to as a male, and I know it will feel weird having to correct yourself when it comes to these things. I expect it, and I'm fine with it. I also expect questions, lots and lots of questions, and I want them to be asked without fear. I'm an understanding person, and I understand how weird this might be for some of you; I want to minimize that as much as I can for everyone's sake.

I'm writing this to all of my family, friends and colleagues, but it is the people that I've known the longest that this will affect the most. People who I've known since my childhood, who have seen me grow as a person, and seen me change in many different ways, but never like this. I do feel like I should say sorry to you for keeping this a secret for so long, for building up a wall between us that I led you to believe didn't exist. I'm not sorry for who I am, but I am sorry for who I made you believe I was.

We only get one short life, and everyone deserves the right to live it as their authentic true self. Since coming to terms with all of this, I'm already a happier person. I am taking my life into my own hands, and I'm going to live it the way that I deserve to live it. This is my life, my story, and this is the next chapter, I hope you will all be part of it.

Thank you for reading

Amy-to-be, Ian-for-now

Reading that back as I added it to this chapter brought tears to my eyes. Not tears of sadness, but tears of pride for getting through the toughest fight I've ever faced. I can look back over five long years at the journey I made, and the changes that made Ian fade away and Amy come to life. This undertaking was far beyond anything I'd ever faced in my life before. It was a process that saved my life but ultimately, my life would have been far easier if I had been comfortable with the gender to which I was born, leading a happy life without ever considering or doubting my gender identity. Nobody chooses to be transgender, it's just something that some of us were born with. Whether we transition at some point in our lives, or take our secret to the grave, none of us chose this, our fate was sealed before the umbilical cord was even cut.

September 22nd, 2015

Last Friday, I came out at work. I was so nervous, but the reaction from my team was amazing, and they have offered me so much love and support. The rest of the teams found out yesterday, and the story has been much the same. I have received nothing but love and understanding. I feel so happy at the moment; it feels like forty-three years of pain have been washed away with one act of bravery. It has given me hope that my family will also come to terms with it, but only time will tell. My mum moves into her new home in two weeks' time, so I am waiting to tell them all when the move is over.

My apprehension over coming out at work turned out to be unnecessary. The majority of my colleagues were incredibly supportive. The next morning, as I walked into the canteen to get my usual latte, some of the women from the office (whom I barely knew) approached me to tell me that the letter had made them cry, and that I had their full support. This of course made me cry. A couple of my fellow trainers popped into my classroom at various points of the day to tell me that they had no idea what I was going through, but that they had my back, which was lovely. One colleague called Nick awkwardly commented that I had, 'balls of steel for doing this' to which I replied that it was a shame that I didn't need them. I could literally see him making a conscious decision in his head over whether it was appropriate to laugh at my joke or not, and at that moment, I knew that I'd never be treated the same again. Even now that my transition is over, guys talk to me like they're humouring my choice to live as a woman. They will address me as a female and treat me with respect, but they don't instinctively see me as one. This is clear in their behaviour. A good example is my colleagues at work. The guys will joke about rude and sometimes pretty twisted things in the break room while I'm around but if another woman from the office comes in, they change the subject and act very differently around them. Following my coming out at Volkswagen, some of the guys that I'd known for years whose careers had crossed paths with mine on many occasions were clearly struggling with it, giving me a wide berth at all costs. I had expected worse and

I tried to be positive about it, but those relationships never healed. On the whole, the reaction was a positive one. I felt like I was flying for a couple of days, but I was about to receive my first reality check on just how hard transition can be.

October 2nd, 2015

Today I came out to my best friend Tristan, after a day out at the cycle show in Birmingham. I was hoping he would understand, but it seems he is having difficulty coming to terms with it. I have sent him several texts but I've received no reply. I knew there would be casualties when I came out, and I hope he will come round in time, but I suppose this is something I have to accept as part of being transgender. I am planning to tell my whole family, and also my partner's family this weekend, so I guess it will be a pretty crappy weekend. I will write an update next week on how it went.

My best friend, golf buddy, fellow biker, drinking partner, and guy who I helped throughout his career, even saving him from screwing up on his stag night (I was his best man), turned his back and walked away. It's been five years since I last spoke to Tristan; the day he got out of my car clutching the letter I had just given him, and the day I needed my best friend more than ever, was the last day I saw him.

A few weeks later I arranged a curry night with my other friends Shaun and Andy. By now Wayne was pretty much off grid and we never saw him, so I had assumed that friendship was taking its last breath anyway. I explained things to them in the same way that I had with Tristan and explained why he was absent. They seemed to take it pretty well, but a few days later, Andy called me to say he was having a hard time with it and he didn't want to see me. This is the guy I grew up with, went to school, and later college with, worked on countless race cars with, and performed the role of best man for. Like Tristan, I haven't seen or heard from Andy in five years. Shaun on the other hand was pretty decent about it. It was obvious that he wasn't comfortable with it, but I could sense that he could tell I was having a hard time, and he put our friendship above his own feelings or prejudices. Shaun moved away not long after that, and we have since lost touch, but I give him respect for standing up and being a decent man when I needed a friend the most.

Coming out to my family was by far the hardest thing I had to face back then. I grew up in a traditional home with traditional values and old-fashioned thinking. My dad used to refer to gay people as "woofters", and my mum would laugh along with him. I'm not judging them, they just come from different times, and the world is waking up to the realisation that people who are considered different, are just as valid as those who consider themselves "normal", whatever that is.

October 5th, 2015

This weekend, I told my whole family, including my Mum, that I am Transgender. This was so scary, and I felt sick the whole day until it was over. I couldn't get round to everyone in one day, so I had to tell my brother James, and my partner's parents the next day (Sunday). My mum and my sister were so supportive, and although my brother Graham looked like I'd just handed him a live grenade with a missing pin, he did what he thinks is expected of him as the oldest sibling of the family, offering me support even though he said he didn't understand it. My partner's family were also supportive, except for her mum, who at first looked shocked, but then sort of glared at me like I had wronged her in some very deep way. Despite these mixed reactions, I'm so happy to be finally out to more or less everyone, although I still haven't told my daughter and two of my close friends. I will wait to tell my daughter until after Christmas, and my friends I will tell soon, over a curry night. It seems that Tristan and I are done, there is still no word from him, but his wife messaged my partner to say that he is not coping with it and doesn't want to see me. I'm sad of course, because he is a close friend, but at the same time, I'm really disappointed in him for his reaction. If it is short term shock, or even grief, I can understand that, but if this is just because I'm transgender, then he really isn't the person I thought he was, and as such, I'm not sure I want him in my life anyway. Only time will tell, and he may come round. I hope so.

I can still see the look in my brother James's eyes when I told him. I knew from that very moment that I would never see him again. Both he and his wife ask my sister about me from time to time, usually commenting on how they just can't understand how my sister can call me a she. They are dinosaurs, they chose not to even try to understand, they just don't want to, so they are no longer in my life. My ex-partner's mum had this crazy notion that I'd duped Tracey into a relationship, knowing full well that I was trans, only to come out as transgender four years later. I asked her to explain how I thought it would be of any benefit for me to do that, but she just kept going over the same blame loop, so I gave in and walked away from that one too.

My niece and nephew (my sister's children) are grown-ups and have their own children. My nephew was one of the first to offer support along with his lovely wife and their children. On the other hand, my niece was not coping with the news, saying that she felt that she had lost her uncle. For five years we didn't speak face to face, but recently we have reconnected, and she is now happy to have an aunt who is much happier than her uncle ever was.

The dust eventually settled on my newsflash, and life returned to normal for a while. I was still presenting as male at this point, but I had started to make some subtle changes, like getting my eyebrows waxed and wearing clear nail polish. The plan to give everyone time to adjust before going full time as Amy seemed to be working, aside from the aforementioned casualties. The relative calm was broken when I had a stupid argument with my sister one day, over a silly misunderstanding. We both left voicemails for each other, and we had both misinterpreted the other's intensions. Afterwards, we spoke on the phone, which ended with me losing my temper, and saying some hurtful things. We didn't speak for a few months, but then sometime after I started living as Amy, I contacted her to apologise, and we eventually sorted the whole mess out. During that time, I bumped into my brother Graham, in the foyer of my mum's care home. I was leaving and he had just arrived. I said hi, and before I could say anything else, he started laying into me about how badly I'd treated my sister. He was toe to toe with me, pointing his finger in my face and shouting in full public view. I asked him not to point his finger at me as he was being very aggressive. His reply sealed the fate of our relationship forever. His words conveyed his true feelings, the ones I was sure I'd seen behind that fragile mask of family values, on the weekend that I came out to them all. He said, 'while you've still got them things in your trousers, as far as I'm concerned, you're a bloke, and I've got no problem giving you a good hiding'. He turned and walked away in the direction of my mum's flat, stopping only to say, 'at the end of the day, if it looks like a duck, and quacks like a duck, it's a duck.' There really is no coming back from that. He can never unsay those words, and I'm certain he wouldn't want to. With my head held high, I walked out of there without looking back. I no longer regard either of my brothers as family, and for that, I make no apologies.

Having come out at work, to my friends, and to my family, there was only one task left: my daughter. I had no idea how to tackle this, as she and I hadn't spoken for quite some time. As it turns out, the choice was taken away from me anyway. I naively thought that no one in my personal life was connected to my professional one, but with the power of social media, the news reached my daughter before I had a chance to tell her myself. It seems a colleague at Volkswagen had relayed my news to an ex-girlfriend and former colleague of mine from some years ago. She was still in touch with Louise, my daughter's mum, and the news came spilling out. As it turns out, my daughter wasn't as upset and horrified as I thought she would be. She just wanted some time to work through it, and if anything, I think it helped us to repair the damage that our relationship as father and daughter had suffered. I kept in touch with Louise, and she helped my daughter to process the reality of what was going to happen when I eventually started living full time as Amy. It would be another year before things changed for the better, but I always had hope in my heart that if I gave her time, and respected her space, she would come to me when she was ready.

October 8th, 2015

Today has been one of those thinking days. I am loving being out, and I have received so much love and support from parts of my family and colleagues at work. I've had offers of free makeup lessons, shopping partners, and one colleague is going to put me in touch with a transgender friend of hers who has helped other trans women. I have never felt so accepted and loved, and it is amazing. On the flip side, I also have sad days, and this is one of them, because no matter how much love and support I get, I know the reality is that transition is going to be the hardest thing I will ever do. To be honest, I'm not even sure that I can do it. There's laser hair removal, electrolysis, financial implications, surgeries, and even things like getting my voice right seems so hard. That's before I even think about the social side of transition, blending in and being taken seriously as a woman. I know nothing worth having comes easy, but I am scared that I may not be able to get through this some days. I suppose I will find the courage and muddle through, and probably look back someday and say wow, look how far I've come, but at the moment, I'm struggling to see the light at the end of the tunnel.

November 2nd, 2015

My appointment with the psychologist went really well. It was the second of two appointments needed to get an official diagnosis, which then allows me to access treatment. I got there early, dressed in a women's gingham shirt and simple jewellery. I didn't wear makeup because I was afraid she'd think I was trying too hard. We talked for over two hours, and I broke down in tears several times as I explained how

I have always felt inside, and over the last year, I have begun to understand why I always felt so disconnected and sad. At the end, I was exhausted, but the outcome is that she is happy to refer me back to Dr Stevens to begin the process of hormone replacement therapy, and eventually, gender affirmation surgery. This means that I have my complete diagnosis of F64 - transsexualism (catchy isn't it), and I no longer have to worry that they won't believe me or tell me that I can't transition. Now I have reached this point, I can really begin to make plans for the future. In my head, driving to the appointment, I had already decided that I would find a way to transition with or without their help. Self-medicating is strongly advised against and can be very dangerous, but for someone who has considered death as a better option than life in the wrong body, this isn't much of a deterrent. I would have done whatever it takes.

I didn't write any more entries in 2015. There was nothing more to say. Those who supported me were there for me, and those who didn't had made their feelings clear, and I had disconnected with them for my own self-preservation. I knew there would be a lengthy wait before the gender clinic would send me another appointment to discuss my next steps, but I felt like for the first time, there was real hope. I could achieve anything I wanted to, if I could just pluck up enough courage to get through transition. Although there was now hope for the future, there was still the present to deal with. Christmas 2015 was looming just a few weeks away, and with the situation with my partner Tracey hanging by a thread, it wasn't shaping up to be a merry one.

Chapter Nine
What would Audrey do?

Christmas 2015 was the last festive season I would spend as a man. Having been diagnosed with gender dysphoria, and coming out as trans to everyone I knew, there was nothing to stop me from planning the beginning of my transition. While I waited for more news from the gender clinic, I had a strong urge to be pro-active, to take some control of my gender identity for the first time in my life. I began planning my very first day as a woman. I decided that I would present myself to the world as Amy Kate on May 4th, 2016. Why that date? You might be thinking that I planned it to coincide with Star Wars day, and although it's a happy coincidence, it was never my intention. It just happens to be the birth date of the late Audrey Hepburn. I have idolised her since I was a teenager: her beauty, her presence and her effortless femininity always drew me to her. She was a devoted humanitarian as well as an incredibly talented actress. May 4th just felt like a good place to draw a line in the sand for a transformation of this magnitude. I could have picked an earlier date, but I needed to give myself plenty of time to prepare. I still had to buy a whole new wardrobe of clothes appropriate for work and socialising; I needed shoes, wigs, make-up and breast forms (prosthetic breasts) too. There was so much to be done.

Audrey was famous for her quotes. One of my favourites is: *"Nothing is impossible, the word itself says 'I'm possible'!"* This became my mantra in the time leading up to the day that I would take my first real steps into the world as a woman.

Amongst all the planning and list making, everyday life continued. I'd love to say it continued as normal but that would be underselling it, because nothing would ever be the same again since I dropped my atomic bomb of a newsflash on everyone. Christmas was horrible because I couldn't be with my family as I always had in the past. My news had created some division, and as such, some of them didn't want anything to do with me.

New Year's Eve came and went with little fuss. I spent it at the opposite end of the sofa to Tracey with a bottle of single malt and Jools Holland on the telly. We barely spoke except to comment on the guests performing on Jool's show. We headed off to our separate bedrooms and I polished off the rest of the bottle, having my usual chats in my head with my dad. With each glass poured from the bottle, I told him how much I missed him, and how I wished I'd been a better son. I also asked him for a sign that I was doing the right thing, and I wondered if he would have been proud of me for being brave enough to transition, or devastated because his son turned out to be a girl. This year, 2016, would be one of the most important of my life, so there was little point in making a token new year's resolution like giving up Curly Wurlys or Wagon Wheels. This was it, the year

I'd unknowingly been waiting for my whole life. Looking back on my life, there was so much pain but yet still there was denial and overcompensation. I'd spent half my life working hard to be a man, trying to fit in with people's expectations of me. It saddens me to think of all those wasted years, all the wasted money and time that could have been spent living my life as a woman: as me.

February, March and April seemed to fly by. I buried myself in my work and came home as late as possible to avoid the awkwardness. Before I knew it, I was just a few weeks away from May 4th, my Hepburn-inspired self-imposed deadline. I'd bought some clothes, not many but enough to have a few changes of outfit. I found work clothes to be the easiest, with a simple black skirt and a white blouse being my go-to outfit. There is so much to think about when you begin transition. It's difficult to know where to start. Essentially, the process of transition or "journey" as it is often described can be split into two parts, physical transition, and social transition. Physical transition consists of many different aspects, depending on what an individual needs in order to achieve their transition goals. For a male to female transition this will include essential facial hair removal and possibly hair from the body too depending on how cruel puberty was to them. It will in most cases involve taking hormone replacement therapy (HRT) to feminise the body and create a better sense of well-being and congruence with one's internal sense of gender. Many transgender women also need voice therapy to learn how to modify or adapt their voices to sound more feminine. The success of this voice adaptation training varies as each individual will have a different vocal range to begin with. Think of it like this, A trumpet has small tubing and makes a reasonably high-pitched sound. A tuba has large diameter tubing and makes a low-pitched deep tone. The male chest cavity is larger than that of a female so the resonance in the chest produces a deeper tone. This makes it much harder to adapt the voice to bring it into the female pitch range. The training is not all about reaching a certain pitch though. For those of us that were not blessed with trumpet like tones and were instead saddled with a tuba like I was, the importance is in the intonation and pronunciation. Women generally speak in a very melodic way, using a rising and falling range of tones and accentuating certain words or parts of words. An important part of the voice training is to learn this melodic vocal delivery. Get that right and the tone becomes slightly less important although I still get misgendered pretty much every time I make a phone call. For this reason, I still dread having to use the phone, instead opting to text or email wherever possible.

Depending on individual needs, many transgender women will undergo surgeries such as hair transplants to reverse male pattern baldness, breast augmentation, facial feminisation surgeries and vaginoplasty (the creation of a vulva and a vagina). There is a lot of stigma attached to transgender surgery. People have on many occasions come right out and asked me if I have "had the op", or whether I am "fully a woman". If I'm in a good mood I'll joking diffuse the situation by saying something like 'yes, I had my tonsils out when I was eleven'. If I'm in a bad mood, I'll say 'none of your fucking business'. And there is the point: it really isn't anyone's business but trans people are seen as fair game. They are a novelty, something unique and in many people's eyes misunderstood. For that reason, this curiosity is considered acceptable, but trust me, it is not. Let's put this into context. On any given day, people all over the world undergo surgeries to enhance their bodies. If a woman chooses to have a new nose or have her breasts enhanced, no one would bat an eyelid. She has made that choice to feel more feminine and to reduce feelings of dysphoria about her body and face. If a transgender person makes that very same choice, also to reduce dysphoria about their body and face, it is seen as wrong in many people's eyes. Go figure!

While this all sounds quite daunting, in reality the physical transition stuff sort of takes care of itself, and you can opt in or out of any of them, depending on what you need and what you can afford. Social transition, on the other hand, is by far the most challenging part of becoming your true self, and that is because a fairly large proportion of our society, doesn't seem to want you to.

You don't have to go far these days to read about transphobia and intolerance of transgender people. I'm not on a one-woman crusade to change the world but I am so sick of reading all the nonsense that is written about trans people, by people who have no idea what being trans is like. Probably the biggest drive for me to write this book was a desire to put the record straight, to tell it like it really is. From what toilet I should use to what sport I'm allowed to play, it seems that everyone has an opinion, but few want to listen to the opinions of the trans community themselves. Suffice to say, discrimination is par for the course if you are transgender. As the days ticked by in April, I was blissfully unaware of the highs and lows that I was about to subject myself to in the pursuit of inner peace, and of becoming my true self.

Around mid-April I decided it was time to change my name by deed poll, and so I set about spending the next three weeks ringing every single company, institution and organisation I had any links with, to change my name to Amy Kate Carter. In most cases this was pretty simple. The easiest to my great surprise, was HMRC. I expected Her Majesty's Revenue & Customs to be a complete nightmare, probably requiring a sample of blood, a retina scan and a sacrificial offering of a virginal goat. Essentially, all I was doing in their eyes was changing a few fields on their records at this stage. My national insurance number hadn't changed, just my name, my gender marker and my title. This turned out to be the case with many of the organisations and companies that I'd had night terrors and panic attacks over. The only company that made the process difficult, was my credit card company. I won't name them, because they don't deserve the notoriety. Also, they have access to fancy lawyers whereas the only official legal advice I've ever received is that speed limits are not just a suggestion. No matter what I did, how much evidence I provided, they simply didn't believe me. It was almost as if they wanted me to fail in my quest to become a woman. There was blatant discrimination from the staff I interacted with. Even after going into the store locally and presenting them with my birth certificate, driver's licence and passport, they were reluctant to change my details. After some mild threats of a strongly worded email to the financial ombudsman, and an episode of Watchdog being devoted to them, they relented, and the account details were amended accordingly. I cancelled the credit card the very next day.

April 18th, 2016

This is the last time I will write in this journal as Ian. In a few weeks' time I will be presenting to the world as Amy Kate on a daily basis. In short, I will be living full time as a female. I've got to master makeup and dressing as a female correctly, including accessories, bags etc. The girls at work have been so helpful and have arranged their timetable so that they can be there to support me, which means the world to me. Lately I have been in a bit of a mess and have had serious doubts about transition. I know in my heart that it's the right thing to do, but it is such a huge undertaking that sometimes I feel like I'm out of my depth and I can't cope. I'm sure once I've been living full time for a few weeks it will settle down and I will start getting used to life as a female.

I may have spent half my life feeling like I was a woman, but that does not automatically prepare you for what living as a woman is like. I've worked so hard to be taken seriously as a female, and not just a man who likes dressing up. I've been abused in the street, over the phone and literally laughed at in bars, shops and social spaces. It still amazes me that we, as a society, don't seem to have moved on from this type of shaming and discrimination. Probably the hardest and most daunting part of transition for me, (especially at the very beginning of my transition) was knowing that I was putting myself at much greater risk. I was purposely placing myself in harm's way. I knew from that moment on, that life would never be the same again. Not just because I'm transgender, but because I was becoming a woman. Discrimination comes in many forms; online trolling, slut shaming, body shaming, homophobia, transphobia, racism, sexism, the list is endless. It's easy for the keyboard warriors of the world to cause hurt, pain and suffering to people who are different. It's not always easy to hide the fact that you're transgender. Male to female trans women can be easy to pick out of a crowd, especially in the early days of transition when they are still trying to find their way with hormones, makeup and clothes. Some people are even bold enough to stop you in the street to point out the big mistake you are making. How dare you leave the house dressed in clothes that align with your gender identity and not your birth-assigned sex? How dare you wear clothes, makeup and jewellery that make you happy and provide a sense of comfort and self-worth? All they see is your birth assigned sex, which instantly puts a target on your back. My sense of subconscious safety quickly disappeared. I suddenly felt very vulnerable and afraid. Before transition I would have thought nothing of meeting my friends at a bar or curry house, having parked my car in a poorly lit street away from the safety of CCTV and other people.

If I'd asked my male friends back then to describe what they did to feel safe on a night out, they'd have said 'make sure I've got plenty of condoms' (so mature). Ask a woman the same question, and the reply will be very different. They'll say things like, 'hold my keys so I can use them as a weapon', 'never drink too much, and always have my drink in sight in case someone slips something into it'. They'd also say 'watch what I wear, vary my route home in case I'm followed, carry a rape alarm, check the back seat of my car before getting in and lock the doors before starting the engine'. Shocking isn't it, to think that when a woman is planning her night out, or even thinking about where she will meet her friends, exercise or even go to relax, that this is what goes through her mind.

Despite my worries and my fears, preparations for my first day as Amy continued at full steam. I had just a couple of days left before I would take the long commute to work and into the Volkswagen National

Learning Centre in Milton Keynes, dressed as a woman, as Amy, as the real me. I had already agreed with Terry, my boss, that I would deliver a diesel engine management course. He gave me the option to back out, saying he could get someone else to do it, and I could dip in and out as I saw fit, but I knew that if I took that option, I would lose my courage. I had to walk into that building with my shoulders back and my head held high. I was proud of myself even at that early stage because while transition had only just begun, I had already come so far and achieved so much. I'd narrowly avoided suicide, finally realising I needed help. I'd told my entire family, friends and colleagues that I was transgender. I'd begun treatment for gender dysphoria, and I was well on the way to receiving hormone replacement therapy (HRT) which would begin the process of feminising my body. I was finally starting to realise who I really am, and what I needed to do to achieve my goals.

Speaking of goals, one of the things I found hardest back then, and I still do if truth be told, is makeup. I never wore it, even on the rare occasions in my life when I'd cross-dressed. The last time I'd worn makeup was when I went to Transformation for my makeover, and that was applied by someone else. I was in trouble, I started to panic about it. I had a thousand other things to panic about but makeup was the thing that was troubling me the most. I got myself into a real tailspin over it, so I decided to consult YouTube. This was a mistake. I scrolled through endless videos of fresh-faced teenagers with dewy skin smoother than a baby's backside applying makeup effortlessly as if I had missed out on some big secret. In a way I had. I grew up a boy, with a sister who had left home way before my female instincts kicked in, and a mother who only wore makeup on special occasions. I was completely disheartened by my research, so I resorted to just trying a few things out in the mirror. The results were less than perfect.

"Makeup can only make you look pretty on the outside, but it doesn't help if you're ugly on the inside. Unless you eat the makeup."

Audrey Hepburn

I love this quote, and I was mindful of it as I sat at the mirror trying to turn my face into something that didn't look like a badly drawn Pokémon character. I realised just how powerful makeup really is. Don't get me wrong - it wasn't exactly an epiphany. However, I believe that Audrey's quote does make a valid point; you cannot make someone a beautiful person, but you can make them look beautiful. As the saying goes, "you can't polish a turd, but you can roll it in glitter". So, does real beauty all boil down to what kind of person you are? I hope so because as much as I was starting to realise the confidence and self-worth that makeup can give a person, I would hate to think that we are all so shallow that we can't be that person without it.

I must confess that I envy women who are amazing at applying makeup, and I long to possess the same skills. I just don't have the vocabulary let alone the ability to do it. I read Cosmopolitan and I'm baffled by some of the articles on makeup products. Pore minimisers, I don't know about you girls, but I can keep loose change in my pores. Contouring, highlighting, baking, BAKING! What's that, sticking your head in the oven to set your makeup? Then there's the makeup counters in the department stores. Rows and rows of brightly coloured counters staffed by similarly brightly coloured men and women who look like they're auditioning for RuPaul's Drag Race. They ask questions like, 'what is your moisturising regime?' Regime? Are we trying to look attractive or are we staging a coup? Is this about beauty or a military intervention?

What I have learned from those early days of transition, right up to the present day, is that when I go out with minimal makeup, I get stared at a lot more. I see people making comments, I even hear them as they're usually very indiscreet. 'Look that's a bloke' or 'there's a tranny over there', are some of the more notable ones I've overheard. It's almost as though they feel that I owe it to them to make a huge effort to appear female, or I don't deserve to be taken seriously. Whether I'm wearing a cocktail dress and heels or a hoodie and trainers, I'm no less a woman. Trans women don't owe anyone hyper-femininity.

After a few attempts at applying foundation, powder, blush and mascara, and looking like the drummer of a 1970's glam rock tribute band on more than one failed attempt, I sort of mastered the basics of everyday makeup. I'm going to share my beauty secrets with you. Don't thank me, you're welcome.

Moisturise

I like to use "I can't believe it's not butter" for this but if it's not available, the value brand "I can't believe it's not better" (available in all good budget supermarkets) also works. Failing that, lard or cooking oil will do the job.

Concealer

To fill the fine lines in my face (or cracks if you want to be picky) and smooth out those blemishes, I use tile grout. I find a spatula is the most effective way to apply this but if you don't have one to hand then a trowel will work just fine.

Foundation

Two parts sand to one part cement and mix with water to create the perfect base. I buy in bulk to avoid running out. You can do this by purchasing a trade card from your local builder's merchant or hardware store. Baking the foundation on is optional but does not under any circumstances involve putting your head in the oven. To bake on your foundation, simply apply at least fifty layers of foundation until your face is sagging under the weight of it, then let it set until it feels like you've got Bell's palsy. Finally, dust off the excess with a powder brush.

Eyeshadow

Try to use colours that will complement your eyes. Apply eye shadow with any instrument you see fit to use but avoid sharp objects which may cause blindness. The rule of thumb for eyeshadow is to apply the darker colour to the crease, which in my case completely disappears as it's more of a slot than a crease. Then, the lighter colour is applied to the eyelid. If you have hooded eyes like mine, this will also disappear instantly as soon as you blink. Finally, the lightest colour goes under the browbone to highlight the horrific mistakes you made when plucking your eyebrows. I know what you're thinking, eyebrows are sisters, not twins. I completely agree but they should at least look like they came from the same face.

Mascara

Apply two thick coats of mascara to your lashes. Be very careful not to poke yourself in the eye with the brush as this will induce temporary blindness, and it feels like your eyes are being held open and squirted with lemon juice. If like me you are unfortunate enough to have less than full lower lashes, simply collect as many dead spiders as you can from your home and remove the legs. Glue them to your lower lash line with Pritt stick (other PVA based glue sticks are available) and discard the mutilated corpses.

Eye liner

Simple eyeliner is usually applied with Kohl pencil for the under eye and liquid or gel liner for the top lid (get me, I sound like a pro). If you have a steady hand, you'll be fine, but if you don't, your eyeliner will look like it's been applied by your pet hamster. Then there is winged eye liner. This comes under the "advanced makeup techniques" category. There are two basic styles for the winged eye liner look. Neat and symmetrical, or Amy Winehouse. The latter is the easier of the two, as the eyeliner can be applied with a child's crayon.

Blusher

Applying blusher is harder than it looks. Too much and you look like rag dolly Anna, too little and the effect is lost. If like me you are not proficient in the application of blusher, simply get a friend or colleague to slap you around the face every five to ten minutes throughout the day, to maintain that warm reddish glow. Remember to do both cheeks evenly.

Lips

The secret to balanced make-up is this; Dramatic eyes, nude lips. Bold colour on the lips, go easy on the eyes. This tip can be completely avoided if you work behind a makeup counter in a department store. In this environment, anything goes.

Fixing spray

This is designed to keep your makeup looking fresh all day. There is no other product that can replace fixing spray. After seven hours in A&E I can confirm that "Gorilla Glue" spray adhesive is not a suitable alternative.

Disclaimer: Don't try any of this at home!

After a while I reached a point where I felt that I could at least get away with it when it came to makeup. My clothes, shoes, hair and breast forms were all sorted, so I was as ready as I'd ever be. I thought about my journal quite a lot back then. What should I do with it? Should I carry on and document my transition, or stop, because it was really only there to provide me with an outlet for my sadness and frustration as I slowly started to realise that I was transgender, and what I needed to do about it. In the end I decided that as my last post on 18th April 2016 had been my last as a guy, then it was a good time to draw a line in the sand and stop writing, so that I could focus on the job in hand. This didn't last long though, because I found the writing cathartic, as I could pour my heart out on a page much easier than I could in person. Not long after finishing with the journal, I started a blog called Afternoon T with Amy Kate. This ran for three years, documenting my transition and providing me with endless material for this book. I closed the blog at the end of my transition. I felt at the time that there was nothing else to say. How wrong I was.

The day had come. Wednesday May 4th 2016, the day that I presented to the world as my true self for the first time. I got up uncharacteristically early, showered and dressed excitedly albeit with a fairly large dollop of 'oh shit what the hell am I doing'. I put on my makeup as I'd practised (a lot!) and headed downstairs. Breakfast was discarded as a bad idea because I was close to throwing up with nerves already. I had a fifty-five-mile commute ahead of me and the last thing I needed was to be pulling over to see my Coco-Pops for the second time. The drive to work was horrible, not for the usual reasons like traffic, bad weather or being stuck behind a tractor, but because I was dreading the moment that I stepped out of the relative safety of my car, walked across the car park, and into the foyer. My stomach was on the spin cycle, I was crying, which was not helping my freshly applied makeup, and I was almost at the point where I wanted to turn the car around and go home. Just as it was all getting a bit too intense, I turned off the A5 and headed for the car park. I sat in my car for what seemed like ages before finally plucking up the courage to head into the building. I felt sick as the doors of the foyer swished open. I walked in, and was immediately greeted by some of my female colleagues. They were hovering around the reception desk waiting for me to arrive. They had been so supportive on the build up to this day and seemed even more excited than I was. I started to feel at ease as they took turns to hug me and compliment me on my makeup (they are pathological liars, but I love them). They headed off to their respective office desks or classrooms and I made my way to mine. I sat at my desk in the classroom staring out at the neatly laid out tables that I had prepared. I took deep breaths to calm my nerves but it had little effect on the waves of panic that were by now washing over me like waves on a windswept bay. Taking a final walk around the horseshoe shaped desk layout I straightened every pen and lined up every book with the edge of the desk with the precision of a master engineer. This somehow calmed me and I began to feel my pulse return to somewhere near normal. When the time came to begin the course, I went over to the canteen to collect my group of learners. I didn't know if I could do this, I was more scared than I'd ever been. I sheepishly called out the course code, and a group on a table not far away all started to push their chairs back and head in my direction. I decided not to say anything, and just lead them to the classroom. I'd figure out how to address the elephant in the room once they were all settled in their seats.

'Welcome to Audi diesel engine management', I said nervously as the group looked at me expectantly. Some looked calm, some looked like they were trying to work out exactly what I was and if there were hallucinogenic drugs in the coffee machine, and some were sitting there, arms folded looking mildly disgusted. At that moment, my instincts as a trainer took over from my nervousness at presenting for the first time as a woman. I started with 'so lads, I have something to tell you. Strap yourselves in, this is going to sting a bit.' I told them a brief potted version of my story before explaining that being transgender isn't contagious, and that they'd all be absolutely fine. This raised a few giggles and the mood in the room seemed to soften a little. By lunchtime, it seemed as if they'd forgotten that I was transgender altogether.

Lunchtime also provided the first knock back of the day. Things had been going so well and my confidence was beginning to grow. As I stood in the queue for lunch, one of the servers who I didn't know at all said, 'can I ask you a question? So now that you are a woman, are you gonna start sleeping with men?' I was shocked, totally shocked. I didn't know what to say. He seemed to be trying to push my buttons, and before I knew it, I felt my anger kicking in, but I held back and politely said that I really didn't want to answer that question. He then went on to his next question, 'So what do you plan to do with your balls?' At this point I lost my shit completely. 'Well, you're the chef, I was hoping you could knock up a stew with them.' My colleagues, who had overheard the whole thing, were obviously shocked at my outburst but equally appalled at this guy's comments. I left the canteen with tears streaming down my face, heading straight to the car park where I sobbed and cried until one of my colleagues came to find me. With her help, I pulled myself together and headed back to my classroom to finish the day.

As the class finished for the day, the learners all headed off to their homes or hotels, but one remained, sitting in his chair. 'Is everything OK?' I asked. He said that he'd been very worried when I'd told the group that I was trans, but actually he thought I was just the same as always, but with a skirt. He explained that as he had known me for several years, having attended many courses with me, he was worried that the situation would be too weird. He was relieved to learn that I was just the same person, 'the same chocolate bar, just in a different wrapper' as he so eloquently put it. I drove home with tears in my eyes, having had a mixed day. It was mostly positive, but I couldn't shake the comments that the server had made at lunch. It plagued me for days, but I didn't report it because I knew that if word got out that I had and he was disciplined for it, no one would want to talk to me in case they said the wrong thing and ended up in trouble. I decided on a different approach, the next day I took him to one side and explained why his questions were not only hurtful and inappropriate, but poorly timed considering we were in a very public space. We actually became friends after that, which just shows that anyone is capable of changing their mind if they really want to.

As the weeks went on, I settled in to work as Amy and most of the learners and my colleagues seemed quite comfortable around me. Word had started to spread around the dealer network that one of the trainers was now a woman, and of course comments were made, both good and bad. Things at home had really become unbearable for Tracey and me, and we finally made the decision to split. It was heart-breaking but there was just no way around it. We both wanted entirely different things from our lives. We even tried counselling. The poor guy sat there listening to our story, taking in both sides and debating a solution which would be beneficial for both of us, but I could see in his face what was coming. 'Let me clarify the situation. You want to live your life as a woman, and she doesn't want you to. What advice do you think I can offer in this case?' He basically suggested we go our separate ways as there was really no middle ground to be achieved. Our living arrangements weren't ideal either. Neither of us could afford to move out of our rented home back then so I had moved into the spare room a while back and we made the best of a bad situation. Realising that you're trans while you're in a marriage or a relationship is awful. The very last thing you want to do is hurt your partner or children. This is just another point in proving that no one chooses to be trans. Who would choose to hurt the ones they love like that? The choice to transition is never taken lightly, and it certainly isn't a fad, a phase or a whim.

May rolled into June and my birthday was approaching but I still hadn't heard from the gender clinic regarding my hormone replacement therapy (HRT). Then, out of the blue a letter dropped through the door. My eyes were wide with excitement. The endocrinologist had approved me for HRT and my GP would be in touch to arrange my first testosterone blocker injection. For transgender women, HRT usually consists of two medications. An anti-androgen or testosterone blocker is given which suppresses the male body's ability to produce testosterone from the testicles. Then, oestrogen is taken in the form of what is called oestradiol, to replace the testosterone that would normally have been produced in the male body. In some cases, transgender women may just take oestradiol, and don't need the testosterone blocker, it really depends on the individual's needs. The blocker injection is usually received every twelve weeks, and this continues until the person has undergone gender affirmation surgery, as it is no longer needed once the testicles are removed. Of course, if the individual chooses not to have surgery, they will usually take the injection indefinitely.

Taking this form of HRT causes some remarkable changes in the body and also the mind. Essentially, it forces your body to enter a second puberty. Many trans people refer to this as the "right puberty". It's important to note that HRT is not a magic wand. Much of what is needed for a male to become female is up to the individual to progress by themselves. For example, male pattern baldness may improve slightly but it is not reversed by taking HRT. Facial hair does not disappear just because you are taking it either. Ever wondered why your granny has a moustache? The effects of HRT are subtle, taking several years to complete, just like the first puberty. Breasts will grow, but they will usually be small. Fat will be redistributed around the body as it would be in the female body, and body hair becomes softer, finer and sparser, especially in areas where a male would have lots of it. I was very relieved to learn this, as body hair was definitely the biggest source of my dysphoria. I hated it with a passion. I started shaving my arms, legs and underarms at the age of fifteen, and I never stopped. My chest was a fire hazard, a full Axminster shag. Thankfully, with time and a little laser therapy, that situation is close to being resolved. Let's face it, no one wants hairy boobs.

    A week before my birthday, I received a phone call from my GP and the injection was booked in. I would also pick up the prescription for oestradiol at the same time, and that would be it, a lifetime of medication, but good medication. Life changing, lifesaving medication. The day arrived, my birthday, June 23rd 2016, also coincidentally, the day that the country would decide on Brexit. I went to my GP for the injection, no big deal, needles don't bother me, but when the packet was opened, I did wince a tiny bit at the size of it. It's called a depo injection, which means it is delivered into a large muscle and stays there, slowly dissolving into the blood stream over a period of around twelve weeks. It is delivered by a needle that looks more like an Olympic javelin than a medical implement. Despite that, it was relatively painless and over in seconds due to the skill of the lovely nurse who administered it. I picked up my prescription and went off to vote before heading home to take stock of this momentous occasion (for me at least). Swallowing that little blue pill was such an insignificant thing in itself. I was used to swallowing pills like Paracetamol, antibiotics and even multivitamins so large that they looked like a choking hazard but this was different. This seemingly innocent little blue pill would change my life forever, it would change *me* forever. There was a very long path ahead of me but I had taken the first and most important steps. All that I needed now was the courage to see it through.

Chapter Ten
Riding the Dragon
(10 things they don't tell you about HRT)

Whether you have taken HRT (Hormone Replacement Therapy) or not, most women can testify to an alarming array of hormone-induced mood changes as her menstrual cycle comes and goes. The same can be said of women in pregnancy, and of course, women going through the menopause. Oestrogen, (the American spelling is estrogen) has a direct effect on the part of the brain that regulates mood, in particular the release of serotonin, the feel-good happy hormone. There will be days when murdering someone for looking at you in a funny way seems perfectly rational, and there will be days when your dog has peed in your favourite shoes and his sorrowful look has you in floods of tears. Then there are food cravings, weight gain, stomach cramps and brain fog. Some days, a woman can experience all of these things together, rendering her barely able to function as a human being. Although trans women don't experience a menstrual cycle in the way that a natal female does, the emotional effects of oestrogen changes in our bodies have similar effects. Suffice to say, "riding the dragon" seems an appropriate term for the effect that oestrogen and HRT has on us poor women, however we started out in life.

HRT is an incredible thing. The principle is fairly straightforward; it replaces a deficiency of hormones in the body, which helps it to function correctly. Hormones control a number of functions within our bodies, including metabolism, reproduction, growth, mood and sexual health. In the case of trans people, HRT (often referred to as cross-sex hormones when used in transgender health care) is used to induce a second puberty, making the body change to become more feminine or masculine depending on the hormones being supplemented. Once this second puberty is complete, which usually takes around three to four years, the individual will need to continue taking HRT for the rest of their lives. This is because the body cannot make sufficient quantities of oestrogen or testosterone, depending on which way the person is transitioning.

You may have read in the news recently that puberty blockers had been restricted for children under sixteen. This was successfully challenged by Mermaids, the charity for gender diverse children, and the NHS Gender Identity Development Service (GIDS) at the Tavistock and Portman hospital in London. After a lengthy court battle, they won their appeal to have the decision overturned. I can understand the argument from someone who has no understanding of the pain that gender dysphoria inflicts upon an individual, but as someone who lived with that pain for over forty years, I can say with confidence that this treatment is vital to supporting young trans and gender diverse children. I want to set the record straight on this, children are NOT being prescribed HRT, they are simply given access to hormone blockers. These hormone blockers suppress the dominant hormone in the body and thus delay the onset of puberty until the individual has decided that transition is right for them or not. If they change their mind and stop taking the blocker, they will go through puberty normally with no lasting effect. If they choose to transition, it will give them a significant advantage, allowing them to more successfully transition into their correct gender. For example, if a person who was assigned female at birth identifies as a trans man, and goes through puberty, they will grow breasts. This is disastrous for this person and they will often use a binding material to strap their breasts close to the chest to appear flat chested. This can be very dangerous and has even resulted in death in some cases due to asphyxiation. In addition to this, surgery will be required to remove the breasts at some point in the person's future. This double mastectomy is often referred to in the trans community as "top surgery". A person assigned male at birth but identifying as female would grow facial and body hair which will be devastating for them, but far worse than this is the breaking of the voice. This is not reversible with HRT and for me personally it is one of my biggest hang-ups. I actively avoid phone calls even to close friends, opting instead to text them. I am a professional voice user in that I am a trainer, and while face to face speaking is less of an issue for me than the phone or internet, it is still the only real problem that I focus on in my training delivery. As such, If I could go back to being a teenager and have another go at life, I would have done anything for those hormone blockers to stop my puberty. Around 72% of young trans people have self-harmed including cutting, one in four has attempted suicide, and over 90% have had suicidal thoughts. These are children - how can it be wrong to help these kids by providing them with hormone blockers which offer nothing but time for them to make a life changing decision? Yes, this is a highly emotive subject for me. I know many young trans children and their parents, and I know how important it is to support them. That support would have completely changed my life, but it simply wasn't available back then. So now I've got that little rant out of my system, (ahem) let's take a look at HRT in more detail.

What exactly is HRT?

Put simply, it replaces the sex hormone that should be released naturally in your body via your reproductive organs. In some people the level of hormones in the bloodstream is insufficient to keep them healthy, such as women in the menopause. For transgender people they need the dominant hormone to be suppressed, and the hormone that aligns with their gender identity then replaces it.

Where do our sex hormones come from?

For men, testosterone is produced mainly in the testicles, and for women, oestrogen is produced mainly in the ovaries. Other glands around the body also secrete these hormones, but in very tiny amounts. Recent scientific studies also prove that the hypothalamus, a part of the brain responsible for the self-regulation (homeostasis) of the human body, and a direct link between the nervous system and the endocrine system, can also produce large amounts of oestradiol (the dominant component of oestrogen). We all have oestrogen and testosterone in our bodies in varying amounts depending on our birth assigned sex, and one or the other will be the dominant one.

HRT is incredible, but taken incorrectly it can be very dangerous, even deadly. Please be aware that what you read in this chapter is purely my own observation of my body and mind and is in no way a reference guide for anyone else, or to be taken as medical advice. For accurate medical advice regarding HRT, always consult your doctor.

When I had finally jumped through the burning hoops of fire that granted me access to HRT (which took over a year), I was given lots of information in the form of leaflets and stern verbal warnings from the endocrinologist about how it would probably kill me before I reached the end of my transition. As if that wasn't enough to put me off, I was also told not to expect too much due to my age (cheeky bugger). Words like deep vein thrombosis, stroke and heart disease were mentioned as well as increased risks of certain types of cancer. This is fair enough I thought to myself, as I sat in front of the endocrinologist at the gender clinic thinking 'I may not make it through next week let alone transition'.

These medical professionals are duty bound to explain the dangers of any treatment as well as the positive effects. But what about the things they don't tell you? What about the things that only someone who has experienced HRT first-hand could possibly know? I've watched a lot of YouTube videos of trans people making wild claims of amazing results on HRT. From flat chested to a DD cup in 6 months, A bottom like J-Lo's within a year, wild claim after wild claim. This is not only misleading, it is also very damaging to any trans person watching these, and then comparing the results to their own. Having taken HRT for nearly six years now, I can confidently report the changes it made within my body and mind, from the obvious changes like breast growth and fat redistribution, to the less obvious effects of HRT that the medics and celebrity YouTubers don't tell you about. So here are 10 things they don't tell you about HRT from my own personal experience.

Before I start on the list, please understand that while I like to write with humour wherever I can get away with it, some of the points I'm about to write about are pretty dark. I could have omitted them but then it wouldn't be a true reflection of my experience on HRT, and I am always brutally honest about my transition. I cannot hope to show people what it's really like to be transgender and go through transition, if I don't tell the whole truth on every single page of this book.

#1: Body hair

If like me, a trans person developed more body hair than an average sized mountain goat during puberty, they may naturally be concerned that when they begin transition, they will be too hairy to expect a successful outcome. This was one of the fears that stopped me from pursuing transition much sooner. I used to have my back waxed by a team of professionals armed with more wax strips than it would take to wallpaper my lounge. The strips were dipped into a vat of boiling liquid with the consistency of Marmite before being applied to my already whimpering skin. Once the pain of the hot wax had started to subside, a beauty therapist / skilled torturer ripped the offending wax strip off, making it look like an emergency landing strip that had been ploughed in the middle of a field. As a former mechanic and Thai boxer, I have a very high pain tolerance, but the pain that ensued when the wax strip was removed often made me cry out, sometimes involuntarily. It even led to the invention of new swear words at times. This was a painful but necessary part of my grooming routine as a man. After six years on HRT my back has a few fine hairs around the bottom of my spine and there are a few on my chest. Although by no means completely clear of hair, it is at a point where laser treatment will get rid of what is left. My leg hair grows very slowly now and is much finer. In fact, it hardly grows at all below the knees. My thighs do need regular shaving but the amount of hair and density of it has significantly reduced. The same can be said for my arms, with the hair being finer and lighter. One area where HRT does not have an impact, is the reduction of facial hair. The growth is slightly slower, but the overall amount of hair did not change. The only way to get rid of facial hair is with laser treatment or electrolysis, both of which are painful and expensive. The downsides to this are that laser is not permanent and the hair does eventually return although finer in most cases. Electrolysis is the individual treatment of each hair, killing it at the root and is the only treatment considered to be permanent, however this can take years and the financial cost is very high. It also hurts, a lot! Imagine if you will the process of electrolysis. A tiny needle is inserted a few millimetres into the hair shaft (painful) and then an electric current is passed through the needle into the hair bulb (also painful). This produces heat, and the area is now feeling like a hot poker has been inserted into your face (very painful). After a few seconds the machine that has administered this torture makes a welcome bleeping noise which means the treatment of that hair is done. The needle is removed, and the dead hair is tweezed from the skin, sometimes making a little popping noise as the hair bulb pops through the skin. Imagine how long it takes to clear a full beard, and the pain that a transgender person will go through. I may be labouring the point here, but it is the essence of why I wrote this book. No one in their right mind would choose this, whether a child or an adult. No one is crazy enough to put themselves through the process of transition unless they feel that it is that or suicide. It is not a want, a whim, a phase or a fad. It is a need.

#2: Fat redistribution

This is one of the areas where I thought I wouldn't see much of a result due to my age. I have to say that I was surprised at the results, even after just one year on HRT. Men tend to carry body fat mainly around the middle and as they get older it can develop into the classic "beer belly". In women it is far more evenly distributed around the bottom, the upper arms, torso and thighs. We've all heard of "apple bottoms and bingo wings". Over the years on HRT, I have also seen a significant decrease in muscle mass and strength. This was a welcome surprise for me having spent many years lifting weights to overcompensate, trying to be ultra-masculine (that went well). When I think of all the time, energy and money that I wasted building all that muscle purely to try to be a man despite my instincts that I was a woman, I could cry. It also makes me wonder why the so-called experts in sport cannot see that trans women are not necessarily at an advantage due to their former male bodies. Back when I was lifting weights and doing martial arts training, I could easily do fifty push-ups, but now I struggle to do ten. I used to bench press around 100kg for six to ten repetitions in the gym. Now I struggle to lift my shopping bags out of the car. These changes might seem like a disadvantage but to me they were very welcome because I associated my size and strength with masculinity and as such, I was happy to shed as much of it as possible.

Another area where HRT has worked its magic is my bum. It is definitely quite a bit bigger than it was before transition, and I love the shape of it and how it flows nicely into my thighs which have filled out promisingly. Subtle changes that I didn't consider are things like facial fat, which is responsible for filling out the cheeks and giving a softer appearance to the jaw line. In this area I didn't really see noticeable results in the first few years, but when I compare photos from my early transition with now, it is very clear that my face has changed shape considerably. Having said that, as a woman in her late forties, my face is plagued by the effects of gravity, and I am developing a selection of chins to complement it.

A few of my friends have reported changes in their shoe size. I am a UK size eight (euro 42) which I'm very happy with, but friends have told me that they had dropped a shoe size as they reached the latter part of their transition. HRT cannot and will not change a person's skeletal structure. The bones in my feet cannot shrink, but the fatty tissue, tendons, ligaments and cartilage can alter, and this is what may lead to a change in the size or shape of feet for some. After nearly six years on HRT, I have not dropped a shoe size, but my feet look more slender and more feminine.

The one thing that should be in capital letters, in bold print on the medication packaging, is a warning about weight gain. Before transition I used to be able to eat anything without putting on weight. As a young teenager I weighed eight stone (50kg). There was more meat on a lamb chop than on my entire body. Since taking HRT my body seems reluctant to shed weight, even if I work out like an angry Power Ranger and eat fewer calories than a pet tortoise. I have never been a fan of diets as I don't think they are effective, not in the long run anyway. If you want to lose weight, you need to move more and eat less. Good nutrient-rich food and plenty of water and sleep take care of the insulin and cortisol levels in your body, and in turn, that takes care of the fat burning, along with regular exercise. Motivation and willpower, however, are not things that come easily to me, and that is often my downfall. It never ceases to amaze me how I am highly motivated to get in my car and drive several miles to the shops to buy chocolate and wine, but a drive of similar distance to a gym or swimming pool is something I would only do under heavy protest or at gunpoint.

#3: Sex drive

The fact that sex drive is greatly reduced when you start HRT is a bit of an understatement. I was warned by the clinician at the gender clinic, but I wasn't prepared for what actually happened. Within a few days of starting HRT, my sex drive (which was pretty low to begin with) became non-existent. Nothing turned me on, nothing even interested me sexually let alone excited me. It was as if sex no longer existed. I wasn't in a relationship so it didn't really matter to me but if you are trans, then you might want to plan ahead for this and speak to your GP prior to starting

HRT. The effects of this lasted around nine months in my case, despite being told it would wear off after three or four. Although I still wasn't in a relationship, my sex drive did begin to return to normal eventually. When it did finally return, it brought about a very unexpected change in how I felt about my own sexuality. As I mentioned early on in the book, sexuality and gender identity are not directly linked. Just because you identify as a gender other than which you were assigned at birth, it doesn't mean that you are going to change who you are attracted to. That said, in some cases, mine included, a person's sexuality can change. I think it is much more than that though. My theory is that my sexuality didn't actually change at all. I've always been attracted to women, and as such I identified as straight, but I believe that I also had an attraction to men which I suppressed to such a point that it wasn't even obvious to me. So, imagine my surprise when I started perving over Chris Hemsworth and Ryan Reynolds whenever they appeared on the tellybox. Coming to terms with a shift in your sexuality is often hard, but in my case, it actually brought relief. I began to feel free of the binds that had forced me to believe that it was only acceptable to be straight, having lived my life according to the confines of my birth assigned gender. I am now a proud pansexual woman, meaning if I feel a physical and emotional connection with someone, their gender doesn't matter to me. It really is that simple.

#4: Sensitive boobs

The gender service is very clear in setting expectations for breast growth. It is unlikely that a trans woman will develop large breasts. An A to B cup is what can be expected in most cases. I am very happy with my fairly pert B cup boobies. What they didn't tell me however, is how painful my boobs would be during the growth process and indeed forever whilst taking this miracle medication. Even now I get days when my nipples are both painful and sensitive. They don't hurt all the time, just when you bump into or press against something or someone, even very gently. A few years ago, long before Covid or "The Rona" when it was ok to hug people, I went to stay with my brother from another mother whose name is Mark. On leaving the next day, I hugged his lovely wife Kate and then Mark took his turn. Mark is a heavy-set chap, with a vice like grip and the hugging capability of a grizzly bear. As he squeezed the oxygen from my lungs, there was a moment, a very brief moment, where I thought a sniper had shot me through both nipples. As my boobs were crushed against his chest, a burning pain shot through me that took my breath away.

A more welcome effect of HRT on my boobs was the sensitivity of my nipples. Prior to my gender affirmation surgery, they were pretty sensitive already and certainly played a large part in self-pleasure (purely for research purposes). The best way to describe it is an increase in intensity. It feels as if they are directly connected to my naughty bits. Following my surgery, and after some months of recovery, the intensity grew even stronger. Definitely a welcome effect of HRT.

#5: Male pattern baldness

You're probably thinking what the hell has this got to do with HRT? I added this because I've heard some pretty wild claims on this subject, again from YouTubers who've apparently regrown all their hair as a result of HRT. I have no doubt that a few lucky people will see some regrowth when taking HRT but actually, all that is happening is that testosterone is no longer causing or contributing to male pattern baldness. HRT will prevent any further male pattern baldness, that much is true, but if like me you are balder than one of Sir Lewis Hamilton's tyres after qualifying, then you'll need to look at treatments. The most common treatments are minoxidil and finasteride. Minoxidil is applied directly to the scalp and finasteride is taken orally. If you are trans, it is best to speak to your GP if considering either of these treatments as they can have some side effects. Sadly, in my case the hair just never came back, so my only real option is to wear wigs, which is probably the source of the only real dysphoria that I now have. Some advantages are that I can change my hairstyle or hair colour in a moment. Disadvantages include the fact that wearing a wig is like wearing a woolly hat - all the time. Its fine in the depths of winter but not so good on a hot summer's day. On really hot days I can get quite dizzy as the temperature under my wig begins to reach dangerous levels. There is always the possibility of hair transplants, but this is very expensive and there is no guarantee of a successful outcome.

#6: Feelings & emotions

To be fair I was warned by the clinician at the gender service that things would be rough in this area. I was told to expect mood swings of epic proportions as my second puberty developed. They said I would experience tantrums akin to that of a twelve-year-old girl high on Skittles and Fanta. Oh, how they underestimated that one. My range of emotions was significantly wider than ever, going from "move or I'll kill you" to "I love you, give me a hug". I can experience empathy, love, hate, and primeval rage within a five-minute window. The thing that I love the most aside from my temper tantrums is that I feel so much more in tune with my emotions. I rarely cried as a man, except in the last few years before transition when my emotional state was at rock bottom. Even at my dad's funeral I didn't break down in the way I thought I would. Now I cry at everything, literally everything. A cute bunny rabbit eating a banana on YouTube - crying. A story of bravery in the face of adversity - crying. Someone took the last Jammy Dodger from the biscuit tin at work - crying. You get the picture. Songs, poignant memes, you name it - crying. When things get really tough, I can also feel utter despair and heartbreak. I have felt close to the edge at times during transition and although I have never returned to the feeling that I want to end my life, it can at times feel as if there is no hope. I have felt so lonely over the last six years, and someday I hope to meet someone who I can share my life with. In my old life I welcomed time alone, but now I despise it, I fear it, because those old feelings of despair can creep back into my head, an echo of the past and an unwelcome reminder of the life I lived before transition. As dark as these feelings are, I have to acknowledge them, I cannot hide them or push them away like I used to be able to. Transition is such an intense process, and it can be so hard to fight day in day out. Sometimes you fall down, and you just have to say, 'I'm not OK'. In contrast, when things are good, they feel great, I feel in awe as I walk through nature, feeling the leaves brush against my skin and the long grass tickling my legs. My senses are heightened, particularly my sense of smell, and I feel more connected to nature. Joy is heartfelt and feels more real. I never really knew what happiness was in my old life, I would just smile when I thought it was appropriate, but now, I find that my smile is autonomous, I have very little control over it, just as it should be.

#7: Memory

Ever heard the phrase "women never forget anything"? This is actually true, to a point at least. Women have a higher rate of blood flow to certain parts of their brain, including those that control language. This is why there is overwhelming evidence that women have better immediate and delayed recall of the spoken word. Scientists have found that although a trans woman may have been born male, their brain more closely resembles that of a natal female. HRT seems to further enhance these heightened neural pathways. I have always had a pretty good memory, especially for faces and reciting lines from films. One area I was not so good at was remembering minor details. My memory after six years on HRT is far sharper than it ever was before. I can recall tiny insignificant details with ease that before would have escaped me after just a few minutes. This is something that my male colleagues at work consider to be a downside of HRT.

#8: Body odour

Such a pleasant subject, but again I report good news. If you've ever had the misfortune to enter the bedroom of a teenage boy, or a men's locker room at the gym, then you will know that the odour that hits you as you enter is not dissimilar to that of your local landfill site. Put simply, boys stink. I should know, I was once one of these foul-smelling individuals. Much of this is due to our old friend testosterone which releases pheromones through the sweat glands in the skin making men irresistible to women. Irresistible? IRRESISTIBLE? Let me tell you this, if a man wants to get into my knickers, he needs to smell like soap and expensive cologne, not like the contents of a gym bag. Just a few short weeks after starting HRT, one of the first tangible changes I noticed was that I smelled far more pleasant after exercise or after rising in the morning. I had that good stank. Amazingly it also seemed to have an effect on foot odour. I never really had smelly feet as a guy except when wearing my steel toe-capped boots all day as a mechanic, but this also seems to be far better since I started taking HRT.

#9: **Orgasms**

I was once given some great advice by a wise old mechanic from my hometown of Leicester. He said there are essentially two types of people in this world, wankers and liars. Don't let anyone call you a liar. Well as you know I have been brutally honest with you so that must make me a… Hey! Okay so we all do it right? Okay maybe not nuns or Tibetan monks but most of us. My gender clinic doctor actually told me to "use it or lose it" regarding my little sausage, as HRT significantly reduces size and ability to maintain an erection. Well I can't say I followed that advice to the letter, but once in a while Chris Hemsworth was on the telly and I couldn't be held responsible for my actions. Enough said.

So, what has changed? The answer is quite a lot really. It is hard to explain but the feeling of orgasm is more intense than it was with male orgasm or "boygasm". It's also more prolonged and seems to spread across my whole body. Unlike the old days before transition where once orgasm had been reached, I was out of action for at least half an hour while the little sausage reloaded, I'm ready for another go in just a few minutes now. The real change came after gender affirmation surgery. My clitoris, once fully healed, became very sensitive, and I can now masturbate like any other woman. Unlike my former male sexual urges, I find now that I really have to be in the mood. I can't force it, I'm either horny as hell or I'd rather eat Marmite on toast. It can strike at the most inopportune moments as well. There I am minding my own business reading a book or watching TV and suddenly, it all starts to get a bit fizzy down below. My mind starts to go into overdrive and that's it; it has to happen right there and right then. If that isn't possible due to my location or circumstances, I'm going crazy until I can find that moment of release and pleasure.

#10: Confidence & self-worth

I saved this one until last because it is probably the hardest one to explain. I've read several accounts from trans people and watched many YouTube videos where the individual mentions feeling like they are "in bloom". A sense of wellbeing and euphoria is also often referred to. It took at least a year before I felt like I had experienced that. When it did finally arrive, I felt a sense of inner peace like I was blossoming into the woman that I truly am. As it turned out, I didn't find real inner peace until I'd had my gender affirmation surgery. After that, I started to feel physically the way I felt emotionally and spiritually, and this made me feel more relaxed, more confident and even more sassy than I was before. This isn't the case for everybody though. Not every trans person needs or wants the surgery. It's a huge commitment and it can never be reversed so you must be absolutely sure that it's the right thing for you. In some cases, just taking HRT alleviates the gender dysphoria enough to make it manageable.

I haven't added this to the ten things listed above but I thought it would be wrong for me not to at least mention the negatives of taking HRT. Menopausal women are advised to take the medication no longer than is necessary due to an increased risk of heart attack, stroke, deep vein thrombosis and liver damage. Additionally, the person taking the medication has a higher risk of developing some cancers. Trans people on the other hand have to take the medication for their entire lives once they have decided to transition. Cross-sex hormones for trans women come in three forms (four if you live outside of the UK). In patients under forty, oestradiol is usually prescribed in tablet form. This of course passes through the liver and can have a damaging effect over time. Once past forty, the patient is often switched to oestradiol in the form of a gel or a patch, similar to a nicotine patch. I was asked to switch to patches but they were an absolute nightmare; always falling off which caused my oestradiol level to plummet and I suffered health problems as a result. In America and other parts of the world it is possible to have the oestradiol in the form of an injection, but this is not usually offered in the UK. I now use oestradiol gel which I just rub onto my arms each morning after my shower. Easy and simple.

Much of the concern around health risks from HRT, particularly oestradiol, exist because there is not enough strong data to understand the long-term effects. Back in the forties when it was developed, it was called Premarin. Breaking the name down unveils a sinister fact. Premarin is made from the urine of a pregnant horse - Pre (pregnant) Mare (female horse) In (chemical substance). This type of drug has since been proven to be dangerous to humans. Basically, the liver doesn't understand what the substance is, so it identifies it as toxic and this causes serious health problems over time. What is also very disturbing is that the mares are specifically raised for their urine. They are confined in cramped conditions and kept in a constant state of pregnancy. The foals usually end up at the slaughterhouse.

Thankfully, modern science has found a synthetic alternative which has been available for quite some time now. It avoids the animal cruelty that its predecessor was guilty of (although I suspect some companies would have tested it on animals prior to release). The problem lies in the fact that very little research has been done into the long-term effects of taking HRT, particularly in transgender people. One of the main reasons for this comes down to good old-fashioned profit margins. There simply isn't anything in it for the big drug firms. Trans people make up less than 1% of the global population. Spending millions on extensive tests and research to better understand the long-term outcomes of such a drug is unnecessary in their eyes. Their argument is that in its mainstream form (prescribed primarily for menopausal women), it is only prescribed for a few years to tackle the worst symptoms of the menopause, and they have the data they need to understand the risks and side-effects. Due to this lack of data, endocrinologists can only advise the trans patient based on what they know; and much of that information comes from the older oestradiol Premarin.

After six years on HRT I have experienced significant changes. These changes may not be so obvious to other people, but they definitely are to me. My mind, body and soul are connected for the first time in my life. While things aren't perfect, like my voice and my hair, I feel no uncomfortable feelings about my body like I used to. My mind is at peace and I am able to concentrate on my work and my relationships with my friends and my family. My body will never be able to make its own oestrogen; not in sufficient quantities to sustain my health at least, so I will need to take this medication for the rest of my life. To me this is a small price to pay because thanks to this miracle medication, it is a life I look forward to living.

Chapter Eleven
Puberty 2.0

As the summer of 2016 started to fade and the nights began to draw in, I was starting to settle into my new life. HRT had become part of my daily routine since June, and there appeared to be no negative side effects. My second puberty was in full swing, and although the physical changes were subtle at this point, emotionally I was changing every single day. At the end of July, I decided that it was time to get rid of all "his" clothes. Every time I opened my wardrobe door, they were just hanging there, unwanted like old Christmas decorations in mid-February. They were a daily reminder of who I used to be: a sad and angry man who had been broken physically and mentally before finding the courage to set himself free. One Saturday morning, I decided that enough was enough. I laid out a few black bags on the bedroom floor and set about removing any traces of the old me from my new life. First it was the shoes; five pairs of various trainers and a pair of black work shoes. This did make me giggle a little bit. Most of my female friends will admit to at least a mild to moderate shoe obsession, and a couple of my male friends collect trainers (sneakers), but the majority of my male friends could list their shoe collection on one hand. Work pair, DIY pair, trainers, motorcycle boots, posh pair (weddings and funerals). Then there's me: I am incapable of walking past a shoe shop without at least going in for a browse. I'm not sure if I'm proud or ashamed to say that I have around thirty pairs of shoes at last count. I may have a teeny-tiny shoe problem, but I could quit any time, honest (I need help!).

With a bag filled with shoes and work clothes, I moved on to the rest. Jeans, motorcycle t-shirts, gym stuff, hoodies and a couple of suits. I had barely filled three bags. It wasn't much to show for a person in their forties, and it reminded me of how I rarely went clothes shopping as a man. I just didn't see the point, I hated the clothes, I hated the clothes shops. I never tried anything on, no care was taken over colour choices or co-ordinating things with other garments. I couldn't care less; clothes kept me warm and stopped me from being naked, they served no other purpose. As I loaded the bags into the car, I thought of all the times in my past when I had purged all my feminine things from the secret box under my bed, telling myself I didn't need them and that I could make it as a man if I just tried harder to fit in. I made the trip to the charity shop so many times over the years, always with the same mantra. 'I'm a man, I don't need these things, I'm a man, I… want these things.' It was so hard to let go of them but every time I did, I forced myself to believe that I was doing the right thing, what was best for everybody.

Driving to the charity shop in my heels, skinny jeans and a nice white top, I imagined doing a drive-by, dumping a body out of the car door before speeding away in a cloud of smoke and screeching tyres like in the movies. It felt like a metaphor for the future. I had bumped off my former self and now I was dumping the body, the "body" being three large bin bags full of men's clothing. I pictured TV news at the scene, a police helicopter circling overhead, an old lady's legs clad in wrinkled American tan tights and fluffy slippers protruding from beneath a large pile of black bin bags. An eyewitness saying, 'she only came out to buy cat food and a copy of Woman's Weekly'. I shuddered at the thought of the carnage as I parked my car on the high street. The shop was full of people thumbing through racks of stale smelling clothes, occasionally holding them up to check for moth holes. I nervously approached the counter, and a lady of considerable years took the bags from me while making no attempt to hide the fact that she was trying to decide whether to use a male or female pronoun to address me. I didn't wait around long enough to find out. I was halfway out of the shop when I heard her shout after me, 'thank you Sir'. It wasn't the first time I'd been misgendered in a shop but nevertheless, my heart sank.

As mid-autumn set in, I was beginning to make new friends, both at work and in the local area of Milton Keynes. Through a friend, I got involved with a fantastic LGBTQ+ charity called Q alliance. Meeting people like me and being part of some very exciting projects gave me a real buzz, and I looked forward to the monthly meetings at a coffee shop near my work. It didn't even bother me that after the meeting finished, I still had a sixty-minute drive home to Leicester. Actually, the late finish did both my ex-partner and me a favour. It was very awkward at home since we had split, and we still argued from time to time. She was understandably hurting, and I had apologised until I was blue in the face, but I couldn't make the situation any better no matter how hard I tried. Around that time, she met someone new, a really nice guy and someone who could give her all the things I couldn't. While her life was starting to blossom with her new relationship, mine was beginning to flatline. The excitement of May 4th and the months that followed had all but faded away. This was it: I was just Amy now, just me. That in itself wasn't an issue, in fact I liked the ordinariness, and how quickly I adapted to life as a woman, but at the same time I felt very lonely. I looked a mess and I knew that no one in their right mind would be attracted to me while I was in the early throes of transition and a second puberty. The reality that I could spend the rest of my life alone started to dawn upon me.

  I really wasn't looking forward to Christmas. I was eight months into my transition and although some of my family had been incredibly supportive, there were others who would have had me tried for witchcraft and burned at the stake if they could. I was resigning myself to the prospect of spending my first Christmas as my true self alone, when out of the blue, I received an invitation from my nephew to spend Christmas day with him and his family. It felt so lovely to have been thought of, and the icing on the cake was that my sister would be there too.

To me, Christmas is a joyous time. I can eat all the Twiglets I want, and drink enough wine to sedate an elephant without someone suggested an AA meeting. Far more importantly though, it's about spending time with my friends and family, enjoying the sense of occasion that it brings. A few days before Christmas, I was at the Milton Keynes LGBT breakfast club enjoying a chat and a coffee with my trans and gay friends. A gay man whom I'd never met before passed round some small packets of the most beautiful homemade biscuits. He'd been up until the small hours the night before, making them for everyone who was there. He didn't save them only for his friends or people he was familiar with; he gave them to everyone, without prejudice, without question. That is the true spirit of Christmas, and they were delicious biscuits too.

I didn't care if I got a single present that year. I'd already got more than I ever wanted. I had the freedom to live my life in a body that was beginning to feel right. I'd made new friends, and many of my old friends had accepted me for who I am. I had a family who had not completely turned their back on me, and above all else, I had hopes and dreams. Christmas day was wonderful. I visited my mum in the morning at her care home. She gave me a Christmas card with "Daughter" on it which made me cry. We hugged for what felt like ages and she told me how proud she was of me for being true to myself no matter what the family or my so-called friends thought. She also said that even though I had only just started my journey, she could already see how I was becoming happier and more confident. Later, I arrived at my nephew's house. His young children accepted me as if they'd only ever known me as Auntie Amy, and his lovely wife made me feel so welcome in their home. My new name, "Auntie Amy", felt so good. It made me feel all warm and fuzzy, and a tiny bit tearful every time it was uttered. My sister and I chatted about the past, and about the challenges I would face in the upcoming new year. It was a lovely time, and a day I'll treasure for years to come.

By February 2017, my ex-partner and I were totally fed up with the situation at home. Neither of us could afford to move out so we were forced to live in a kind of limbo. She started to spend more time with her new partner, and I was trying to figure out where I wanted to live once we did eventually move out. I knew that I definitely didn't want to stay in Leicester. The town just felt dead to me. It was Ian's town, not Amy's. All that was left here was my mum, my daughter and my sister. For the first time in my life I had the world at my feet. I could do anything, go anywhere. I imagined Audrey Hepburn, jet setting all over the world as a glamorous actress, spending summers in St. Tropez and winters in the Swiss Alps. I wished I could be just like her, and in my daydreams, I was. As well as the sense of freedom, I had so much energy too. Physically, I felt fantastic. My breasts had begun to grow, although the side effect was that my boobs were sore and tender literally all the time. My skin was becoming softer and my body hair was slowly disappearing or becoming lighter and finer. It wasn't all good news though; my mood swings were horrific. I would throw full on teenager tantrums at times, usually followed by floods of tears.

Another area where things weren't going so well was my hair. I lost my hair to male pattern baldness in my mid-twenties, and I've shaved my head ever since. I started to let it grow after a few months on HRT to see if the lack of testosterone would allow it to regrow but sadly it didn't. I resigned myself to the fact that I would probably need to wear wigs for the rest of my life, and this doesn't come without its challenges. The positives are that I can change my hair style or colour in just a few moments, but the downsides far outweigh that. They are heavy, they make your head itch and it's like wearing a woolly hat in the mid-July sun. Also, getting it wet exposes the webbing of the cap and tells the world that you wear a wig, so keeping your hair dry is essential. You also need to ensure that the cap is adjusted right so that it fits tightly but doesn't cut off the blood supply to your scalp. I learned this the hard way while walking past a parade of shops one day. With a sudden gust of wind, it took flight like a peregrine falcon. Off down the high street it flew with me giving chase like a scene from a Benny Hill sketch. Thankfully, it was a quiet afternoon with only a couple of elderly women gossiping outside the chemist. They watched the chaos unfold open-mouthed as if they were witnessing a landing from Mars. I gathered up the fleeing hairpiece and returned it to my exposed scalp before running to the safety of my car in embarrassment.

I can recount several embarrassing wig stories, so it's no wonder that I am self-conscious about my hair. I went out on my motorcycle with some friends recently. I turned up on my black Royal Enfield Interceptor looking super cool in my skinny black riding jeans, black leather jacket and biker boots. I got off my bike, removed my goggles and strutted towards my friends with my best Marilyn Monroe swagger. As I pulled off my helmet, my wig came with it, nestling inside my helmet like a ferret taking a nap in an old man's cap. I could see that they were trying their hardest not to laugh, but in the end even I burst out laughing, and we all fell about giggling like school kids. Despite the laughter, it was very embarrassing and I hated that it had happened, but all I could do was laugh it off.

The thing I miss most when it comes to my hair is spa days. Even before transition I've always loved to have a pampering day, with sauna, steam and facials followed by a nice massage with essential oils. The last time I went to a spa was around four years ago. It was a complete disaster, and I haven't had the courage to go since. I went with a friend to a local spa. We had booked a couple of treatments for the afternoon, after a morning of swimming, sauna and steam and then a nice lunch. We were feeling very relaxed after a jacuzzi session, so I decided to take a swim in the heated pool. I was so relaxed that I wasn't really thinking too much, almost daydreaming as I swam. After swimming a few lengths of the pool, I noticed something floating in the water ahead of me. I couldn't quite make out what it was. Was it a box jellyfish? A Portuguese man o' war? Should I swim for my life? No, it was my wig, which had slipped from my head as I gracefully did the breast stroke and was now bobbing up and down in the water like an abandoned plastic bag. I grabbed it quickly and ran to the changing rooms. That was my last spa day.

May 4th, 2017, my first birthday. I had survived my first whole year of transition. It had been a tough year too. I lost count of the times I was misgendered, mostly by shop assistants who didn't seem to care if they offended me or not. At work people made the odd mistake but quickly corrected themselves with minimal fuss. The learners that I taught were also very respectful and I even received compliments on how I looked from some of them. Despite this, I began to feel like something wasn't right at work. There were still a few of my colleagues who took greater steps to avoid me than to avoid stepping on a land mine, but I was okay with that, some you win, some you lose. What it actually boiled down to was that after six years as an Audi senior technical trainer, I no longer felt that the job was right for me. I loved the cars, I frequently had the pleasure of driving Audi R8 V10s and RS6s, and I loved the events we covered too like the Goodwood Festival of Speed and the British Motor Show, but still something wasn't sitting right. After a lot of soul searching, I decided that I needed to explore my creative side. I needed a more feminine career path (or so I thought). A position became available as an instructional designer within Volkswagen Group UK. I decided to apply just to see if I even had a chance of an interview, and to my surprise I was offered one that same week. As I do with most things, I researched, planned and prepared like my life depended on it. The day of the interview came round and although I was nervous, I knew I could do no more to prepare. It all seemed to go very smoothly. I answered all the questions and the interviewers seemed to like what I had presented to them. I left the room feeling like I'd done my best, and all I could do was await my fate.

A few days later, I received an email from one of the managers in the design team. I had been successful! I was so happy that I'd been offered the job, not only because I had been the strongest candidate, but because I had got myself a new job as a trans woman. According to recent reports, one in three UK employers would actively avoid hiring a transgender person, regardless of their suitability for the role. Thankfully, Volkswagen Group UK are not one of them. The following day I had a meeting with my line manager Terry, and my new boss Kate. A transitional period was discussed and agreed upon and I went back to my work. Over the next few weeks, I was given small projects to ease me into my new role as an instructional designer. It was harder than I expected, and for a while I thought I'd bitten off more than I could chew. When the day came to finally say goodbye to the Audi team, I was very sad to be leaving them behind, but equally excited for my future in a new role.

June 5th, 2017, my first proper day on the job. I was given a desk next to one of the other designers, Serena, who I'd got to know quite well since starting my transition. She helped me so much in the first few months, and we became close friends. My boss Kate, who is without question the best boss I've ever had, was patient and understanding with me, especially when I couldn't see the wood for the trees, and I was having trouble meeting the client's needs. She taught me so much about the process of instructional design and I did eventually get the hang of it. Unfortunately, the more I learned about the role, the more I missed my old role. I missed training, I missed cars, it's in my blood, it excites me. I confided in Serena about my problem, and she advised me to give it a year before making any big decisions, so I got my head down and tried my best to meet my targets and keep my clients happy.

The change in job role meant a change in my benefits. I kept the company car, but I lost my fully expensed fuel card. Without it I wouldn't have been able to live in Leicester and work in Milton Keynes, so losing it was a big blow financially. The reason I agreed to the package that was offered was that I fully intended to be moving away from Leicester in the summer so I wouldn't have to carry the extra cost of fuel for very long. I spent most of May and June glued to Rightmove and Zoopla in the search for somewhere to live. Tracey had arranged a date to move in with her new partner and so we came to an agreement on when we should leave the house. Our agreed deadline was end of July. I looked at a few flats in and around Milton Keynes, but nothing stood out, they were either in a bad area or they needed renovating. I found a lovely one-bedroom flat only ten miles from work. It was well within my budget and when I viewed it, I fell in love with it. It had a 1920s art deco feel to it despite it being built in the 1980s. It was filled with light and was in a lovely area with a village feel to it. From my lounge window there was a view of an enclosed woodland area with a few trees and wildflowers growing there. It was everything I'd wished for, and the rent was very affordable too. 'I'll take it' I said enthusiastically, as I completed the viewing with the letting agent. The paperwork was signed and now I had four weeks to arrange to move.

Tracey had already arranged to move out on Saturday 29th July so I had to get my skates on as I still had so much to do. My letting agent informed me that the flat would not be vacated by the current tenant until the first week of August, but this didn't tie in with our leaving date, and I didn't want to pay another month's rent for the sake of a week, so I was in a jam. At work, a friend called Karen kindly offered to let me stay with her and her partner Chris at their beautiful home in Milton Keynes. I had already lived there over several weekends throughout the year as I'd been their live-in cat-sitter when they went to visit family in Wales. That arrangement had worked out great because they knew the house was safe and secure, and the cats were well cared for. The bonus was that Tracey and I could get a break from each other and the awkwardness of our situation at home. As well as lodgings for a week I was also offered the use of their garage to store my things in readiness to move across town to my new home. Now that I knew what my plans were, I could start buying furniture as there wasn't much that either of us wanted to take from our old house. With my credit card in hand and my Skoda estate car turned into a makeshift van with the back seats folded flat, I ram-raided IKEA in Milton Keynes. Sofa, wardrobe, dining table and chairs, storage cubes and bookcases purchased, I stored them all in the garage at Karen and Chris's and moved on to the next challenge.

A few runs to the council tip and a visit from the British Heart Foundation took care of the contents of our house in Leicester. Tracey had already taken most of her stuff in her partner's van, so the house was pretty bare already. As the final weekend approached, Tracey was living with her partner fully now, so I had the job of locking up for the final time and handing the keys back to the landlord. By the time Friday 28th July came around, the house was empty aside from my clothes, shoes and some other stuff which I'd already packed into my bulging estate car. I ordered a pizza and had a few cold beers as I sat on the floor of the living room saying goodbye to the old place. We had lived there for the last four and a half years and even though I was excited to be moving and starting a new life in a new town, I was also sad at what that empty house represented. I remembered all the good times we shared there, me, Tracey, my daughter and her son all having fun in the garden or eating takeaways on a Saturday night as we shouted at the terrible contestants on Britain's Got Talent. I started crying. I knew I had to be true to myself and that meant moving away and starting a new life but the cost was losing Tracey and the future that we'd planned. I'd already lost my daughter over a year ago and with my only communication with her being a few updates from her mum, it felt like everything and everyone I loved had been lost. I cried myself to sleep that night as I lay in my sleeping bag on the cold floor of our empty lounge.

  The next morning, I showered and put on some makeup before loading the last of my things into the car. With one last look around the place and a final tear running down my cheek, I said goodbye to our once happy home and locked the front door. I drove to Milton Keynes with my suspension crying out for mercy and my rear-view mirror filled with my shoe collection nestling on top of several suitcases and bags. I still felt that same sense of loss, but as the miles ticked away, hope started to fill my heart and my head. The week I spent with Karen and Chris was so lovely. I was able to relax knowing that everything was taken care of. My things were in storage in their garage, all the paperwork was sorted for my new home and all I had to do was move in next Saturday. I will never forget Karen and Chris's kindness. It made a difficult situation so much easier to deal with and it meant I wasn't alone, for a week at least.

Saturday 5th August: moving day. I had asked the letting agent if I could decorate as the whole flat was in need of a refresh. Every wall was painted in disappointment beige. For the first week in my new home, I had a sleeping bag on the floor, my tools laid out in the lounge, and that was it. Everything else remained in Karen and Chris's garage until the work was done. By the middle of the week I'd finished painting. The lounge and kitchen were finished in a nice pastel mint green. It was very subtle but it made a striking contrast with the fresh white gloss of the doors, skirting boards and windows. The bedroom was painted in a soft lilac and the bathroom in a pastel sea blue. It looked fantastic, and I was very proud of myself. Even more so because I'm no professional decorator, everything I know is self-taught. My dad's decorating skills were questionable to say the least. He once painted around a picture hanging in the hallway of our old house instead of removing it. He was great with engines but terrible with a paintbrush.

Now that my lovely little flat was sparkling with fresh paintwork and cleaned from top to bottom, it was time to move the furniture in. Box after box filled my poor Skoda and several trips were made until there was a pile of flat pack furniture as tall as me in the bedroom. Some people hate flat pack furniture, but I love it. It's a big puzzle to me and I love following the instructions, watching it take shape with each completed step. After a few evenings the furniture was all assembled and placed in position, pictures were hung on the walls and ornaments adorned the shelves and windowsills. I had finished creating my first home. Over the next few months, I was very happy there, having friends around to eat and even stay over on occasion if they'd had a few too many glasses of wine. My friend Laura came to stay for a few days when she lost her job and needed cheering up, and I had a few sleepovers with my girlfriends now and again. After three months I had my first letting agent inspection. I was hoping they would be okay with the changes I'd made, but I needn't have worried as the only comment that was made was to ask why I hadn't considered a career in interior design, which made me very happy.

Christmas 2017 was fantastic. I was invited to spend it with Serena and her two grown-up children. We had such a laugh, partly because Serena and I bring out the wicked side of each other's sense of humour, and partly because we were drinking heavily. We decided to play a game of Cards Against Humanity. I laughed so much it hurt. I also learned the depths of depravity that my best friend is capable of (scary!). That Christmas was so much fun, and I hope we get to do it again someday.

In early January, I had an appointment with the gender clinic to discuss being referred for gender affirmation surgery. The surgery involves the creation of a vagina, using skin and tissue from the male genitalia. It looks and functions very much like a natal female vagina with just a few exceptions. Firstly, it does not have the ability to self-lubricate, as there is no mucosa in the vaginal wall which would secrete lubricating mucus in a natal female. Secondly, it does not lead to a cervix and a womb so of course, childbirth is not possible. This also means that there is no monthly menstrual cycle, as there is no lining of the womb to shed. In every other way it looks and functions the same, including the function of the clitoris and urethra.

It wasn't my first visit with Dr Dhalsim. He is lovely, and we have chatted before as my transition has progressed, but the stakes were high today. I had my game face on, and he knew it. He asked me the question I had been dreading. 'How much do you weigh?' I knew as the answer left my mouth what his response would be, but like a prisoner in the dock awaiting sentence, I let him speak. Out came the calculator and while chewing the top of his pen and making involuntary humming noises, he looked up at me – 'I'm sorry, your BMI (body mass index) is 32.5. We need you at a minimum of 28. I cannot refer you for surgery at this time. I will make you a new appointment for three to four months from now, and we can weigh you again.' I don't think the gravity of his words really impacted on me at that point, I just let them wash over me. I responded politely and before I knew it, I was in the corridor facing the exit to the car park. As I sat in my car processing what had just happened, my anger spilled over and I punched the steering wheel with both fists as the tears formed in my eyes. Why didn't I take control of my weight sooner? Now I had a simple choice to make; give up and be a victim, or kick some ass. By my calculations, I had around two stone to lose. I knew what I needed to do. I fastened my seatbelt and started planning "Operation Fat Fighter".

One thing I had definitely ruled out was a fad diet like the ones you read about in Cosmopolitan or Vogue. I looked at the options, the maple syrup diet, the cucumber diet, intermittent fasting, the Himalayan starvation diet (I made that one up). There are so many crazy diets out there if you're prepared to go to extremes. I was not keen on eating dust and drinking my own urine to lose weight, so I adopted the "stop eating crap diet". I was eating pizza, McDonald's, curries, chips, and ice cream far too often, and in portion sizes that were far bigger than the recommended amount. I needed to eat smaller portions, reduce my carbs unless exercising and drastically cut back on my sugar intake. White bread, white pasta and white rice were all swapped for wholegrain alternatives, and I limited my alcohol consumption, cutting out wine and beer and swapping them for gin & tonic. I chose food with colour: lots of veggies, fruit, nuts and seeds. I reduced my meat intake and ate more fish, and I cut my dairy intake to a minimum. Exercise was next to be introduced to my daily routine, with power walking and Muay Thai boxing, as well as aerobics and yoga. I was focused and determined, I just had to hope that it would be enough.

A week or so after the devastating news that I had been refused surgical referral, I received a phone call from my friend Kelly. I met Kelly back in early 2017 through a friend at Volkswagen, and we became friends instantly.

Kelly – 'I have a proposition for you, how do you fancy three days at a mind spa with me and Caroline?'

Me – 'Let me move some stuff in my diary and I'm in.'

I had no idea what a mind spa was, but with complete trust in Kelly, we met at the venue at an equestrian centre in the Warwickshire countryside. We were greeted by two facilitators whose real names I'd rather not share, but they looked like Richard Madeley & Judy Finnigan, so let's go with that. I'm not going to give any details about them or their company for reasons which will soon become clear.

The course began on Monday morning with Richard & Judy sitting on tall chairs smiling widely out at the room as if to spread warmth, peaceful vibes and wellbeing. So far so good I thought. I was sitting in a comfy chair, I had coffee, and the room was nice and quiet despite the thirty or so delegates. I am a trainer/facilitator by trade with twenty years of experience, so when they announced that there was to be no presentation, no activities, no learning, and no agenda, I was shocked but at the same time intrigued. How did they plan to get away with this I thought? Perhaps I would learn some amazing new delivery style, which spiked my interest even further. As it turned out there was no hidden secret, no Jedi mind tricks - nothing. What actually happened was that Richard & Judy sat at the front of the room, mostly in silence, while we all sat in awkward silence staring at our feet so that we didn't have to make eye contact. Once in a while a topic of discussion would be raised or perhaps a question would be quietly asked by a member of the group. This would break the silence for a while and allow the nervous ones to sneak out to the toilet almost unnoticed. The course consisted of intentionally long coffee breaks (up to forty-five minutes), two-hour lunches which Kelly, Caroline and I used to our advantage by going to the pub, and 4.00pm early finishes. As training goes, Richard & Judy had got it made. Nice work if you can get it.

The first and second days were finished off with the group sitting in our comfy chairs wrapped in blankets (because the temperature in the room was sub-arctic), while listening to a recording of a mindfulness seminar for half an hour on YouTube. At this point Richard & Judy had sloped off to the cafeteria (no doubt to count their pot of gold earned by duping us into thinking this was in any way value for money). Needless to say, the course had no impact on my thoughts, feelings or the wellness of my mind, but it was still worth the journey every day because I got to spend three days with Kelly and Caroline and we had a right laugh.

By early Spring 2018, I was beginning to see real results in life as well as in my second puberty. I hadn't had any kind of depression since 2016 and my concentration and memory seemed to be greatly improved. My body was changing subtly with my hips and bum filling out a little, and my boobs were beginning to take shape too. My skin was soft and smooth, and my body hair was beginning to disappear in places. The gender clinic was very happy with my progress too, except for my weight which had thrown a spanner in the works regarding my surgery. Social transition was also going well, although I was still being misgendered almost daily, unless I went out wearing a lot of makeup. I was building up a lovely circle of friends in and around Milton Keynes, some were trans or at least fitted into the LGBTQ+ community somewhere, but many were women I worked with at Volkswagen. We had afternoon tea in Woburn, went out clubbing at Pink Punters or we'd eat at our favourite restaurant Nonna's in Woburn sands. My second home was the Starbucks near the train station. I often met friends there or would sit for hours working on my work projects with a slice of fruit toast and a Venti Latte.

With my confidence growing steadily day by day, I decided to get involved in more social events. I saw an advert on social media for a creative writing workshop in Brighton with the insanely talented Travis Alabanza. Travis is a performance artist, theatre maker, poet and writer, and I have for some time now been mesmerised by their work. They identify as a gender non-conforming trans feminine, using the pronouns they/them. This was an opportunity not only to meet Travis but to learn from them in a small setting with just a handful of people in a trans focussed creative writing workshop. The workshop drew from Travis' book, "Before I step outside [you love me]" and we worked our way through some really interesting exercises as the afternoon went on. I felt a deep sense of creative energy in that small space, and I was both moved and impressed by the work that we collectively and individually created. As the session drew to a close, I bought a copy of Travis' book and they signed it for me and gave me a huge hug (which was lovely as Travis is VERY cute.)

After that I took the opportunity to head to The Nuffield hospital in Brighton, where I would eventually have my gender affirmation surgery at some point in the future. It's in a beautiful location on top of the hills overlooking the sea just outside of town. Sitting in the car park staring at the building which would someday change my life forever was a strange experience, and I found myself crying. They were not tears of sadness; they were tears of self-acceptance and love. I had been to hell and back throughout the first two years of my transition, but it seemed that I was beginning to find an inner peace which had eluded me up until then.

In May 2018 I had a follow-up appointment with Dr Dhalsim to discuss my surgical referral for the second time. I was refused the referral in January due to my BMI being over 32 with a target of 28. At that time, I had formulated a plan; not just any plan, a plan that Hannibal Smith of the A-Team would have been proud of. I started Operation Fat Fighter with a weight of 92.4kg. I needed to weigh in at 80kg or less to achieve a BMI of 28 to satisfy the criteria for full vaginoplasty (surgery to create a vagina). Fast forward three months of eating less than a Guinea pig and I achieved my target, weighing in at 80.3kg on the day of the appointment.

I sat in the waiting room, very aware of the nervous beads of sweat forming on my lower back. My future happiness was riding on the outcome of this appointment. Doctor Stevens called me in, and we made small talk about the weather, his garden and how he had recently adjusted the handbrake on his wife's Volvo. He was happy with my weight and happy to give me my referral. One down, one to go. I sat there already working out that this meant at least another three to four months of waiting for an appointment to be seen again to get the required second referral. Cue super doctor! Doctor Dhalsim, who had refused my referral back in January, just happened to knock on Doctor Stevens' door while we sat chatting. He had only come to ask a fairly trivial question, but Doctor Stevens pounced on him like a lioness on a wounded gazelle, asking if Doctor Dhalsim would mind giving me a second referral while I was there. He happily agreed and summoned me to his room for a chat.

We went over the same questions and information as the last appointment, and then he confirmed my awesome weight loss (personal achievement unlocked). After typing his notes on the computer, he looked at me and said, 'I have one final question. Owing to the nature of this surgery and the fact that it is not reversible, do you feel that you may at any point regret it?' All I had to do was say no and smile. I got halfway through no, before my lip went wobbly and my eyes started leaking. I was crying uncontrollably in front of this poor defenceless doctor. Eyeliner stained my cheeks as the tears flowed. He could see that I had lost my composure and he was running out of tissues fast, so he put me out of my misery and said the words I had been waiting so desperately to hear. 'Miss Carter, I am happy to refer you to the surgical team at Brighton.' He smiled as the words hit my brain and my emotions went into overdrive. It was like being handed a gift that you've waited your whole life to receive. A gift like no other; the gift of inner peace, and a body that aligns with your internal sense of gender.

Daventry isn't too far from Leicester, so I visited my mum, who was thrilled with the news. She hugged me and we both started crying. Then I drove to my friend Kelly's house in Wolverhampton to share the moment with her. She hugged me too, and we both started crying. I called some close friends to share the news, and I cried then too. By the end of the day, I was emotionally exhausted and somewhat dehydrated from the uncontrollable crying. All happy tears though, not the tears of sadness and despair that I had been so accustomed to over the years. With my two referrals completed, I waited with childlike excitement for the day that the letter would drop through the door, inviting me to go to Brighton to meet Mr Charles Coker, the man who would perform my life affirming surgery.

Chapter Twelve
The mid-transition blues

In early June 2018, I confided in Serena for a second time about how I still felt completely out of my depth in my job as an instructional designer. I would wander off to see the technical trainers after staring at my screen for what felt like hours, just to get away from the work. I was envious of the trainers and I knew my heart belonged in teaching. Serena then dropped a huge bombshell on me: she had handed in her notice. She had found a job closer to home with better prospects and had made the brave decision to leave Volkswagen. That was the kick up the backside that I needed to deal with my own problems so I had an informal chat with the Audi training manager about a possible return to technical training. There seemed to be no appetite to have me back, so I started to look elsewhere outside of Volkswagen. In the meantime, Serena's last day came around, and as everyone cheered her on with cakes, flowers and gifts, I had to leave the office because I couldn't stop crying. Serena had become my best friend over the course of the year and my heart was breaking to know that she would not be there next to me at her desk every day. On the following Monday I spoke to Kate about the difficulties I was having getting to grips with the job and she completely understood. I thought she'd be angry with me after investing so much time in trying to help me fit in with the role and the team, but she was kind and compassionate as she always is.

Through the grapevine, I heard about a technical trainer job at DAF trucks in Haddenham, Buckinghamshire. Two of my former Volkswagen group colleagues had left to work there and there was space for one more trainer. I applied, and an interview was arranged. The interview was slightly awkward. I could tell that there was a nervousness about me being trans, and the interviewers were being very careful with the language they used. They had been totally honest in saying that they'd never interviewed a transgender person before, and they were keen to make sure they got things right. I gave them the assurances that were needed, and the questions moved onto more technical subjects. After grilling me over the function and operation of an exhaust gas recirculation valve and its effects on combustion engine emissions, they were satisfied that I had the necessary skills. Next, I was given a tour of the building by Mark, my potential new boss. He asked me to complete a practical assessment, diagnosing an electrical fault on a circuit board. This was child's play in my old job as a Senior Audi technical trainer, but I was rusty. I hadn't picked up a multimeter in over a year. Panic swept through me and I froze, but after a few seconds of staring at the circuit, my instincts kicked in and I quickly found the fault. A few days later I was offered a second interview. The brief was to deliver a fifteen-minute training session to the whole training team at DAF, but I could not talk about trucks. The brief was very vague saying that I should use my imagination. I love a challenge and training comes pretty naturally to me so after a good thinking session I decided to do a training session on strawberries. Why? Well, it was scheduled for Friday afternoon in late June so the strawberries were in season, and who wouldn't want to finish the working day and indeed the working week with fresh strawberries and cream? (Except maybe those with severe lactose intolerance or strawberry allergies). I created a beautifully colourful presentation with close-ups of fresh strawberries dripping with dew and a few fun facts thrown in for background. For example: Did you know that there is a strawberry museum in Belgium? No? Me neither but there you go - every day is a school day. The main focus of the session was to teach the team how to "hull" a strawberry. This means removing the centre stalk that runs through the middle of the fruit that has the tiny leaves on it. There are several ways to do it, but the easiest way is to push a drinking straw through the middle of the strawberry which removes the hull. The session went down very well, and while my new prospective colleagues enjoyed the fruits of their labour (see what I did there?) with their freshly hulled strawberries and fresh cream provided by yours truly, I discussed the terms of my new career at DAF trucks with my new manager.

With my notice handed in and a hug from Kate, I set about wrapping up all my outstanding projects at Volkswagen. One of those projects was a training session on transgender awareness requested by the human resources department of Volkswagen Group UK. I'd been approached by the head of HR some weeks earlier and had prepared the session and set it aside while I concentrated on my other projects. I was really nervous because I'd never met any of the thirty or so people in the room and I wasn't sure if what I had to say would be well received. I needn't have worried; Kate was there for moral support and she enjoyed the session. It seems that others did too, as some of them took the time to email me to thank them for giving them an insight into what being trans is like, and how they can be better allies to future colleagues or friends. I was on a real high that day, and part of me wondered if I'd made the right choice, but the next day when I went back to my normal projects, I knew I was doing the right thing. People seemed quite shocked that I was leaving, and many said they'd be sad to see me go. Over the next four weeks I received so many hugs from my female friends in the office, and despite my excitement to go back to teaching, I felt very sad to be leaving them behind.

There was just one more problem to deal with before I left: transport. I had a company car with Volkswagen, but my new job didn't have a car scheme. I had no savings as I was still paying for all the furniture and moving costs, so I had no choice but to buy a car on finance. I only needed something small, so I narrowed down my preferences, and top of the list was the Fiat 500. I love them; they are cute but surprisingly spacious and so much fun to drive. I struck a pretty good deal on a convertible in metallic grey with a red fabric roof, and I decided to call her

"Flossy". I couldn't wait for the day I could pick her up.

All my to do list boxes had been ticked by the time my last week at Volkswagen came around. Friday, 27th July would be my last day, and I was having very mixed emotions about leaving. Serena was doing really well in her new role and she was pleased to hear the news of my new job. Despite my treachery, Kate was still being the best boss ever, helping me to close my projects and handing the larger ones over to other designers.

Fridays at Volkswagen Group UK start with a fry-up in the onsite restaurant if you are a trainer. It's tradition, and even though I was no longer a trainer, the lads and I sat down to one final breakfast. It was good to chat with them for the last time and as I said my goodbyes, I could feel a tear forming in the corner of my eye. I had very little work to do for the rest of the day because I'd cleared up all my projects, so I spent the day anxiously twiddling my thumbs and watching the clock. I was anxious because I knew what was coming and I was dreading it. Around 3pm, people started to congregate around my desk. Not closely, just moving into the general area. 'This is it, here we go' I muttered under my breath as a pile of gifts appeared on Kate's desk and more people seemed to flock to the scene. I knew what was coming because I had been one of those people, hanging around the office waiting for the signal to pounce on the poor unsuspecting leaver on so many occasions. After being showered with praise and gifts, (which made me cry) I was asked to say a few words, but I couldn't get anything out that made any sense, so I just quietly thanked everyone, and they all clapped before starting to disperse. With one final hug from Kate, I said my goodbyes to the Volkswagen National Learning Centre, where I'd worked for the last seven years.

July 30th, 2018. The thirty-mile drive to my new job was quite picturesque, taking in several of Buckinghamshire's finest villages. I was greeted by Mark when I arrived and shown to my new desk. I'd already met the team at my second interview so I felt really at ease. I was full of excitement as I made myself familiar with the big trucks in the workshop and discovered the whereabouts of all the tools and diagnostic equipment I would need to use. Even on my first day when my nerves were unsettled and I felt out of place as the newbie, I knew I'd made the right move. This was the fresh start that I needed. Of course, I missed Kate and the team, but I knew I'd never be happy doing a job that doesn't excite me like teaching does.

Hindsight is a wonderful thing, so do I regret taking the instructional design job at Volkswagen? No, not for a second, because not only did I gain some very useful skills, it also taught me a lot about who I am. It allowed me to see that my job did not define my gender and my gender did not define my job. There was no reason why I couldn't work as a technical trainer as a woman just as well as I had as a man. I was very naïve to think that leaving the senior trainer role for a design position would in some way make me feel more feminine, or at least make others see me as more feminine. Looking back to that time, the first two years of transition, I was very naïve in general, and I made a lot more mistakes than that. I truly believe that everything happens for a reason, and that job forged my friendships with Kate and Serena, two incredible women whom I'm certain will be life-long friends.

A few days after starting at DAF, I received a letter in the post. It was marked "Nuffield hospital, Brighton". This was it, the letter I'd been waiting for since May, when I had finally been granted my surgical referral. I tore it open like an excited child and there it was, my appointment with Mr Charles Coker, August 10th 2018. I booked the day off with my boss and began counting the days until I would head to Brighton.

Have you ever been on the precipice of some big life changing event, and then something bad happens which you immediately see as a bad sign? I was leaving work on Thursday, 9th August, minding my own business as I drove out of the car park at a sensible pedestrian pace, when one of the other staff members reversed his black BMW right into the side of my brand-new car. He didn't even look, he reversed with such speed that I had no time to react or get out of his way. I got out all flustered and looked at the large crease in my rear quarter panel and dislodged rear bumper. 'Sorry 'bout that, didn't see you. Your car looks pretty new.' 'Yep, three weeks old' I replied as I held back tears of anger. I needed the car for the next day so I checked to make sure the wheel wasn't rubbing on the damaged body panel and after exchanging details, I left for home. I called my insurance company later that evening and arranged for the car to be repaired. Still angry and upset, I went to bed hoping to get some sleep before the long drive to Brighton the next morning.

August 10th arrived and as I rubbed the sleep (or lack of it) from my eyes, I could feel my heart beating against my chest. I was certain that gender affirmation surgery was what I wanted, but I wasn't fully ready for the magnitude of what was about to happen. I have spoken to many trans women about how they felt about having gender affirmation surgery, and almost all of them say the same thing: I couldn't wait, it couldn't come soon enough. I never really felt that way. Of course, it had been an important part of my physical transition, and undoubtedly the next and final logical step, but if I were given a choice between gender affirmation surgery or facial feminisation surgery on the NHS, I'd have chosen face every time. It's not that I didn't want a shiny new vagina, of course I did, but it wasn't what defined me as a woman and as such it wasn't my biggest priority at the time despite the effort that I'd made to get the referral in the first place. I could easily tuck the little fella away, especially since he was ravaged by the effects of hormone replacement therapy. After two years on HRT, there were slugs in my garden that had more physical presence than my penis, and that was fine by me. My face is the thing that everyone sees, in the street, in the queue at Starbucks and when I'm being served in a shop, restaurant or bar. This is one of the biggest sources of my dysphoria, and the thing that often attracts unwanted attention and abuse from total strangers. Facial feminisation surgery costs thousands of pounds and is completely out of reach for me. It isn't offered on the NHS, understandably, because it is seen as cosmetic and not life threatening, but ask any trans woman if they would sell their soul for a new nose or a softer jaw line and the answer will always be yes.

As I pulled into the car park in Brighton, it began to rain. This was no whimsical summer shower, this was rain of biblical proportions, the kind that would have got Noah hurrying to finish that ark. I made it to reception but not without getting drenched. Was this another bad sign? An omen? A lovely lady took me through and did all the paperwork with me before we were joined by the surgeon Mr Coker. I sat there listening to him explain the surgery in graphic detail and the risks and potential outcomes. It sounded like a scene from a horror film but still I knew I wanted to go ahead. As it turned out, he had bad news for me. My weight had crept back up during the summer, what with the stress of the new job. I'd lost focus on my goal and I'd been making excuses for it too. I had gone back to my original weight of 90kg, 10kg too heavy for the surgery to go ahead safely.

The strict BMI is to minimise the risks during surgery. I had two options, full vaginoplasty or cosmetic vaginoplasty. The cosmetic would mean that I'd have a functioning clitoris and urethra, but the vaginal entrance would be sewn shut, making it look like a vagina but without the ability to experience penetrative sex. The advantage of this is a faster healing time and no need for regular dilation to keep the depth and girth of the vagina. I had opted for full vaginoplasty. The reason was not because I expected lots of sex with my new equipment, but because I felt that I needed to have a vagina as close to a natal female one as possible. For this surgery to be as low risk as possible, a low BMI ensures that visceral fat around the organs and lower abdomen is as minimal as possible, allowing the surgeon to see where he is going and to reduce the risk of penetrating the bowel with his scalpel which would be a nasty situation resulting in months of additional recovery.

Appointment over and armed with all the information, I felt overwhelmed and very angry with myself. As it was a Friday, I had booked myself a hotel for the night, 'might as well make a little trip of it' I thought. I went to my hotel, a music themed guest house near the beach. Each room had a different theme from music history. I was given the "Pressure sounds" Reggae room. Walking into the room I was greeted by a large mural of Bob Marley with palm trees in the background and an ocean with waves lapping the shore. It filled the whole wall and was facing the bed. Distracted by this, and in a classic

Amy move, I stubbed my toe on the bed, instantly breaking my middle toe with a resounding and confirming click. Pain, PAIN! Ouch. I knew it was broken because I'd broken three toes in Muay Thai fights in my past and the clicking noise and the pain were all I needed to confirm it. After some cold water and much swearing, I headed out for some food and a few drinks, mostly to drown my sorrows. I wasn't really in the mood for going out but Brighton has a way of cheering me up. Within twenty minutes I was in Bar Revenge dancing with a Lesbian couple from Berlin and having a great time. The next morning, with an enlarged black toe, a hangover, and Bob Marley staring at me while I put on my makeup, the reality of what the surgeon had said began to properly sink in. It all felt so overwhelming and I was struggling to deal with it. There wasn't much I could do about it at that moment so I headed out to hit The Lanes for a bit of mandatory shopping. My head was a bit worse for wear so I decided that a hearty full English in the Druid's Head would sort that. As I sat there alone in the pub, I started crying. What the hell? Why was I crying? I should've been the happiest person in the pub but I was miserable. It wasn't the weight loss, I'd done it before and I could do it again, it was something more that was troubling me but I couldn't think of what it was. I tried to put it to the back of my mind as I wandered round the shops but I couldn't.

Later that day as I drove home the tears just kept flowing. The thing that I couldn't put my finger on that had upset me in the Druid's Head, was suddenly becoming clear to me. Doubts had crept in; I wasn't ready for this surgery. I got home, ate a full pint of Ben & Jerry's Cherry Garcia ice cream and went to bed. For a few months afterwards, self-loathing, indecision, sadness and depression hit me hard. Why the hell was I rebelling against my plans to have surgery? The plan that I had wanted so badly and worked so hard to achieve. I began to have nightmares, which was very out of character for me. I rarely dream, but these were horrible. It centred around my dad's death in hospital. I kept picturing the tubes and wires that he was connected to when I'd last seen him alive. For some reason, my brain associated his death with my surgery. I had never feared hospitals before but now I had developed an irrational fear of the surgery, in particular, the count backwards from ten as the anaesthetic courses through your veins and you drift off to sleep.

While my nights were filled with broken sleep and uncontrollable bouts of crying, I spent most of my days learning new training courses for my new job at DAF Trucks. I hadn't worked on trucks since I was in my early twenties, so I was rusty to say the least. Being a woman in a male dominated environment can be scary enough as it is, so imagine how I felt as a transgender woman, delivering training to a class filled with all male truck mechanics. The learners were actually very sweet. I didn't hear any nasty comments and they were generally very happy to be attending courses delivered by me. After a while the word spread around the dealer network that I seemed to know what I was talking about and I built myself a good reputation with the learners and the service managers. My bosses were happy too and my evaluations were all positive.

At the beginning of my transition, I thought that I needed to shed any trace of my old self. I used to joke that I once knew a miserable guy called Ian, but I didn't like him, so I killed him. In essence that is exactly what happened as Ian faded away and Amy came to life. I tried my hardest to remove any trace of my former self from existence so that people would see that this was permanent, and not a phase or a whim. I thought that in order to be taken seriously as a woman, I had to be hyper-feminine all the time. I thought I had to wear makeup every day, avoid wearing jeans or tracksuit bottoms in case I got misgendered, and I always wore expensive perfume. When I was out, either alone or with friends, I was constantly thinking about how I came across. I'd make sure that when I walked, I wiggled my hips and bum like Marilyn Monroe. I walked with my head held high, my shoulders back and boobs thrust forward. I doubt anyone would have noticed the boobs though because after two years on HRT, they still looked like a contoured map of Holland. Despite this, to me they were like Patriot missiles pointing at my enemies, warning them not to mess with me.

What I eventually came to realise, is that trans women shouldn't have to pander to female stereotypes or wear overtly sexualised clothing to even be considered female. My femininity should not be in question. My clothes, makeup and hairstyle are not what defines me. My "transness" is not what defines me. Women are judged for pretty much everything in society. For things like whether they have children or don't have children, whether they go back to work or not after having children, for being too fat, too thin, too ambitious, not ambitious enough, too flirty, not flirty enough, not good looking enough, or even too good looking. I'm just scratching the surface but I'm sure that this will resonate with a lot of readers. This is also true of trans women, although the extra layer of judgement is almost always based on whether or not you are still in possession of a penis, which apparently invalidates your right to be considered a woman.

This judgement is often aired publicly, as many of my trans friends can confirm. We all have stories of a time when someone in the street has stopped them to ask if they've had "the op". The suggestion that I am not a woman until I am in possession of a vagina has been made on many occasions, by friends and strangers alike. There was no real malice intended, it's just that society considers gender to be linked directly to our anatomy, and in particular our genitalia, and that is simply not true. Consider this scenario if you will. A man has an unfortunate accident and his penis is severed, and the surgeons can do nothing to re-attach it as it fell into a meat grinder (I know I'm reaching here but stay with me). Once recovered, would he still consider himself to be a man despite the absence of his penis? Yes, of course he would because that is his gender identity so why should it be different for a transgender person? Our gender identity is who we are, how we express ourselves and how we feel about our gender, not what lurks in our underwear.

Now is a good time to pass on a handy tip: If you find yourself curious about what a trans person has lurking in their underwear, DON'T ASK. It is nobody's business but theirs. Would you feel uncomfortable if a stranger asked you what genitals you had? I imagine you would. It would be completely inappropriate, and therein lies the issue. Trans people are generally seen as fair game. We've put ourselves out there, transitioning very publicly (what other way is there to do it?) so people think they have every right to ask you embarrassing and very personal questions. Actually, they don't. Trans people are still people, they deserve the same respect as anyone else.

I stopped trying to prove my femininity when I finally realised that I couldn't. As with all women, trans or not, people were going to judge me no matter what I did, so instead of trying to achieve an impossible standard, I began to learn to just be myself. Nowadays I don't wear makeup unless I'm going out with friends, or I just feel like wearing it. I am a woman, and my choice of career, what I choose to wear and what I put on my face is not going to change that.

The same is true of hobbies and interests. I love to read, and my preferred genre is romance and what is often described these days as "chick-lit". I don't like thrillers or horror and I only pay a passing interest in crime novels. This hasn't changed since I transitioned. I would often pick up a Jenny Colgan or a Jojo Moyes for my bedtime reading long before I transitioned, and they are still my favourite authors today. While my reading choices didn't change, I did actively avoid certain pastimes that I used to do frequently. Some of them I did purely to fit in as a man, so I was happy to shed them and never look back. Golf is one of them, stupid game. Another is bodybuilding. I did this for years to be big and muscular so that people wouldn't see the feminine side I was struggling to hide. Now, I still enjoy going to the gym but I prefer things like spin class, aerobics and yoga.

Back in 2012 I gave up motorcycling, my favourite thing in the world (except chocolate). I sold my Triumph Street Triple and put my leathers, helmet and boots on eBay. My debts were becoming unmanageable from buying and selling bike after bike because I needed a new distraction, and Tracey and I needed the money to set up home together. When I began my transition, I thought that I'd forget about motorcycles, but as time went on, I missed my bike more and more. As 2018 came to a close, I realised that there was absolutely nothing wrong with liking things that I used to like in my life as a man. It didn't make me a fraud, it didn't prove that I wasn't transgender, and it didn't change the fact that I am a woman. This revelation might seem pretty obvious to you, but when you have turned your entire life upside down in the pursuit of happiness and inner peace, there is a lot to learn and understand about yourself and what you want from your future.

So, what did I want from my future? I was very happy in my job, but at home I had become very depressed. I loved my little flat, but the commute was becoming a problem, and in the evenings, I was terribly lonely. I discussed my feelings with my GP, but her suggestion was to go back on anti-depressants. I'd spent most of my twenties and thirties on anti-depressants, and this was something I vowed never to do again at the beginning of my transition. I sought the advice of the gender clinic, and this led to a chat with one of their counsellors. After an hour of crying and explaining my feelings, we came to the conclusion that I was suffering from what she called "the mid-transition blues". 'This happens to most trans people,' she told me with confidence. I was less than convinced, especially as there was no magic solution other than to accept the offer of anti-depressants from my GP. 'It will pass eventually' she added, saying that the lack of any tangible progress during the middle part of transition can be very deflating, and it is easy to lose focus on the light at the end of the tunnel. She was right, I had lost focus on that light. In fact, I was beginning to lose focus on everything. Loneliness and too much time to think were beginning to unravel my brain like a ball of wool in the paws of a playful kitten.

Transition is different for every trans person. The length of time it takes to transition is also different. Despite this, some things cannot be rushed. Physical and emotional changes brought on by taking HRT will go at their own pace. Social integration in your new gender role will take time as you become more familiar to those that knew your former self, and you stand out less to strangers as you settle into your correct gender. The things that can vary the length of a person's transition the most are waiting times for clinic appointments, availability of HRT, what surgeries are required, and how they will be accessed and funded. Having made the weight requirement for surgical referral back in May, I should have been on a surgical waiting list, but due to my fear and stubbornness, I had refused to lose the weight, and I'd put surgery firmly on the back burner. This prolonged my transition by at least a year.

In contrast, some trans people have a very short transition. They may not require surgery or may not be eligible for it due to health risks. They may also have accessed HRT via private appointments which will dramatically speed up their progress. In some cases, social transition can also be a lot easier if the person has spent a lot of time in public dressed as their correct or preferred gender prior to transitioning.

In my case, I started with a blank sheet of paper. I barely spent any time in public as a woman, and I had no idea how to find acceptance from society as I learned to settle into my correct gender. I was losing patience with my perceived lack of physical progress, and every negative experience in the wider world felt like a huge setback. I was lost, confused and frustrated in equal measure. My fear of surgery and yet desperation to have it was constantly torturing me, and the loneliness made the depression even worse over time. I was beginning to feel the familiar thoughts that had filled my brain on those long journeys to and from my old job. Killing myself seemed to be the logical solution to being seen as a freak, a pervert and a monster in the eyes of some people.

I was sick of being stared at wherever I went, especially when I needed to go to the toilet. If I had to queue for the women's toilet, which is often the case, I could feel the stares burning into me. Some women (particularly young women) would shout at me. 'Fuck off out of here you pervert' was one particular comment. I remember sitting in the stall, peeing and crying at the same time, scared to open the door in case I was faced with an angry mob of women who wanted to beat me up.

This may come as a shock, but there are no recorded cases of a transgender woman going into a women's public toilet to commit a sex crime. I scoured the internet to find one for balance, but I could not. All we want to do is pee, unless it's a number two but let's not go down that road. It doesn't even make sense, most sex crimes, particularly rape, are about power rather than sexual urges. If a man wants to commit a sex crime in a women's toilet, is he really going to go to the trouble of dressing as a woman to do so? Wearing a disguise might help when robbing a bank but in this case it just doesn't happen. When I need to pee, I walk into the women's toilet with my head down, avoiding any eye contact so that I don't attract any attention or anger anyone. I head straight for the nearest cubicle, even if it isn't the cleanest, and I lock the door and pee as quickly as I can. Once finished, I wash my hands, sometimes not even bothering to dry them, so that I can leave as quickly as possible. In a women's public toilet, I feel vulnerable, I feel judged, I feel unsafe.

Physical transition was going pretty much according to plan, but social transition was proving to be the hardest thing I had ever faced. I was laughed at in a bar in Milton Keynes one night. Not because I'd just done a drunken karaoke or performed some questionable dance moves, but because I dared to stand in line at the bar waiting to be served. The young man in front of me turned around, looked me up and down and then without even looking away, nudged his friend who turned around to stare too. 'What the fuck is that?' was the response from his less than courteous friend, and on that comment, I left the bar, crying all the way home in the taxi. When I got home, the taxi driver purposely made a point of misgendering me as he asked for the fare, saying 'that will be twelve pounds mister.'

What made that bitter pill hardest to swallow was the fact that I felt content in my gender for the first time in my life. Behind the safety of my locked front door, I felt safe, content and at peace. Leaving the safety of my flat was beginning to trouble me so much that I would often make excuses to avoid turning up to social events with friends or colleagues. I decided that I'd had enough of Milton Keynes, I didn't feel safe there anymore and it was thirty miles away from my new job which was less than ideal. In September, I decided to start looking for a place closer to work. I found a nice enough flat in Aylesbury, just six miles from work. I handed in my notice at the letting agent and arranged the move. On the day that I handed the keys to my old flat back to the letting agent, they informed me that the landlord was planning to sell anyway and he had requested that I be asked to leave next month. He moved another female tenant into the flat as soon as I left. He had been to the flat a couple of times to check on the boiler, and although polite enough, it was clear he was uncomfortable being in a room with a trans woman. It wasn't even a shock when I found out that someone else had moved into the flat. As I passed the flat a few weeks later, I saw the LET AGREED sign outside and a woman putting up curtains in what was once my bedroom.

My new flat was very convenient for work, but it didn't feel like home. I missed the old flat, and even though I'd had my share of bad experiences in Milton Keynes, I still had a lot of friends there and I missed them too. After a while I began to hate the flat so much that I'd come home, park outside and sit in my car for hours playing games on my phone or reading a book. The neighbours must have thought I was mad. I used to get fish & chips on my way home from work and just sit there, often crying and feeling sorry for myself until bedtime, when I would go in and go straight to bed.

Around November 2018, I was fighting the black dog of depression hard. It was a battle like no other I'd faced before. It was worse than in 2015 when I had first planned to end my life, because at least back then I had Tracey to confide in. Now, I had no one. I was completely alone and it hurt. At work, I tried very hard to appear as though everything was okay, but it was far from it. To make matters worse, I was facing my first Christmas alone. Out of the blue, I received a text from my friend Kirsty. Kirsty and I had met about a year earlier when I worked with Q Alliance. She had needed some advice on trans matters relating to her job and had emailed the charity asking for help. As the only trans trustee, I was dispatched to assist, and Kirsty and I quickly became very good friends. Kirsty is from a military background. She grew up in bases all over Europe due to her father's military career, and later joined the Navy herself. One of the things she learned growing up on all those bases in strange countries with people they'd never met, was to always show kindness and hospitality. Every Christmas, her parents would set an extra place at the dinner table, for anyone who was lonely or in need of a friend and a good meal. This is a tradition that Kirsty has carried on. Kirsty had seen how depressed I'd been, and she wanted to help, so I was invited to join her for Christmas dinner. I have spent the last three Christmases with Kirsty, and I wouldn't have it any other way. She is one of the kindest people I know, and a wonderful friend.

Christmas 2018 was to be one of the most magical of all. I received a text message from my daughter. We hadn't seen each other since 2015, when she had decided that she didn't want to come to stay at the weekends any more. She had never really given a reason but I had no choice but to respect her wishes and stay in touch, hoping that she would one day change her mind. This all happened before I broke down and decided that transition was my only option. She had been aware for some time that I was in the midst of transition, and had communicated with me by text on and off since finding out. She was actually fine with it, although very apprehensive about meeting me for the first time. I always maintained that the choice should be hers. She would know when the time was right to see me, and my instincts as her father were right. I know my daughter; I know how much things weigh on her mind and make her panic. She is very much like me in that respect, over thinking and worrying about things that are out of her control. Despite her fears, we arranged to meet at my mum's flat, with her mum Louise there so that she would feel comfortable.

The meeting was set for a few days before Christmas. I had spent nearly a week choosing an outfit from my bulging wardrobe. I eventually settled on a tartan skirt and white top with black cardigan which looked quite Christmassy. I bought her some gifts and wrapped them lovingly, remembering all the Christmases past when I'd be up until the small hours wrapping her presents and leaving them out with subtle clues to suggest that Santa had been. I used to replace the carrots we left on the front path with ones I'd chewed off at the top so it looked like the reindeer had eaten them. I'd leave biscuit crumbs on the plate that was left out for Santa, and one year, I even bought some fake poo from a joke shop, telling her that Rudolph had done a poo on our lawn.

With gifts in hand, and my nerves in overdrive, I arrived at mum's flat and paced the room in anticipation. A few minutes later the doorbell rang, and there was my daughter, smiling nervously at me. With tears in my eyes, I hugged her so tightly, feeling the pain of being apart from her slowly dissolve into our embrace. There was so much to say, so much she wanted to learn and understand. We talked for a few hours, and when it was time for them to leave, I kissed her cheek and told her how proud I was of her and how much I love her. That afternoon will be forever etched in my memory. I was lost without my daughter - transition or not, I knew that I could never be truly happy without her in my life.

Writing this chapter has brought back so many memories of a time which was nothing but turmoil. Transition was going okay but it wasn't without its problems. The change of job and home had been stressful enough, and then there was the surgery. It seemed as though I had the weight of the world on my shoulders at times, but having my daughter back in my life had somehow washed away all that worry, depression and stress. Nothing else really mattered, and we continued to see each other as much as we could. Today, my daughter and I have a wonderful relationship. She confides in me about her boyfriends and what's happening at school, and although we don't share lots of time together due to where we both live, our relationship is stronger now than ever. She thinks that it's because I'm happier now, and I no longer have to pretend that I'm a man. Although she accepts me as a woman, she still likes to call me dad. This isn't completely comfortable for me but that is less important than my daughter's happiness, and I wouldn't expect her to suddenly start calling me mum. My daughter is an amazingly bright and perceptive young woman. I could not be more proud of her; I love her more than any words could ever describe.

Chapter Thirteen
Operation Foo Foo

Christmas 2018 was such a wonderful time. Meeting my daughter and celebrating with my friend Kirsty were a real tonic after what had been a pretty crappy year all in all. New Year was never going to top that and rather predictably, it didn't. I was still living in the flat from hell that I just couldn't bond with or call home despite its practicality and easy commute to work, and although mending the situation with my daughter was a huge step forward, I still had so many other issues to deal with. New Year 2019 was a repeat of so many others in my past. I was alone, depressed and my mind was in a mess. I got through the event with my usual tools. A family size pizza for one, a bottle of single malt whiskey and Jools Holland's Hootenanny on the telly.

At the end of January, after celebrating my daughter's birthday with her, I decided to do something about my living arrangements. It was very clear that I'd never be happy there so I began looking for a suitable alternative. There was no rush as my lease didn't run out for another two months, but it was time to find something to look forward to. My depression and the mid-transition blues were beginning to lift thanks to my daughter and the support of my friends. The last six months had been a horrible mix of severe depression and anxiety, amid dealing with one problem after another: surgical referral, job change, and health problems related to

HRT because my oestrogen level was too low. In hindsight, the very low oestrogen level may well have contributed to my depression at the time.

My search for new dwellings was hampered somewhat after a car accident on Valentine's Day. There I was minding my own business, stopped at traffic lights waiting for them to change. They turned green and just as I was about to move forward, there was a huge bang and my head whipped back into the head restraint, shattering my hair clasp into pieces across the car's interior. Still in shock, I got out of the car to be greeted by a young man who was apologising profusely. The fact that he still had his mobile phone in his hand suggested that he was looking at that rather than watching the road properly. He'd seen the lights change in the corner of his eye but hadn't waited for me to move forward. The damage to the car was relatively light but my back and neck had been jarred badly. The next six weeks were spent in pain, attending physio appointments arranged by the insurance company. Despite the advice from my insurance company, I didn't take the matter to court because I had been treated for my injury, the car had been repaired, and that was that.

While I was recovering from the accident I was still working, but physically I was in pretty bad shape. I'd stopped exercising, mostly because it hurt so much but also because I'd lost interest in my weight loss goals altogether. I was still having doubts about the surgery, fuelled by my fear of not waking up after the anaesthetic. My priority for now was to find somewhere to live. My lease was due for renewal and there was no way I would be doing that, so I was glued to Right Move and Zoopla once again. As I hated living alone, I decided that a house share may be a good fit for me. This would reduce my outgoings but also bring some social interaction which might be just what I needed to lift me out of the hole I'd found myself in. I also felt that moving back to Milton Keynes would be better for me despite the bad experiences I'd had previously. I missed my friends and even though I was dreading the long thirty-mile commute, it felt like the right thing to do. I found a lovely house share on a farm on the outskirts of town. The landlady greeted me at the viewing and showed me round the room. Plush purple carpet spreading from wall to wall showed the vastness of the huge room on offer. To the right was a full-size bathroom with under-floor heating, a corner bath and separate shower cubicle. The bathroom alone was bigger than the lounge of my current flat. I was already sold on the idea of moving in before the landlady revealed the room's secret weapon, a weapon that I was powerless to resist. Double doors were opened and there it was, a walk-in wardrobe with shelves floor to ceiling on either side and several rails for clothes along the back. I was in love. 'I'll take it' I proclaimed with glee, and the deal was done. The next four weeks were spent selling all my furniture and arranging my change of address. By the time moving day came in April 2019, I was able to do it in two trips in my little Fiat 500, with my bicycle sticking out of the open top roof and boxes stacked so high I had to peer over them at junctions to check if it was clear to go.

I settled in quickly at the farm, it really was a lovely place to live. I had my own cupboard in the large open plan kitchen and use of half of one of two fridge freezers. There were willow trees by a small babbling brook just by the entrance to the courtyard, and stables which had long since seen any equestrian activity overlooked a small wood which attracted a lot of wildlife. The other residents were all male, but they seemed to take to me with little fuss and we all got along really well. I became good friends with two of the housemates, Glen and Tony. Glen is South African, and had worked in a highly paid job at a cosmetics firm in Northampton before Covid led to redundancy. Tony worked in a warehouse in Milton Keynes, and is a very accomplished runner. His claim to fame is carrying the torch for one of the legs during the 2012 Olympics. The three of us would often organise pizza and movie nights or get takeaway at the weekends, laughing and joking over a gin or a beer. I felt really content there; I'd made the right decision.

Before the move, my friend Vicki announced that she was getting married to her partner Jeff. I was there when they first met two years before and had become very close friends with both of them. Vicki and I had met through the trans community of Milton Keynes when I first moved there in 2017. She and I had quite a lot in common and we just seemed to drift together. Vicki asked me if I would be her maid of honour. I was overwhelmed with emotion, not only for my friend and her forthcoming nuptials, but because I had dreamed of being a bridesmaid since I was a small child. Ironically, I had been a best man no fewer than four times in my previous life, but secretly, I always envied the bridesmaids at each of the weddings.

The wedding was held at the Cock hotel in Stony Stratford. The day went absolutely perfectly. Vicki looked stunning in her peach dress and I had found a lovely dress in blue with a floral pattern and a flattering neckline. There were a few slip ups during the vows due to understandable nerves, but otherwise the bride and groom got through the ceremony in one piece. My speech was well received as was Claire's, the best person. Afterwards, karaoke and dancing ensued which meant time for me to disappear to the bar. My duties were over, I was now free to enjoy a gin or two and relax. Being a bridesmaid totally lived up to my expectations and all those daydreams from years gone by. I felt like a princess, and more feminine than I had ever felt before. It wasn't the dress or the shoes or the makeup that made me feel feminine, it was the responsibility of the role, and my duty as a woman to assist my friend on her special day.

As my birthday approached in June, I decided that it was time to think about dating. I was lonely and I wanted to find someone to share my life with. While my body wasn't where I would have liked it to be before putting myself out there on the dating scene, I felt that as long as I was honest, I still had a chance of finding love. I joined a few of the more common dating sites and made a profile which made it very clear that I was trans and pre-surgery.

Until that point, I hadn't really tackled the subject of my sexuality. I had always identified as a straight man before transition but by the time transition began, I was having pretty serious doubts that I was quite as straight as I thought. After a lot of soul searching, I realised that I was attracted to both sexes. I conducted extensive research by watching lots of films on Netflix, gauging my reaction to the male and female stars on screen. With an extra-large G&T in one hand, and the TV remote in the other, I spent a whole weekend on my research. By the end of it, Chris Hemsworth, Angelina Jolie, Jude Law and Scarlet Johansson had all got me very flustered. Bloody hell, I'm bisexual!

Actually, as time went on and I did more research I discovered that I'm pansexual. If you're not familiar with that term then let me explain. If a person identifies as bisexual that means that they are attracted to both men and women, sometimes equally and sometimes with a bias toward one gender or the other. A person who identifies as pansexual is attracted to a person, not a gender. Put simply, they are attracted to hearts not parts. In the hit Netflix comedy Schitt's Creek, Daniel Levy's pansexual character David Rose sums it up beautifully when he explains that he's, "into the wine, not the label".

In a way, admitting to myself that I am pansexual was like coming out all over again. As I let the revelation sink in it quickly began to feel very comfortable to me, and looking back I'm pretty sure I was always pansexual, but like my gender issues, I repressed them hard for all those years. Needless to say, like being trans, being pansexual is not a phase, a whim or an experiment. It's who I am.

Now that I finally knew what I wanted, and what type of person I was attracted to, I felt more confident in myself. I knew that I was unlikely to find the love of my life in a bar or club like I had done in my old life, because I was now fishing in a much smaller pond. That pond is full of sharks and nasty little piranhas with very outdated and often offensive views on trans women. There are some decent guys and girls out there but they are few and far between in my experience. On the more mainstream sites I regularly received messages based only on my profile picture. They clearly hadn't taken the time to read the profile blurb because as soon as I mentioned I am trans, they deleted the conversation.

On the LGBTQ+ sites, I often received pictures of random guy's dicks, with no accompanying words or even a romantic gesture. Sometimes I'd get messages like "wanna suck my dick?" (who says romance is dead?). Guy's profiles often used outdated nouns from the porn industry like "Tranny", "Shemale" or "Ladyboy" to describe what they were into, which are deeply offensive terms for most trans women. I found all these sites to be pretty much the same. Swipe left if you don't like them, swipe right if you do. I think I developed repetitive strain injury from swiping left. Lesbian women mostly made it clear that they were not interested in dating a trans woman. In some cases, they actually pointed out that they don't recognise trans women as "real" women. Men were generally just sleazy, mostly asking if I'd had "the op". And what is it with guys and their profile pictures? I was often confused at what I was supposed to be looking at. If not confused then shocked, or just disappointed with the male gender per se. For those of you that are considering joining one of these swipe happy dating sites, here are a few handy tips from your Aunty Amy on choosing a profile picture.

1. The picture should have YOU in it.
2. I don't want to see your children. I'm sure they are lovely but protect them from predators.
3. Women don't care about the fish you caught last week, unless they subscribe to Angling Times. On a side note, fishing waders look attractive on no-one.
4. Smile, it's free!
5. Sunglasses may look cool but they hide your eyes; possibly the biggest connection point for a woman.
6. The under the chin angle is not flattering; especially if you have a selection of chins.
7. That pic of you with your arms around your ex isn't helping sweetheart.

8. Why do you look so angry? It's not macho, it makes you look like a serial killer.
9. That's not your Ferrari you're standing next to, is it?
10. Lycra. Just…. No.
11. Why are you half naked in your bathroom mirror? Do you have no clothes? Shall I set up a "Go fund me" page to get you some?
12. Using a pic of you in your twenties when you're fifty-three? Why?

It may seem like I'm bashing all guys here but believe me I'm not. I'd love to meet a nice genuine man who understands that I'm just as valid as any other woman. Unfortunately, on these sites, they are the needle in the haystack. Whoever you are and whatever you're into, be honest, be kind. If trans women aren't your thing, just scroll on by.

My dating profile got a few views in the first week but nothing concrete came of it until one afternoon when I heard the familiar ping of a notification on my phone. A message from a nice-looking man in his mid-forties called Mark. He had read my profile and liked what he saw. We arranged a dinner date for the following evening and a time and place to meet. He looked very smart in his grey suit and open collar crisp white shirt. He was slightly skinny with salt and pepper hair and a broad smile that showed a few age lines at the corners of his eyes. We sat down to dinner and chatted our way through three courses and coffee. He travelled the country fixing industrial machinery. He was married but his relationship wasn't working (that old chestnut) and he wanted to explore the possibility of meeting someone new. Although I was attracted to him, something other than the obvious lie about his wife was bothering me. I decided to ask him outright. I had nothing to lose as I wouldn't be seeing him again anyway because he was married. 'What is it that made you want to message me?' I asked. His response was enough to sour even the crème brûlée that I was about to eat. 'I'm not gay or anything, but I fancy playing with a cock.' I wasn't sure whether to throw my Chablis over him and storm out or hear him out. It turned out that he had a fetish for cross-dressers and pre-op trans women. TAXI!

Guys like this are known as "chasers" or "tranny chasers" to use the full term. The word "tranny" is horribly offensive to most trans women, so we generally shorten it to just chasers. They are specifically turned on by cross-dressers and trans women who have a penis. Speaking of penises, I logged onto the dating site the next day to send Mark a message, and to give him a piece of my mind, only to find three new messages. Two of them contained dick pics, and only one of them had a request, 'fancy a fuck?' What a lovely well-rounded individual. The third was from a man with possibly the hairiest legs I've ever seen, wearing what he described as "his wife's panties". Delete, delete, delete. NEXT!

A few weeks later I tried a new site. It seemed a lot less seedy than the previous one from which I'd removed my profile after a barrage of dick pics from pervy men. I find it ironic that these men will abuse me in the street for being trans and yet send me pictures on the internet of their semi-flaccid genitals behind their partner's back. I came across the profile of a trans woman around the same age as me, called Helen. I messaged her and to my surprise she messaged back the next morning. We arranged to meet in my hometown of Leicester as it was half-way between where we both lived. We arranged to have coffee and a chat, nothing fancy. We didn't have much in common but there was definitely a spark between us. She was in the military which fascinates me, so I was happy to listen to her stories as the afternoon passed. Helen was a no-nonsense straight-talking woman from the north, which would turn out to be just what I needed. We dated for a month or so before she had to go on a two-year sabbatical in Europe. This meant that she would only be home for a few days every three months or so and this put a huge strain on our fairly new relationship.

I am a firm believer in fate. I believe that some people come into our lives for ever, and some come into our lives to make a change, or to teach us something new, or maybe just lift us up when all feels lost. At that point in my life, I needed a straight talking no bullshit kick up the backside, and Helen was the one to deliver it. After many conversations about surgery and my weak explanations of my fear and anxiety, she had clearly had enough. 'Look, you either want it or you don't. Can you imagine being truly happy without a vagina? It's really that simple.'

She was right, it really was that simple. I had to face my fears, I knew I needed to have the surgery and the sooner the better. I'd procrastinated for over a year since my surgical referral, and I should have been done and fully recovered by now. As I waved her goodbye on her way back to the base in Europe, I had a renewed strength and willpower to get the job done.

It was time to sort myself out and get the surgery over with. As I'd done the previous times that weight loss was needed to reach my goal, I came up with a plan: Operation Foo Foo. This was more than just a reference to my surgical procedure. This was a mission, planned with near military precision. I had procrastinated long enough. Battle plans were drawn, commitments made and written down on post-it notes for self-motivation and encouragement. I committed myself to a vegetarian diet with lots of fresh fruit and vegetables, and hardly any processed food. Whole-grain rice and whole-wheat pasta replaced their white counterparts and alcohol and junk food were completely banned. I called the hospital to tell them that I was no longer just floating around aimlessly in their system, and that I had a target to be ready for surgery before Christmas. Nicky, Mr Coker's PA, was delighted to hear this news, and wished me well in my mission. 'Just give us a call when you get near to your target weight and we will arrange to check your weight and book your pre-med.' This was like music to my ears, but I had so much work to do before that day would come.

I exercised twice a day. A combination of Zumba, aerobics, yoga, Muay Thai, power walking and running was getting the job done fast. I had breakfast after the first workout, either a smoothie made from spinach, carrot and mixed fruit, (which tasted like bin-juice) or a bowl of granola which is basically mildly sweetened gravel. Lunch was mainly salads or low carb foods and my evening meal, after the second workout, mostly consisted of steamed vegetables and some form of protein like Quorn or beans. By the end of September, four weeks after starting the diet and exercise, I had lost 2kg, with another ten to go. Game on.

Another topic of conversation that Helen was sick of hearing on our long-distance evening phone calls was motorcycles. I hadn't owned a bike since 2012 and following my recent epiphany that I didn't have to completely avoid the things that I loved from my old life, I was aching to get back on a bike. As she had with the surgery, she gave me a pretty no-nonsense answer to my constant bike chatter: 'for Christ's sake woman, will you just buy a bike then maybe you'll shut up about it.' Fair point, although slightly harsh I thought. My morning routine now included a thirty-minute session on a stationary bike. I used to point it at the telly and get to pedalling, but now I spent my pedal time on eBay looking for a second-hand motorcycle. After a week or two of searching I found a lovely Yellow Honda CBR600F. With a bit of bartering, I struck a deal with the seller and the job was done. I was a biker once again. It was like slipping on a familiar old pair of shoes. I rode that bike every chance I got, and when I wasn't riding it, I was fixing it or making improvements to it. It was given the name "Dorothy" partly after my grandmother Dorothy Kate, and partly a reference to that famous yellow brick road.

At the end of September, I decided to start the process of getting my GRC (Gender Recognition Certificate). This is a legal document that proves that a person has changed their gender permanently, both legally and medically. It can only be applied for if the subject has lived in their correct gender role for at least two years, has been diagnosed with gender dysphoria, and intends to live in their correct gender until death. It does not require the subject to undergo gender affirmation surgery, because this would be discriminatory to those individuals who cannot have surgery for medical reasons or simply don't feel that they need it. After submitting more evidence than it took to convict Ted Bundy, including household bills, payslips, medical correspondences dating back over two years, a signed declaration witnessed by a solicitor, and the non-refundable £140 fee, my case was put before the panel. The judgement is made by a group of professionals such as magistrates, general practitioners and civil servants, who operate under a branch of the HM Courts & Tribunal Service called the GRC panel. If the subject's application is approved, they can then apply for a new birth certificate in their correct gender. Recently, the application fee for a Gender Recognition Certificate was reduced to just £5 to make it more accessible. After a nerve-racking two-week wait for news, I received an email from the panel saying that I had been successfully granted a gender recognition certificate, and I was now eligible to apply for a new birth certificate. I was overwhelmed with emotion; I now had legal confirmation that I am female. My transition was coming to an end with just my surgery to get through, and this marked another important milestone along the way. A week later, two A4 envelopes arrived in the post: my new GRC and my birth certificate. Opening them both and staring at the words – "Gender: Female" had me in floods of tears. I had dreamed of seeing that on my birth certificate for such a long time but here it was in my hand. The process for me was pretty straight-forward. I have heard of some people having a hard time convincing the panel, but if you have lived in your correct gender for the appropriate amount of time and have documentation to prove it, you will be fine.

Operation Foo Foo was going brilliantly. My diet and exercise regime were working better than I'd anticipated and I made the required weight by the end of October. I called the Nuffield hospital in Brighton to give them the good news. Teresa, the specialist healthcare assistant (HCA) asked me to book in with my GP to have my weight checked. I asked if it was possible to come down to Brighton to do it in person instead, as I felt that going to my GP might delay the process after booking an appointment, waiting for them to send the results and so on. Teresa thought I was mad but agreed that I could travel down to them on the Friday of that week.

After a traumatic journey round the M25 (Britain's biggest practical joke), I made it to Brighton just in time for my weigh-in appointment. Wearing my lightest carbon fibre racing knickers and nothing else, I jumped on the scales. 80kg dead-on. Result! With my weight officially recorded on my file, I headed to the beach to collect my thoughts. I love to just stare out to sea sometimes; it is a great way to connect with your subconscious thoughts and emotions. After a few moments I started crying; no sadness, no misery or despair, just tears of joy and relief. All that hard work, all that sacrifice that I'd put in to lose twelve kilos in weight, had come down to this one day. All I had to do now, was keep the weight off until I had a date for surgery. I headed home feeling very proud of myself, but in the back of my mind, those nagging fears about the surgery were still lurking.

Two weeks after my weigh-in, I was laughing and joking with my colleagues at work on our break when my phone rang. It was Nicky. 'Hi Amy, congratulations on the weight loss. Now we need to get you booked in for your surgery. What are you doing on January 17th, 2020?' My heart was pounding with excitement but also fear. This was it, it all suddenly became so real. 'I… I'm pretty sure I can make that date' I said with tears streaming down my face. Nicky tried her best to calm me down, but she was fighting a losing battle. 'I'll send your pre-med pack in the post. Please stop taking your HRT at least six-weeks before the surgery date. Have a lovely Christmas but keep off the chocolate! I'll see you in January.' With that she hung up the phone and I was suddenly aware that my colleagues were all staring at me, wondering what on earth could have been said to reduce me to such a blubbering mess so quickly.

A date arrived with my pre-med pack for me to go to the Nuffield in Brighton to have some checks and swabs done prior to surgery. Checks for MRSA and other nasties are done as well as a general tick list to prepare for the upcoming surgery. I decided to take my motorcycle, which seemed a great idea as the sun shone down on a sunny Milton Keynes morning, but was less appealing on the way back, on a dark, and freezing cold November afternoon.

My pre-med was something I really wasn't looking forward to but it turned out to be really relaxed because the nurse was so lovely and also hilariously funny. Sitting chatting in her office after all the tests and checks were complete, she went through my notes, and then she said this; 'ooh, you've got Mr Coker. You're going to have a lovely fanny!' I was shocked, and for a split second there was silence before we both fell about laughing. She explained that Mr Coker was known for his amazing suture work, leaving minimal scarring. This, I was very pleased to hear. After giving her a hug and waving goodbye, I set off for home. Riding home in the cold and the dark, I should have been miserable. I was bloody freezing and my hands were so cold I could barely pull the clutch lever to change gear. Despite this, in my heart I was so happy; the end was in sight. All those tears that I'd wept throughout my transition had not been in vain. The light at the end of the tunnel was finally ahead of me. By the time I got home to the farm, my hands were blue with cold and I struggled to dismount from the bike. 'Ow, ow, ow, ow, ow' I uttered with each step as my stiff back and legs creaked as I walked to the front door.

      As Christmas 2019 loomed, I started to make plans for my surgery. Time off had been booked at work, but I was cutting it fine. The minimum recovery time is twelve weeks before it is considered safe to go back to work, but I had just nine weeks. I couldn't afford to live on statutory sick pay so I had to hope that recovery went well, and I could get back to work a little earlier than advised. The next step was to sort out how I would get to and from the hospital. My friends stepped in to help with this. Vicki offered to drive me down to Brighton. I had to be there at 6.30am so we decided that it was best to go the day before and make a little trip of it. My lovely friend Gwen offered to bring me home. She and I have been friends since 2015 when I first started working with Q Alliance, the LGBTQ+ charity based in Milton Keynes. Gwen is one of my closest friends, someone who I have confided in on many occasions when the going got tough and I was at my wits' end. Her calm nature and soothing voice are a tonic at times, and I was very grateful for her offer of help. Lastly, I needed a plan for the first few days after getting home. I wouldn't be allowed to lift anything heavier than a spoon, so I needed a little help. Luckily, this had been sorted many months ago. My dear friend Kelly was out with me in Birmingham one day doing a bit of shopping. Out of the blue over a coffee, she said, 'I know we haven't known each other long, but I'd love to offer to come and stay with you for a few days after your surgery to look after you.' I was blown away by her offer. It was true, we had not been friends for long and although it was clear that we would be close friends as time went on, she had no obligation or reason to make that offer other than out of kindness and compassion. The offer was accepted with a grateful smile, and we finished our coffee and went for a makeover in Debenhams. Kelly is an amazing woman and one of my favourite humans. Not only does she do an incredible amount of work for the LGBTQ+ community, she is also a businesswoman and a sister in the NHS, working in sexual health. She is also the sexual health advisor for this book.

At the beginning of December, I stopped taking HRT. For the first week, there were no real side-effects but as week two progressed, the hot flushes hit hard. There is no warning when they strike: one minute you are comfortable and your pits are nice and dry, then next minute, you feel hotter than an active volcano and you are dripping with sweat. It's really uncomfortable and can be very embarrassing too if it happens when you are out. Night sweats came on around the same time, which meant I got very little sleep and I was constantly stripping my bed to change the sheets. After week four, the hot flushes and night sweats calmed down a little, and the only other symptoms I had were tiredness and lack of energy. I had timed my HRT very carefully so that my last testosterone blocker injection, which lasts for twelve weeks, would be due just a week before surgery. This meant I would not need to bother having that, because after surgery, my body would no longer make any testosterone, hence no need for the blocker.

Christmas with Kirsty was as lovely as it had been the previous year, although I wasn't allowed to eat much, and alcohol was kept to a bare minimum to avoid weight gain. New Year was another quiet affair. I wanted to be alone, I had a lot of thinking to do and still so many fears over the surgery. With a glass of whiskey in my hand and Jools Holland tinkling the ivories like his life depended on it, I looked to the heavens and asked my dad for help and guidance. I must have fallen asleep in my chair but when I woke up in the early hours of New Year's Day, a strange sense of calm had come over me. Was that my dad's doing? I'd like to think so.

January 16th, 2020. Vicki arrived to take me to Brighton, and as we loaded the car with my small pink suitcase, she could see that I was nervous. 'You will be fine sweetheart, I promise' she said as we set off on our journey south. After checking in to our hotel, Vicki and I spent the day wandering around Brighton, checking out the shops and stopping for the occasional ice cream or bag of chips. I wasn't allowed to eat much as I had to follow a low residue diet for twenty-four hours prior to the surgery which basically consisted of white bread, pasta or rice, mashed potato, carrots and clear soups. While Vicki tucked into her sausage & chips, I looked on in envy with my plain chips with no salt & vinegar.

Back at the hotel I said goodnight to Vicki, and she went off to call her husband Jeff before settling in for the night. I stared out of my window for what seemed like hours. There was no point going to bed, the chances of me getting any sleep were slim to none. I tossed and turned all night worrying about what lay ahead. The fear and worry that I wouldn't wake up from the anaesthetic, or I'd bleed to death on the operating table were still very real to me.

At around 5am I showered and dressed and then packed my bag ready for hospital. At 5.30am I knocked on Vicki's door.

It was only a short drive to the hospital, and we arrived a little early. I didn't want to wait around because I knew it would only make me more anxious, so I hugged Vicki (who was going back to the hotel for some more sleep and a well-deserved full English breakfast) then I left the warmth of her car and headed for the reception doors. There I was, a frightened trans woman nervously knocking on the doors of the hospital on a dark and very cold mid-January morning. After a few moments, the doors swished open and a nurse with a very kind face asked my name and then ushered me into the warmth of the waiting room. There was another equally nervous-looking young trans woman sitting there, and after checking us in, we were escorted to the ward and shown to our rooms. I was given room 22; a light airy room with a view of the sea. I placed my suitcase on the bed and began to unpack.

Just as I finished arranging my underwear and nightwear into neat piles in the closet, (OCD is a terrible thing) the nurse returned with a gown and some attractive-looking compression stockings which I was informed would stop me from dying of a blood clot (dramatic). Before I was allowed to adorn these stylish garments, I had to have the dreaded enema. This is to ensure that the bowel is completely purged before the surgeon gets intimate with your inside bits. I lay on my side, wishing the ground would swallow me up while the nurse fairly roughly shoved a laxative suppository deep inside my tortured rectum. 'Hold it in for at least ten minutes then go to the toilet', she said as she left the room. No problem I thought, as I lay on my bed staring at the sea view from my window trying not to think of the recent violation of my bottom. Within thirty seconds I heard the rumbling, then the bubbling, then, oh god! It felt like my insides were being jet washed. I held my nerve, trying my hardest to follow the nurse's instructions. Ten minutes! There was no way I was going to make ten minutes. I had reached four minutes and I was already at DEFCON 5, imminent attack! By now I was in considerable abdominal pain and the instructions of the nurse had gone out the window completely. This was it; it was happening. I sprang from my bed and launched myself into the small bathroom in my room. Gripping the sides of the toilet with both hands, I braced myself for what was about to happen. With the gentlest release of grip from my overworked sphincter, the world fell out of my bottom! After the pain had subsided, I sat there wondering if I was doing the right thing. Maybe my fears weren't so stupid after all. Even the preparation was traumatic.

After the drama of the enema, I showered and dressed in a surgical gown and the compression stockings before the nurse reappeared. 'It's 8am, they are ready for you, follow me.' The procedure is to follow your own bed to the theatre. At the end of the corridor, the porter pushing my bed turned left into the recovery room and I was ushered into the pre-med room. I lay on the bed and a man with possibly the kindest face I've ever seen greeted me. 'Good morning Amy, I'm you're anaesthetist. By now major panic had set in and I was fighting back tears. It must have been obvious that I was anxious because all the nurses kept reassuring me. After asking my name, address and date of birth, he asked, 'so Amy, what are we in for today?' 'Tonsils' I said with half a smile. He looked at me and said 'well that's not what I have on my paperwork', with a giggle. I said 'just kidding, can I have a vagina please?' At this point I couldn't hold the tears back any longer, I was crying uncontrollably. A lovely nurse held my right hand as the canular was inserted very painlessly into my left. The anaesthetist told me that in a few seconds, I would feel as if I'd had several Gin & Tonics. I was frightened and felt more alone than I had ever felt in my whole life. In just a few seconds I started to feel very weird, like I was completely hammered. I heard him say 'here we go', and that's the last thing I remember. I came round in the recovery room sometime around 11.30am.

During the one hour and forty minutes that I was in surgery, Mr Coker had worked his magic, creating my shiny new Foo Foo. When I was researching this chapter, I was alarmed to discover that like me, so many women have names for their genitalia. Front bottom, growler, flange, cha-cha, mini-moo and tuppence were among the most popular, but I like to refer to my shiny new front bottom as my Foo Foo (I name everything. Even my vacuum cleaner has a name. He's called Steve McClean). The surgery is pretty complex, depending on which choice the recipient has made. As I mentioned previously, the two options are a cosmetic vagina, which has a functional clitoris but no vaginal passage, or full vaginoplasty (such a sexy name), where there is a functional clitoris and a vaginal passage which once healed, can accommodate penetrative sex. I'm no expert so this explanation is in layman's terms at best, but the basic procedure is to first remove the testicles and throw the troublesome little buggers in the bin, then invert the penis, so that it becomes a tube, a bit like turning a sock inside out.

After this, a small piece of the head of the penis containing the nerves that are required to achieve orgasm, are positioned at the top of the vagina to form the clitoris. The urethra is shortened and positioned between the vaginal entrance and the clitoris, and the vaginal passage is anchored with stitches inside the abdomen. Finally, scrotal skin is used to create the labia majora. A pack is then inserted which is essentially a swab, and then drains and a catheter. Job done.

I only lost 100ml of blood during the surgery, about a third of a can of Coke, and everything went perfectly with no issues. I had no pain and no need of strong pain-killers. The sense of relief was immense as I lay there with an oxygen tube in my nose, and once again I found myself crying. This time, the tears were not because I was frightened, or because I felt desperately alone. They were relief, happiness, and pure joy. I lay in bed feeling very tired and groggy from the anaesthetic, but smiling like I'd never smiled before. Later that day Vicki visited me before heading home to Milton Keynes. She smiled and said that I looked completely at peace. That night I was starting to feel human again and I was beginning to take stock of where I was and how I felt. I was so happy, relieved and content. I had very little pain and certainly nothing that paracetamol couldn't deal with. I was told not to move too much for the first two days so I lay flat on my back watching TV or staring at the sea from my window. Directly across from me is a Kestrel nesting box. The hospital has a CCTV camera trained on it with night vision. If you turn on the hospital TV system you can watch the Kestrels as they come and go. This provided me with hours of entertainment as I love birds of prey.

    The next morning, I woke up to a cheerful looking nurse who had brought my pain relief. Nothing heavy, just paracetamol. She also gave me a bed bath and we chatted as she carried out her tasks. After she left, I lay there relaxing, watching the clouds roll across the sky, when I suddenly felt a very strange sensation. Confused, I tried to engage my brain to work out what on earth was going on, but it didn't make any sense. I had an erection, or at least my brain thought I did. I call this phenomenon "Phantom Winky Syndrome" or PWS. I no longer had a penis, but my brain was still figuring that out, and it was taking its time to rewire the circuits. Over the next few days, I had quite a few phantom erections, and on a few occasions, I felt like I'd been kicked in the nuts too, but this was all part of the process of the damaged nerves repairing themselves, and my brain trying to work out its brand-new anatomy.

    At the hospital, surgery day is referred to as day zero. On day one I started to get trapped wind in my abdomen. They gave me peppermint capsules and peppermint tea but to no avail. This pain was really bad and the only real pain I experienced in my entire stay in hospital. On day two I was allowed to get up and sit in a chair. Within a few minutes the trapped wind was gone and all was well again. After that I had no pain at all. I was given paracetamol four times a day and a little codeine but that's it, and I'm not even sure I needed that. On day three I sat in the chair on two separate occasions for around half an hour each time. On day four my drains were removed and I had a visit from my dear friend Emma, who drove all the way from her home in Malvern to Brighton just to see me. I was so glad to see her, not only because she had driven such a long way, but also because she had brought me a Terry's Chocolate Orange, my absolute favourite. That night I didn't get much sleep because I had a strange feeling that I was bursting to go to the toilet despite having a catheter in. The nurse checked it and it was filling the bag correctly so she just said she'd keep an eye on it. At 3am on day five, my catheter let go and I wet the bed. I had no control over it and I was very embarrassed to say the least. The nurse helped me to get up, and she changed the bed. The catheter had collapsed, and was no longer doing its job, but it didn't really matter because it was due to be removed in a few hours anyway.

Day five was the big day! My outer dressing was coming off and my internal pack removed. I had been assured that this was a relatively painless process followed by a lesson in how to dilate my shiny new vagina. My outer dressings came off easily and my failed catheter was finally removed. This wasn't painful but very uncomfortable (I hate catheters). The lovely ward sister Catherine described the process of dilation to me as she worked, asking me to repeat each step as she explained it. While this was going on I could see that she was rummaging around down there like she was looking for a set of keys in a kitchen drawer. 'There, all done, your pack is out.' she said. I couldn't believe it. I didn't even know she'd started. I knew she was distracting me purposely by asking me to recite her instructions but I at least thought I'd feel some discomfort. She then taught me how to dilate my new vagina correctly. Dilating the vagina is necessary to maintain its depth and integrity. This process starts with three dilations a day for the first three months then it goes down to twice, then a few months later once a day and eventually after around a year you can do it once or twice a week but it must be done for the rest of your life. After my first solo dilation, I douched my vagina with Videne iodine solution and took my first shower in five days. Don't get me wrong bed baths are lovely but there's nothing finer than a good hot shower. After this I had no tethers, no drains, catheters or cannulas left in me so I went for a wander down the corridors. My legs were a little wobbly after being unused for the last six days but I soon found my balance and soon after I found the coffee machine and the cookie stash. By now I was on a normal diet and I'd had some lovely cheese and pickle sandwiches, Halloumi and kale salad and even sticky toffee pudding and custard (I love being vegetarian). By bedtime I was exhausted from the emotions of the day, having seen my vagina for the very first time, learning the process of dilation with Catherine and pottering around the ward. I slept better than ever that night but on waking the next day my heart was heavy with sadness, I wasn't ready to go home.

I had met some wonderful people who cared for me amazingly. You might say it's their job to do that, and of course you'd be right, but people make the difference. While Mr Coker had worked his magic in creating my new female anatomy which I am eternally grateful for, these nurses, doctors, caterers, administrators and healthcare assistants had all played a part in looking after me and I didn't want to say goodbye. As I write this, I'm crying just thinking about them. I have so much gratitude for all that they did for me.

I started day six with a dilation and a shower then packed my bags and took a box of chocolates and a thank you card to ward reception. Walking down the ward nurses were hugging me and saying they'd miss me. A trans friend who'd had her surgery a few years before me once said that if she could do it all again, she would. I thought she was bonkers at the time but now I've been through the experience, I totally agree with her.

At around mid-day my friend Gwen arrived, and I said an emotional final goodbye to the Nuffield hospital as we headed home to Milton Keynes. I will never forget my stay there, and I will never be able to repay the amazing team for what they did for me.

Chapter Fourteen
It's like riding a bike

January 23rd, 2020, I'm going home. After a very emotional final day in hospital, hugging all the staff and crying like a baby, I shuffled across the car park toward my dear friend Gwen's car. The general consensus from others who had undergone this surgery was that the journey home was going to be an unpleasant one. It's a little over a hundred miles from Brighton to Milton Keynes so I'd braced myself for bad times as we made our way over Britain's largest off-road track, known more commonly as the roads of Buckinghamshire. As it turned out, the journey couldn't have been smoother. Gwen is an excellent driver, her Toyota Prius is very comfortable, and my tortured nether regions were further comforted by the addition of two large pillows that Gwen had thoughtfully brought with her. Roughly three hours after we left the hospital car park, we arrived at the farm where I lived. I was glad to be home although I was still missing the safe comfort of my hospital bed and all those wonderful people who had looked after me for those incredible six days. There was no key to the front door of the farmhouse we all shared, just a keypad. It had only been a week since I last used the code but I couldn't recall it. After staring at the numbers for a while it suddenly came back to me and we were in. The stairs were a little tricky, but without even thinking, I wrestled my small pink suitcase up to my room. Gwen told me off for carrying it and of course she was right, but I find it hard to accept help from people, I always have. I'm so used to hiding my true feelings and dealing with my own shitstorms that I almost feel guilty when I'm offered help of any sort.

Gwen stayed for coffee then with a hug, she left for home. Even though I lived in a house share with four other people, at that point I was alone in the house and it felt really strange. I'd had constant company since the moment I left for Brighton with Vicki. Either a nurse, a doctor, a caterer or a friendly visitor had been in and out of my room at some time. So, there I stood in the lounge of the big farmhouse. I started to cry. I'd done a lot of that in the last week, not only because of the emotional turmoil of the surgery, but while I was in hospital, I had also received the tragic news of my dear friend and colleague Gary's passing. This was different though; I couldn't understand why I was crying. Looking back, I think it was a little bit of relief to be finally home after a pretty traumatic week, and a little bit of sadness to have left the hospital behind and all the wonderful people who had cared for me and made me smile or sat with me when I was upset.

Later that afternoon, my friend Kelly arrived by taxi. I was so happy to see her as she walked up the drive. She'd thoughtfully ordered pizzas from the train station and they arrived at almost exactly the same time that she did which was wonderful as I was starving. I gave her a huge hug (she gives the best hugs) and we tucked into our food as I told her all about my week in hospital.

Kelly and I had a wonderful three days, chatting and laughing. It really cemented our friendship and I can say without question that she is a friend for life. I'd do anything for her, I'd drop everything for her. Every time I meet up with Kelly, we have so much fun. The business meeting that ended up being a shopping trip and makeover, the mind spa experience, taking a course on working with trans youth at the Tavistock and Portman hospital, meeting our heroes Fox Fisher, Owl, Romario Wanliss, and Caroline Paige at a trans seminar, or being a guest on her radio show at Gorgeous FM - we always have fun. I love that girl like a sister.

There is a lot of pain in the early weeks after gender affirmation surgery. It is considered to be pretty major surgery and as such there is a lot of healing to be done. Most of the pain is from sitting, but walking can also cause pain in the deep tissue of the lower abdomen. Walking wasn't painful as such, I think a more accurate description would be discomfort, sharp pulling pains is the best way I can describe it. The pain when sitting is by far the worst. I couldn't sit on any kind of hard chair or bench for several weeks because it felt like someone was trying to insert a fence post into my vagina.

For the first few days I struggled to lift anything heavier than a tin of beans, and I tried not to move around too much. The dilation routine was going okay but my god does it take up a lot of time. Don't get me wrong time was something I had plenty of but dilating three times a day with each one taking

approximately an hour can become tedious really
quickly. Nonetheless it was a necessary process if I
wanted to heal quickly and get back to work and start
enjoying life. The dilators are made of clear Perspex,
and look a bit like a vibrator, around seven inches in
length. There are two of them, one with a smaller
diameter and one larger. I affectionately named mine
Ronnie and Reggie, after the notorious Kray twins.
My reasoning was that like the Krays, these two little
buggers were going to be nothing but trouble. The
dilation routine post-surgery consisted of cleansing
with disinfectant wipes, lubricating the area with a
water-based gel, then dilation with the small dilator
(Ronnie) for ten minutes followed by a further ten
minutes with the larger one (Reggie). This is followed
by douching the vagina with a mix of Videne
antiseptic solution and water to prevent infection.
After this a shower using aqueous cream to clean the
whole area and suture lines. Then came the fun part, I
had to lie on the bed, legs akimbo with a hair dryer.
This was to ensure that the wound was completely
dry in order to reduce the chance of infection. I don't
know if you have ever lain on your bed blow drying
your vagina, but I can tell you it's a very surreal
experience. Once in a while when I was bored of the
routine, I'd go into full hairdresser mode, asking my
vagina if she was going on holiday this year of if
she'd like some highlights or a perm. This routine
was repeated three times a day, morning, mid-
afternoon and just before bed. After three months of
this trio of daily tortures, it went down to twice a day.
After six months it went down to once a day, and

eventually, I was able to dilate just once a week. I didn't feel daunted by this task because to me it is just part of the female care process that any woman would go through. Okay most women don't have to dilate their vagina, but feminine care is still important in whatever form it takes.

January 27th, 2020, the day after Kelly had gone home. I was preparing to dilate in the evening around 10pm. In my bathroom, where I did all my dilations, I lay on the waterproof changing mat that the hospital recommends you to use and opened my legs ready to begin dilation. Before I'd even started, I suddenly noticed blood pouring from my vagina at a fairly quick rate. I'm first aid trained so I packed a towel into the wound as tight as I could and called 999. I'd heard stories from other trans women of major bleeds from the surgery particularly around the urethra where there is a good amount of vascular activity. The ambulance crew arrived in less than ten minutes. While I waited for them, I knelt on the towel packing, pushing it hard into my wound with my heel. I was crying uncontrollably and poor Glen had come from his room to see if he could help. I rang my sister, who was trying to keep me calm as I wept. The ambulance crew were let in by Glen and came into my room to assess the situation. They were both women and seemed quite relaxed in comparison to my mild hysterics and declarations of 'I don't want to die'. I had convinced myself that I was bleeding to death, and there they were sitting on the floor complimenting my deep pile purple carpet and walk in wardrobe. My bathroom looked like a crime scene, there was blood on the floor, blood on the walls, blood in the bath and blood on the sink and mirror. After doing some routine observations, they decided that although the packing had worked and the bleed had almost stopped, I needed to go to hospital to see the gynaecologist. So, after a fairly uneventful ambulance ride (no blue lights or sirens), I was transferred from the care of the lovely ambulance crew into A&E at Milton Keynes University Hospital.

I lay there in the triage room waiting to be seen. By this time the bleeding had stopped, and I was beginning to calm down. I was also pretty tired as it was now just past 1am. Another hour passed before the gynaecologist arrived to take a look at me, armed with a clear plastic speculum that looked like it was designed for medieval torture rather than gynaecological care. My "neo" vagina was a bit of a novelty it seemed, as neither the gynaecologist nor her understudy had ever seen one "in the flesh" as she so eloquently put it. She inserted the speculum and after a quick poke around she said that there was no tear or broken stitches, but she could see that a large clot had been dislodged from my urethra. She was certain that this was the cause of the bleed and there was no further clotting that she could see. She reassured me that everything should now be ok and asked if I minded if her understudy took a look too. Since I began transition, I have been quite shocked at times at the inexperience that medical professionals outside of gender care have. GPs generally don't know much about prescribing HRT so will often refuse to treat a transgender patient. They have usually never seen a trans vagina before either so seem to think that it is in some way unique or different from that of a natal female vagina. I explained my frustration to Catherine at the Nuffield hospital on a recent visit and I could see her blood boiling as I explained what my GP had said regarding her lack of knowledge of my front bottom. 'IT'S THE SAME AS ANY OTHER VAGINA!' she said, with her fists clenched and anger spilling out of her. She is right to be frustrated too. There really is no difference essentially. My vagina is just like a vagina belonging to a person who was assigned female at birth except for a couple of differences. Firstly, it doesn't have a mucosa, which means it can't self-lubricate, and secondly it doesn't lead to a cervix and a womb but in every other way it functions and looks the same. To help the transgender cause I agreed to let the understudy have a poke around too, after all, how else are they going to learn.

While I lay in triage waiting for the gynaecologist, I called the Nuffield Brighton ward to ask for advice. One of the lovely nurses who'd looked after me just a week ago answered as she got back from her rounds. She gave me advice, telling me what to ask the doctor to check for and that I would be absolutely fine. This was yet another example of the wonderful care that they give. At 3am, I was allowed to go home. I got a taxi back to the farm and when I got in, I sat on the sofa in the lounge and fell asleep. I was woken by my housemates coming down for breakfast wondering why I was fully clothed and asleep on the sofa. Glen filled them in as he could see that I didn't have the energy to tell them the full story.

The next day I had no confidence to dilate because I was scared that I'd start bleeding again. I called Nuffield Brighton again and spoke to the wonderful Liz. She explained what had happened to me and informed me that there was a clot mentioned in my discharge notes which is why they were not surprised. She advised me to take a day off from dilation but to get straight back into it the next day. After this everything was back to normal and I had no further problems.

For the first two weeks post-surgery you are advised to self-quarantine, staying at home to reduce the risk of infection. During the second week, after Kelly had gone home and the blood clot incident was no longer causing me problems, I started to get bored. My car had been sitting in the car park at the farm for a couple of weeks, so I thought I'd start the engine and charge the battery a little. I ended up driving it to the top of the farm track which is around a quarter of a mile. That, was a big mistake. I couldn't actually press the brake pedal properly because it caused severe pain in my pelvis and the wound. The clutch wasn't much fun either so experiment over, I parked the car and went back inside to watch more Netflix. The only pain I was really experiencing throughout those first few weeks was from sitting. If I sat in a normal chair, I had to sit on one bum cheek then after a while switch to the other. The pain could get quite intense if I sat for too long, so I spent most of my time lying on the bed or sofa.

Around four weeks after coming home I started to drive my car, but I could only manage short journeys. A week later I drove from Milton Keynes to Leicester to see my mum. The drive itself went well, with only moderate pain from sitting and operating the clutch and brake. It was lovely to see my mum as I had only seen her once since leaving hospital when Helen drove me to Leicester to visit her. At that time in my recovery, the biggest issue for me was a lack of energy. I was extremely tired all the time. I vacuumed my room, needed a sleep. I drove to the shops, needed a sleep. I cooked a meal, needed a sleep. Driving back from Leicester after seeing my mum I started to feel really tired. Somewhere near Towcester I found my eyes getting really heavy and before I knew it, I was on the wrong side of the road. Thankfully the road was quiet. I pulled over, opened a window for some air and pulled myself together. My body had been through major trauma and it now needed all the energy it could get to heal itself.

At around eight weeks I was able to stop using the post-natal pads that had filled my knickers like an adult nappy. I'd developed a sort of "John Wayne" style walk to accommodate the girth of these absorbent monstrosities. I'm certain that these could be employed in areas where flash flooding is a threat, they would soak up the rainwater in no time. It was so freeing to switch to a regular panty liner, one that wasn't capable of draining the Suez Canal. While it may have been freeing, it did take some getting used to. The post-natal pads had no adhesive, so you just pulled your bulging knickers up and they stayed in place, but these regular ones are stuck to your panties with a layer of adhesive to keep them from slipping. All fine I hear you say, but the first time I used one, I put it into my panties the wrong way round. I pulled them up and got on with my day, pleased with myself at the progress I was making. Later that morning, nature called, I needed a wee. No problem, off I went to the bathroom, dropped my knickers and sat down. Something was wrong. There was no panty liner in my knickers. Where could it be? Had it been stolen by the vagina elves? Had the surgeon given me a vagina so cavernous that it swallowed feminine hygiene products? Nope; it was stuck to my still swollen and very poorly looking flange, including all my suture lines and exposed stitches. Bugger! With a few deep breaths and some motivational internal speech, I ripped the liner from my tortured flaps as fast as I could. I could hear my mum in my head saying, 'it's like pulling off a plaster, it hurts less if you do it quick'. No - it doesn't. A pain that felt like molten lava being rubbed into my vagina with a cheese grater coursed through my nether regions, and a little tear formed in the corner of my eye. I'd love to say I never made that mistake again, but this was the first of three such occasions. Will I never learn?

In late February I started to feel very low. I couldn't put my finger on why. I had everything I'd ever dreamed of; my destiny had been fulfilled, but it felt like a void was opening up. This period of depression only lasted a couple of weeks and from the research I did it seemed quite common. Physically I was healing well and all on track so there was no reason for depression other than the fact that I had been building up to this huge goal for so long and then all of a sudden, it's over; done. Not only this, but my brain had also had to rewire itself to understand my new physical anatomy. I was still experiencing phantom winky syndrome from time to time and on occasion, it felt like I'd been kicked squarely in the nuts, which was very unpleasant. It took some getting used to before I felt like I was back in the saddle and able to start planning the next stage of my life. By the end of February, life seemed to be returning to normal, except it wasn't. The global pandemic had begun to take a grip on the world and every news programme was focused on it. We were still able to go about our business at that time, so I visited friends and family as normal, but all this was about to change.

The post-surgery depression was dragging its heels and just wouldn't lift so I decided it was time to pull the covers off the motorcycle and go for a little spin to blow the cobwebs away. Motorcycles have been an important part of my life since I turned thirty and decided to learn to ride, and even though I'd taken a seven-year break from riding, they were never far from my thoughts. Pulling the cover off my shiny yellow Honda CBR600 was like opening my

Christmas presents as a child. As the cover came off and the yellow paint was exposed, my heart rate started to increase. I wasn't nervous, I was excited. Being a sports bike, it was pretty light in comparison to some bikes I'd owned but even so, wheeling it out of the stable where I kept it was a struggle while I was still healing. I thought I'd just take a steady run up the drive and back, only half a mile, but it would tell me whether I was ready to ride or not. To my surprise, it was more comfortable than driving my car. The seat was narrow, but the riding position took most of the weight off my pelvis and transferred it to my bum and thighs which helped. I knew that I wouldn't have the stamina to ride far but it was a start. The old saying is true, you never forget, it really is just like riding a bike. Now that I knew that I could ride if I wanted to, it was time to get back in shape. Not just me, the bike too. It wasn't in the best condition when I bought it but that was reflected in the price, so I set about restoring the old girl ready for some long summer rides.

Nine weeks after surgery, I had no choice but to go back to work. I had no more time off available and statutory sick pay wouldn't even cover the rent. Physically I felt much better, but my energy levels were still very low. I arranged with my boss to come back the next week on half days to get used to working again but as it turned out, we were all asked to work from home on the day I was due back in. After what felt like a million conference calls and online meetings over Microsoft Teams, we had a plan and we started to revamp and tidy up our entire curriculum. Each trainer had their own courses to look after so we all had plenty of work to do. The next week on March 23rd, the country went into the first of its lockdowns. Panic was spreading fast over Covid-19 and the horrifying stories shown on the news from around the world were shocking. A week later, our boss put the whole training team on furlough because we simply didn't have enough work to do at home, and the DAF building was closed until further notice as so many others were across the country. This was both a nightmare and a blessing in disguise. On one hand I was keen to get back to work even though I knew I would struggle to make it through the day without falling asleep at my desk, but on the other, furlough offered me the opportunity to take my time to relax and heal at my own pace.

So, what's a girl with too much time on her hands gonna do during lockdown? Well first, I stripped the bike in the stable and did a full service. I fitted new brake pads, brake lines and a new exhaust system and had the seat reupholstered. Next, all the bodywork was removed and cleaned. I filled my bath with car shampoo and hot water and gave the bike's bodywork a good soak. My other housemates thought I'd gone mad, but it worked a treat and twenty years of dirt and grime were removed from the fairing, nose and tail piece. Over the course of the next week I slowly rebuilt the bike until it was finished and ready to ride. I did a short shakedown run to the shops just to see if everything was working as it should and that was it, the bike was done. What next? I was getting very bored as my own lockdown had started in mid-January, long before the rest of the country was forced to stay at home. I read a few books from my favourite authors but still I felt restless and bored beyond belief. At the time my mind was already going over the last few years and what I'd been through as my transition unfolded. I started thinking about writing it all down, maybe it was time to share my memories. At first, I thought a blog, or a journal would be the best way to do this but as I began to write, plot and plan, it became clear that there just might be a book in all this. As it turned out there was: this one.

With writing becoming a daily distraction in the spring sunshine, under the shade of the willow trees by the little stream at the front of the farmhouse, I began to feel much better. My body was healing fast now, and the phantom winky syndrome had all but disappeared. Finally, my brain was starting to understand its new anatomy, and the rewiring of my nerves was clearly working at last. I was watching TV one night when I suddenly started to feel something funny between my thighs. A kind of fizzing sensation. This developed as the night went on and although it felt very nice, it was also very intense. It felt like I was having an orgasm, but all the time. I actually started to get worried. What If I was like one of those people who couldn't stop sneezing for years? What would it say in the papers? "Milton Keynes woman talks about her three-year orgasm ordeal". This was a problem. I took some Ibuprofen to see if it might take the edge off and thankfully it did. A few weeks later and the feelings had subsided. I now know that what I was experiencing was the reconnecting of the nerves in my clitoris.

There are no guarantees that the clitoris will have any feeling after the surgery let alone the ability to achieve orgasm, and some women are left with no feeling at all and as such will never experience female orgasm. This is not due to surgical negligence, it is just a luck of the draw thing, it either heals fully, or it doesn't. That worried me too, so it was time to test the equipment. After a cheeky fiddle while dreaming up a Chris Hemsworth sex fantasy, it was clear that although there were stirrings, my little button wasn't quite ready to be pressed. Over the next few weeks, I tried again once in a while but with no success until one day around the end of April, it finally happened, my first girlgasm! During my usual routine I found that what I was doing was really starting to hit the spot. The tension was building and my nether regions seemed to tense up in anticipation of what was about to happen. And then…AND THEN! OH - MY - GOD!!! A wave of pleasure tore through my body making me grip the sheets and arch my back. This was like nothing I'd ever experienced before. A male orgasm would have been over in a few seconds but this went on and on until I lay exhausted on the bed. I was so happy, not just because I'd had the biggest, most intense orgasm of my entire life, but also because I was thankful that the surgery had been successful, and I'd regained the sensation in my clitoris. Regular testing of the equipment has been carried out since for er, maintenance reasons.

June came around and Helen was still away in Europe, so I had a quiet birthday at home. I was beginning to feel very lonely and the long-distance thing with Helen really wasn't working. We decided to split in early July because she still had at least another year out there and our relationship had been non-existent for some time already. It was a relief to be single again, not because Helen was a horrible person, actually she was the exact opposite, but we both wanted different things from our lives and we couldn't even be in the same country so there was no point in prolonging things.

At the end of August, a letter arrived from Brighton. It was an appointment to see Mr Coker to sign off the surgery and discharge me from their care. The appointment was for October 16th, at 10.30am. As I sat there reading it at the breakfast table a strange sadness came over me. I had been so intensely moved by the whole experience at Brighton, and this letter was confirmation that it was over, and I would never need to go there again. It should have been a letter that brought relief and joy at the end of such a long and arduous process, but instead it brought sadness, I felt like I was grieving.

To cheer myself up I went for a long ride on my bike. We were coming out of lockdown and it was now ok to ride without a purpose such as fetching groceries or medical supplies. After a long ride out through Buckinghamshire and into Northamptonshire, I found myself at a Royal Enfield dealership. I love classic British motorcycles, but owning one is an absolute chore. They leak oil, they break down, it's hard to find parts for them and they are expensive to buy. I prefer things that are new but look old. Neo retro I suppose you might say. The Triumph Bonneville is a classic example, with similar styling to the original model but with modern technology. Royal Enfield are another old British motorcycle manufacturer, who since the 1970s have produced all of their motorcycles in India. I've always loved their simplicity and "what you see is what you get" nature. I found myself drooling over a black Interceptor 650cc, and after a short chat with the salesperson, a test ride was offered. I rode up to Santa Pod Raceway, not too far from the dealership, and then around some twisty country roads. Oh, I was in love. I almost felt like I was cheating on the Honda, but this was a much more connected experience. The Honda is blisteringly fast and takes all of your concentration to ride it safely, but this was like being connected to nature, taking in the sights, sounds and smells of the Northamptonshire countryside with a 270° parallel twin engine thumping away as my soundtrack. Once I was back at the dealership, I knew I had to have it. A deal was done and a week later I handed over the keys to the aging Honda and picked up my shiny new black Royal Enfield Interceptor. Riding home I was thinking of a name for it. I had a song stuck in my head that was playing in the dealership, "Paranoid" by Black Sabbath. I love this band as I do all classic rock bands and then it struck me, Ozzy! Ozzy Osbourne is known as the prince of darkness. My bike is painted in beautiful classic black. Perfect. Ozzy and I are still very much a team today. I ride as often as the weather allows and I never tire of watching men stare at the bike and then I see the shock on their faces when I take off my helmet and they see that I'm a woman. At least I hope that the shock is because I'm a woman, and not because they are trying to work out whether I'm still a man.

October 16th, 2020, appointment day. After a short wait in the waiting area, I was called in to see Mr Coker and his assistant Teresa. We had a short chat about my healing and how I'd been getting on with dilation, and then they asked about sensation. I was a little uncomfortable describing my testing procedure to a handsome looking man, but then I remembered that he was the one who created my vagina, so he knew it as well as I did if not better. They were both happy with my answers and so we proceeded to the physical examination. With my legs akimbo and yet another clear plastic speculum up my fluff, I could hear some very positive sounds coming from the other end of me. 'Oh yes, look at those suture lines, there's barely any scar tissue,' said Teresa. 'Yes, I'm happy with the depth and internal structure too' said Mr Coker. Like a pair of classmates admiring their science project, they proclaimed that my new vagina, my Foo Foo, was fully healed and ready for active duty.

I really wanted to hug Teresa as she had been brilliant throughout all my treatment, but with Covid restrictions still in place, I blew her a kiss through my mask instead. I wasn't sure I'd get away with that with Mr Coker, so I awkwardly sort of bowed at him as I left the room. I headed into Brighton to enjoy the rest of the sunny day. I decided to retrace my steps from my first ever appointment on August 10th, 2018. I went to the hotel where I'd stayed and broken my toe. Pictures of that Bob Marley mural flooded my mind. Then I parked my car and headed for The Lanes, my favourite place. I popped into the Druids Head for a drink. As I sat there the feelings of grief came over me once again and I started crying. How embarrassing! I couldn't stop crying no matter how hard I tried to compose myself, and I could see that other people had noticed. The waitress looked at me with that "are you OK" look as she headed past with a tray of full English breakfasts for the next table. I smiled weakly at her and turned my face to the wall.

After I had regained my composure, I headed for my favourite shops. I walked for about an hour, finding myself at Jew's Lane, the place where I'd had such an amazing day with Travis Alabanza in their creative writing workshop. As I stood staring at the door of the community projects building, with its black paint heavily chipped and scarred, it brought back memories of that day. I've never experienced that "life flashing before your eyes" moment, despite having had a few near misses on my motorcycles over the years, but standing there, I saw my whole transition playing in fast forward in front of my eyes like I was fast forwarding the adverts on catch-up TV. I headed to the beach. I looked out to sea for a while, trying to make sense of why I felt so sad to have been discharged from the hospital. That feeling of loss lasted for days, and even now I miss all the wonderful people at the Nuffield hospital in Brighton.

In November I decided that I'd had enough of the thirty-mile commute to work from Milton Keynes. Not only that, but all three of the housemates that I'd shared the last year and lockdown with were also leaving within weeks of each other. It was time to go. I looked for another house share near to work but due to its proximity to Oxford, prices are ridiculously high. In the end I found a lovely landlady who wanted a lodger in a village just south of Oxford and only eight miles from work. She lives in a beautiful old stone cottage in the Chiltern hills, just a stone's throw from the Ridgeway, an eighty-seven-mile national trail which is described as Britain's oldest road. My new landlady and I got on really well when we met and we both agreed that I'd be a good fit for her home, so my notice was handed in at the farm the very next day.

In late November I had a telephone consultation with the gender clinic in Daventry. Covid restrictions made it impossible to see them face to face and it was just a routine follow-up anyway to assess what my hormone levels were like. Based on my last set of blood work they were actually way too high which can be dangerous, so we formulated a plan to reduce my dosage and agreed to speak again in three months. The doctor also said that assuming my hormone levels were right, he saw no reason why I couldn't be discharged completely from the gender service next time. Again, I should have been excited, but my stomach turned over and I suddenly felt very emotional.

On December 5th, 2020, I packed up my little Fiat 500 and headed south to my new home. I had to make a few trips over the course of the week but by Friday I had moved almost all of my stuff. My friend Gwen helped me on Saturday with the big stuff that wouldn't fit in my tiny car and then gave me a lift back to fetch my car as I'd taken Ozzy to his new home earlier that day. I love living in this area, with nature surrounding me and with such a short commute to work. It was the right time to leave Milton Keynes, time to start a new chapter.

After Christmas, I was busy with work and busy writing this book. I had very little time for anything else other than the odd ride out on Ozzy. I saw my now eighty-nine-year-old mum whenever I could and my sister and daughter too. I'd had a second set of bloods done to check my hormone levels and they had come back to pretty much where they should be so medically there was nothing more that the gender clinic could do for me. My transition, the five-year journey that had broken me at times but given me so much hope and so many new opportunities, was coming to an end. All that was left was my last appointment, where I'd be officially discharged from the gender service for good.

'Postman has been' proclaimed my landlady, on a frosty mid-February morning. I picked up the wad of envelopes and scanned through them, separating them into piles of mine and hers. The last one to be placed on top of my pile of bills and pizza menus was from the Danetre hospital in Daventry, Northamptonshire.

Opening it right there and then, I read it aloud to myself.

Dear Miss Carter,

I am pleased to offer you an appointment to discuss your discharge from the gender service. Please attend the clinic on Friday, April 30th 2021 at 10.00 am.

Chapter Fifteen

Objects in the rear-view mirror (Are closer than they appear)

Oh my God! How long have I been sitting here telling my story? It's already lunchtime and I have so many things to do. I still haven't called my mum.

(Phone ringing) …

'Hello?'

'Hi mum it's Amy, I've been discharged from the gender clinic. It's over.'

'Hello?'

'HI MUM, ITS AMY!'

'Oh, hello love, your sister is here, talk to her, I haven't got my hearing aids in.'

My mum has very little hearing at the ripe old age of eighty-nine. Phone calls are difficult to say the least so I'm relieved that my sister is there. My sister picks up the phone and we chat about the appointment, and of course I start crying again. She relays the information to my mum and I can hear her in the background, 'tell her how proud I am of her' she says. 'Amy, mum says…' 'Yeah I got it sis, I can hear her' I reply, chuckling out loud. My sister has seen the best of my transition and the worst. She was there for me when I hit rock bottom and she was there when I was the happiest woman alive. Her kitchen table is like her consulting room. We have had so many sisterly chats across that table. She always gives good advice and it's always delivered with a steaming hot mug of coffee. I hope she knows how much I love her; I tell her often enough. With fresh tears rolling down my cheeks, washing away the mascara streaks from my earlier outburst of emotions in poor Dr Dhalsim's office, I put the phone down and start the car. 'Right, pull yourself together Carter. It's a long drive and you've got a busy day ahead.'

With one last look over my shoulder at the entrance doors to the clinic, I take a photo on my phone to remember them by and drop my phone into my handbag (probably never to be seen again). I pop little Flossy into 1st and pull away, leaving the car park for the last time. It seems so strange to think that I will never have to come here again. I'm going to miss it so much, miss them so much; the amazing team that literally change people's lives. I'll miss Lynne sorting out all my appointments and calming me down when things weren't going well. My voice training with Rhiannon the speech therapist. Appointments with the clinic nurses who helped me so much in those rocky early days when I had no clue what I was doing and needed so much guidance. I'll miss the wonderful doctors. Dr Stevens was the first specialist that I met on my first appointment. He is so very kind and such an interesting, intelligent and well-travelled man. Half of my appointments with him were spent chatting about cars, and then we'd get back to the point and discuss my transition progress, before wandering off on another topic soon after. I am going to miss our chats. Dr Dhalsim is so kind, and his voice is somehow soothing, making you feel like everything is going to be just fine. For nearly six years, they have been my support, my stability, my rock. They kept me going when I thought I couldn't go on. As I pull away from the hospital, I feel a sense of panic wash over me. How will I cope without them? One last look in the rear-view mirror, goodbye Danetre hospital, I owe you so much.

As I'm looking in the mirror, I catch my reflection. I look a complete mess. I have black streaks painted on my cheeks from my "not as waterproof as the label suggested" mascara. My eyes are red and puffy, still filled with tears that have yet to succumb to gravity and find their way down my cheeks. My bottom lip is quivering, and a sort of liquid number eleven has formed on my top lip, deposited there by my runny nose (so attractive). I notice the tiny sticker on the rear-view mirror. Was it always there? Surely, I would have noticed it before. "Objects in the rear-view mirror are closer than they appear." Well, that's an understatement. That place, those people, have been as important to me as family over the last six years. Maybe more important. As I drive away and the hospital gets smaller and smaller, the gravity of what happened in Dr Dhalsim's office is really starting to sink in. That's it, I'm done. Transition is over, I can be who I want to be, go where I want to go and do what I want to do (within the boundaries of the law and common decency of course).

Sure, there are things I still need to do. I have at least another three years of very painful and very expensive electrolysis ahead of me to clear the remaining hair from my face and neck. I will need some laser or electrolysis to clear the remaining hairs from my torso too. There are only a few dotted here and there and they are manageable, but no woman should have to shave her boobs in the shower, it's just not right. Most of my tattoos need to be covered up with something more feminine like orchids and butterflies (much better than gravestones and skulls). That process alone will take years and cost a small fortune. I need to lose weight again because I ate a lot of chocolate and drank a lot of gin during lockdown. My clothes are telling me that it's time to address the problem; especially my biker jeans which are not very forgiving in the waist and thigh area due to them being reinforced with Kevlar. If my finances ever allow it, I'd like to have some surgeries in the future too. Firstly, I'd like a new nose. My nose has always been a little on the large side for a woman, and although I can contour it with makeup to make it appear smaller; a smaller cuter nose would make me very happy and give me more confidence. I'd also love to have my boobs done. I said at the beginning of transition that I would never have them done, but as time has marched on and I have reached the full extent of what nature and HRT has to offer in terms of breast growth, I can just about fill a B cup and that's it. That would be fine if I were a size 8 but I'm a size 16-18 and the smallest bra I can get off the peg is a 40b so I can't even fill the cups properly. I don't want to look like a photo finish in a Zeppelin race, but a shapely C or D cup would complement my frame nicely. Finally, above all else I would love to get a hair transplant. It comes with no guarantees and is very expensive but the prospect of wearing wigs for the rest of my life doesn't thrill me. As I've said in previous chapters, there are advantages to wearing wigs, changing style and colour in an instant for example, but the disadvantages far outweigh them. I long for a day when I can ride my bike without worrying that when I take off my helmet, my hair might come with it, or to go swimming without keeping an eye out for my floating hairpiece as it slips silently from my head. I want to be able to blow-dry my hair in front of the telly in the morning and then style it like everybody else. Or to tie it up in a ponytail before hitting the gym or the yoga mat.

All these things are every day first world problems of course. Half of the clients at the beauty salon where I have my electrolysis are women in their fifties. Some of them have more facial hair than I do, and I'm neither joking or exaggerating when I say that. I'm also sure that I'm not the only woman to have had a tattoo and regretted it, although my reasons might be a bit more elaborate than most. The point is, the things that are left on my to do list are things that any woman might need, not exclusively a transgender woman considering them as part of her transition.

Turning right out of the hospital car park, I head south. I still have tears in my eyes and my emotions are close to overload. I feel a deep sense of grief, like I've just been told a close friend has died. Part of me wants to turn the car round and run back into the building, grab the first member of staff I see and hug them. The realisation that it will never happen makes me start crying again, harder than before, making it difficult to drive through the tears. About a mile down the road from the hospital I approach the first roundabout and I'm already getting road rage. The guy in the blue Mondeo behind me is so close to my rear bumper we could share the road tax. He also seems to be texting on his phone. I recently had an accident which resulted in six weeks of painful physio thanks to someone who didn't see me because they were texting on their phone, so this is a situation that I'm keen to avoid. I drop down a gear and unleash all sixty-nine-brake horsepower that Flossy has to offer. I start to pull away from him which seems to refocus his attention until the next roundabout where he disappears left.

Getting out onto the A5 at Weedon Bec, I am reminded of the old route to work from Leicester to Milton Keynes that I did for almost seven years when I worked at Volkswagen Group UK. Some of those journeys were good, some were slower than others due to the traffic, and one very nearly killed me. How could I have let things get so bad before asking for help? How could I have been at breaking point, contemplating suicide on the A5 before reaching out to someone? All those years and all those tears, the heartbreak, the depression, the nervous breakdowns.

Why did it take me half a lifetime to understand that all I needed was to be set free to be who I've always been inside?

What if things were different and I'd gone ahead with my plans? I'd be dead, not a problem for me, but how would my mum, my sister, my daughter and my close friends feel five years later looking back on that day? What would have happened to the driver of the truck that I planned to turn my wheels into? Would he have a family grieving for him? Would there be fresh flowers slowly decaying at the scene; placed there annually by a devoted wife, husband or parent? And for what? Because I didn't have the guts to ask for help. I'm so thankful that I didn't go through with my stupid, selfish plan. Life is so very precious; it should never be taken for granted and we owe it to ourselves to make the best of what we have and live our lives the best way that we can. As Rocky Balboa said, "it ain't about how hard you can hit, it's about how hard you can *get* hit and keep moving forward. That's how winning is done."

That's what I intend to do, live life the best way that I can, take the hits, learn from them and be stronger because of them. Well, I will when I can overtake this bloody tractor. There are so many things I want to do with my life now that every day isn't filled with thoughts of my transition goals, my next appointment, blood test or voice lesson. I hope that I will eventually meet someone who "gets me" and I them. I am ready to settle down now and I feel like I have love to give now that I am learning to love myself. I'm also ready to progress with my career and my hobbies. I am involved in some new initiatives at work around electric and hybrid truck technology and I fully intend to put myself forward to be at the forefront of them. When I began writing this book, it was intended as a way to keep me sane during lockdown, a hobby while I was furloughed from my job and recovering from surgery. It quickly became a far bigger project than I could have imagined and is now a real thing sitting in the palm of your hand. Creative writing will be a lifelong passion for me, and I would love for it to become more than just a hobby. I already have ideas for a novel, but you'll have to wait and see what the future holds on that one.

   The future; it still feels funny saying it out loud. For most of my life it felt as though I didn't deserve to even think of the future. Maybe I saw it as a punishment for planning my own death or maybe I just felt that I'd never make it this far in life, but I have. I am no Joan of Arc, Rosa Parks or Emmeline Pankhurst, but I am a warrior. A warrior who has faced her darkest times and overcome them. A warrior who knows how to fight and how to survive. Don't get me wrong, I'm not deluded. I know there will be dark days ahead of me as there are for all of us, but I am better prepared to face them now. I am battle hardened, emotionally better equipped and my experiences have made me smarter. I know I will be misgendered, often intentionally by people who think I don't have the right to exist. I will face abuse in public toilets as I have before, when all I want to do is pee and get the hell out of there. I will read vile nasty comments on social media, directed at me or at transgender people like me. Sure, I could just stay away from social media, but why should I? Because I'm trans am I the one who must compromise? Should I be the one who has to lose contact with friends who live overseas or who lead busy lives? I cannot begin to tell you how utterly devastating and hurtful it is to read comments like these, let alone have them spat at you with anger and venom in the street. I have experienced all of these personally:

"Pervert"

"You will never be a woman; you are a mutilated man"

"Freak"

"You are either a very ugly woman, or a bloke in a dress. Which is it?"

"Ladyboy"

"Shemale"

"Why don't you do us all a favour and kill yourself"

"People like you should not be allowed to have kids"

"God doesn't make mistakes. You made the mistake of thinking you're a woman."

"People like you should be burned at the stake"

"You do know you're a man, right?"

"If you got a dick, you ain't a chick"

I particularly enjoyed reading that last one when it appeared as a comment on a Facebook post about trans women in sport. Whatever happened to #bekind? Imagine how comments like this can hurt a person. The people who make these comments are utterly evil and have no care, compassion or empathy. At best they are misinformed, or misguided, but their opinions are no less damaging whatever the motivation. Believe it or not, many of the authors of these comments are women; standing up for women's rights in an attempt to keep "people like me" out of women's safe spaces. These people are often referred to as "TERFs", (Transgender Exclusionary Radical Feminists) but they can come from all walks of life. I am a feminist. I strongly believe in equality for all women, without prejudice, exception or compromise. I believe that if you don't fight for *all* women, then you fight for no women.

Then there are the transphobes who use "religion" or "nature" to justify their hateful vitriol. I like to call these the "flat-earthers". It's not my place to question the validity of a person's religious beliefs. I respect everyone's right to believe whatever they want to believe; but I do find it hard to understand how someone can call me mentally ill for identifying as a woman, when they believe that a man in the clouds loves them unconditionally, but under certain conditions.

Lastly, we have the group of transphobes that I call, the "knuckle draggers". They don't have a religious, moral or political argument as such, most of them couldn't even spell those words let alone have an opinion on them. They just think transgender people, transgender women in particular, are trying to trick them. They seem to think that a trans women's sole purpose in transitioning is to dupe a man into bed. Sorry to burst your bubble Kevin, but no man on this planet is worth the effort, time and courage that transition takes.

Transgender people share the same DNA as cisgender people. We bleed the same colour blood, experience the same emotions and want success, love and validity just like anyone else. We just happen to have been born with a condition called gender dysphoria. Is it really that hard to accept? We have no problem accepting that people are born with ADHD or Autism for example. Is the hate and mistrust of transgender people really justified? This may shock you to learn but there have been transgender people on this earth for as long as there have been people. Ancient Egyptian rulers would often seek transgender people as their advisors; believing that they would get a more balanced opinion. Ancient Rome had its fair share of transgender people too.

These comments, opinions, call them what you will, may well have shocked you. I'd be surprised if they didn't, but to me that's just a Tuesday. I read these things every day, I get stared at every day, and on the really bad days I am abused and made to feel ashamed. If there's a day that I don't experience transphobia in one form or another I call that a win. There are days when I don't want to get dressed let alone leave the safety of my room. On any given day I could be in the wrong place at the wrong time, face to face with someone who thinks they have the right to abuse me verbally and physically. The saddest part for me is knowing that those people, the TERFs, the flat-earthers and the knuckle draggers, may have sons, daughters or family members that could one day come out to them as trans, and because of their narrow-minded views, they may well be rejected, disowned, or even suffer violence. I can only hope that I am part of a generation of transgender people who are paving the way for our trans youth to be more accepted and treated as equals, not misfits, perverts or monsters.

With the road ahead now clear I head towards Milton Keynes, my next stop. The weather is lovely today. Warm spring sunshine radiates through the windscreen and there is hardly a cloud in the sky. Although its mid-day on a Friday there are a lot of motorcycles on the roads which is making me very jealous (but don't tell Flossy). I have this strange instinct to nod to the bikers as I would if I were riding my bike, but after headbutting my side window several times I'm reminded that this only works when I'm actually on a bike. Driving through Towcester High Street I pass the beauty salon where I have my electrolysis. A shudder goes down my spine as I think of the many hours of pain and discomfort I still have ahead of me. On the opposite side of the road is the little coffee shop that I often visit after my appointments, consoling myself with a slice of delicious homemade cake and a steaming hot cup of coffee. Leaving the bustle of the town, I pass Towcester Racecourse, and I'm reminded of the last concert I went to, the day before I started my new job at DAF Trucks in 2018. Paloma Faith was amazing. The rain poured down all evening, soaking me and my friends Wendy and Lucy. Where some artists may have gone full diva and cancelled the gig, Paloma just kicked off her heels and danced across the stage barefoot in the rain singing her heart out, giving us the most wonderful concert experience.

Continuing south I pass the Super Sausage café. It's a biker café on the A5 just north of Milton Keynes. I have spent many a Sunday morning there with my biker friends, stuffing our faces with a full English (vegetarian in my case) then drooling over the sea of bikes that fills the car park, before heading out on a ride to wherever the fancy takes us. These cafés are littered all over the country on our A and B roads; a reminder of the old days after the war when there were no motorways and the truck industry needed a place to eat and answer the call of nature. The Ace café in London on the North Circular is probably the most well-known of all these establishments due to the "ton-up" boys of the fifties on their café racers, but Loomies, Jacks Hill café, the H café, and the Super Sausage, are also my favourites and well worth a visit for any biker.

I reach the Stony Stratford roundabout at the top of Milton Keynes. Left is the A508 heading to Northampton, and just a mile and a half up that road is the farm where I lived until a few months ago. It's the place where I recovered from my surgery, wrote most of this book and spent my lockdown. It never really felt like home but in a funny way, it was a very important part of my journey. I'm reminded of spending those brilliant three days with Kelly after I got home from hospital, the night I had a bad bleed in my bathroom as I recovered from the surgery, and all the nights that Glen, Tony and I sat in the lounge drinking wine and eating pizza. We had some laughs; they were good times, but my decision to leave and move to Oxfordshire was the right one. We all moved on with our lives after lockdown.

      Straight on is Stony Stratford, the lovely old town where my dear friends Vicki and Jeff tied the knot, with yours truly as Maid of Honour. Today, I'm taking the second left down the A5 to meet my friend Gwen. I haven't seen her for months due to "lockdown three, the return of Covid". Our favourite Starbucks has re-opened and although we can only sit outside for now, it is so good to be back. I'm really looking forward to seeing her, not just because I've missed her, but because the act of going to a coffee shop with your friends was, until recently, a distant memory.

      Pulling into the car park I can see Gwen's trusty Prius. That same Prius brought me home from the hospital in Brighton, a journey that seems so long ago now. As I walk through the double doors into the coffee shop, the smell of Colombian roast hits me, and the noise of drive-through orders being taken by the staff on the other side of the counter fills my ears. I spy my partner in crime chatting away at a table just the other side of the window to someone who looks familiar to me but I can't quite place. I order Gwen's favourite, caramel macchiato and my usual bucket of latte (a Venti Latte is bigger than Flossy's fuel tank). I'm a bit peckish so I order a piece of fruit toast and jam too. 'What name is it please?' asks the barista from behind her mask. 'Amy Kate' I reply. I'm feeling sassy today so I use my full name. I usually go by just Amy but that's the beauty of my name, I can double it up if I want to. I think Amy Kate sounds really cool, but I am a bit biased: I did choose it after all. A few minutes pass and then I hear a mask muffled shout from behind the counter, 'Amy Kate'. I pick up the cup and read the name written on the side in red marker pen. "Ammy Kate". Oh well, I thought to myself, at least you make good coffee.

    By now Gwen has spotted me and gestures me to come to her table through the glass of the shop window. Her first question is less than subtle. 'Bloody hell, either you've been crying or you've driven here with your head out of the window. How did it go? Are you discharged?' she asks. 'My discharge is none of your business' I joke (crass). Gwen rolls her eyes but this is not her first rodeo. She has been putting up with my terrible jokes for five years now, and probably deserves a medal for it. After explaining what happened during the appointment, managing not to cry this time which is a bonus; I finish my fruit toast and take a sip from the vat of hot steaming coffee. Aaahh, how I've missed you. I am mildly addicted to coffee, especially Starbucks latte, so this is the antidote to the emotional morning I've had. Gwen and I haven't seen each other in quite a while so there is a lot to catch up on. Having chatted for what seems like minutes but is closer to an hour, I finish my coffee, head to the ladies for my second wee, then with a virtual hug, I leave her to her second coffee order and leave.

Next stop is Sportsbike shop in Milton Keynes. I need to pick up an order for a new bubble visor for my helmet, and it's always good to shoot the breeze with the crew in there. I'm a regular, so they know me by name. As I walk in, and before I've even hit the plunger on the sanitizer bottle, I hear 'Amy!' as John, one of the staff members, spots me. Sue, the manager pops her head round from the stock room and smiles at me while continuing the phone call that she's on. John and I chat bikes, lockdown and what's new for a few minutes, while my order is being sorted. Clive and Sue join in the conversation once they have finished dealing with customers. During lockdown, the shop was closed and all the staff were furloughed, so it is so good to see them back in action, helping bikers to stay safe by providing them with all the safety gear they need. John rides a badass black Harley. The exhaust is loud enough to make small children cry. He loves that bike as much as I love Ozzy, my black Interceptor. Ask any biker; it's in their blood; biking isn't just a hobby, it's a way of life, a freedom that driving a car cannot match. It reminds me of my transition. I couldn't give up riding bikes just as I couldn't deny the fact that I am a woman, despite what the midwife saw between my chubby little thighs all those years ago. After I've taken up far too much of their time, I head out and back across the car park to my trusty little Flossy, gleaming in the sun despite the 57,000 dead flies that are stuck to the front bumper.

Bloody hell, it's nearly three o'clock! I have one final stop before I head back home. After winding my way through many of Buckinghamshire's villages, I arrive at work. I have the day off, but I want to tell my friend Sam how the appointment went. She and I have become close friends since I started working at DAF Trucks, and she was responsible for proofreading the first draft of this book. I ease Flossy into her usual parking spot and grab my bag. Walking across the car park I see our boss Ryan on the phone in his office, his classic BSA motorcycle sitting below in the car park with a tiny puddle of oil under it as usual. I swipe my security pass on the pad and the doors swish open. I take a step inside and wave at Mandy the receptionist. From the upstairs balcony I hear 'SANITIZE!' as our building manager prompts me to hit the foot pedal on the sanitizer before taking another step (thank God I was wearing a mask). Heading up the stairs and along the corridor, I pass the classrooms where on any other Friday I'd be teaching. I feel a little out of place in my vintage get-up; ordinarily I'd be wearing my work uniform of navy-blue skirt, black opaque tights, (to cover my tattoos) blue "DAF" blouse and black shoes as I walk through the office.

The DAF academy office is quite small compared to the rest of the building. There's Sam, (my long-suffering proof-reader) Kate, Jim and Becky (Becky designed the beautiful cover of this book). They all listen as I explain how my appointment went and I can feel the tears coming again so I have to stop and regain my composure. I decide to head down to the workshop to see the other trainers in my team. It's afternoon tea break and they're all sitting there with a brew, talking nonsense as usual. There are two Marks in our team, Mark one is the boss, and Mark two, like Deano, is a former colleague from Volkswagen. They both moved to DAF a few months before me, and recommended me for the job, for which I am very grateful. Paul, John, James, Samuel, Martin, Chloe and Deano are all there, the whole training team. I get the usual 'what you doing here on your day off?' from the guys, and after a potted explanation I hit the button on the coffee machine, "strong, black, no sugar" and grab the nearest seat. This is it now, my life is like any other life. It's a life no longer plagued by thoughts of what if? Why wasn't I born a girl? I am a girl, well a woman at least, and I love it. I love that I don't spend my days in sadness and depression anymore, wishing for a better life, wishing I wasn't transgender. I'm respected as a woman here and I'm respected as a professional. And why shouldn't I be? I can strip and rebuild a sixteen-speed gearbox or a thirteen-litre diesel engine as well as any of my male colleagues. What more could I ask for? My hopes and dreams no longer include the many steps of transition, from being diagnosed with gender dysphoria, taking HRT, learning to live as a woman through social transition, and finally gender affirmation surgery. They are about places I want to see, cars and trucks I want to drive and bikes I want to ride. They are about meeting someone special who I can share my life with, and spending time with my friends and family.

I'm smiling as these thoughts go through my mind. Meanwhile, Mark two tells us about the latest piece of Ducati carbon fibre that he's bidding on in eBay, and James lists all the drinks he consumed last weekend, which by the sound of it would have been enough to paralyse a camel. With my coffee cup drained, I drop it into the recycling bin and say my goodbyes. 'See you Monday' says Mark one, my boss. 'Not if I see you first' I say with a smile, as I walk out of the workshop and head for home.

The drive home from work is a short one, just eight miles through the gorgeous Oxfordshire countryside. Leaving the small-town bustle of Thame, I head south towards Chinnor, with the Chiltern hills creating a stunning vista ahead of me. Red kites soar in the sky above me, occasionally swooping on their prey as they hunt in the fields that line the road. I'm so very happy in this moment, and so lucky to be able to live in such a beautiful part of England. As I arrive at the cottage, I notice my landlady's car in the drive. She also drives a Fiat 500 but hers is a subtle mint green colour. She hasn't named her car but I secretly call it "Minty", Flossy's cousin. Walking into the kitchen feeling slightly weary after a long emotional day, I'm greeted with the smell of her cooking. Something involving stuffed peppers if my olfactory senses don't deceive me. As lovely as the dish smells, tonight, I am treating myself to a pizza and a very large glass of Pinot Noir. My landlady and I chat a while as my pizza cooks and the wine breathes. She asks me how my day went and she is not at all surprised when I tell her how many times I've cried. Even though I haven't lived here that long, we have gotten to know each other quite well, and she always knows when I'm upset or I'm having a bad day. With my pizza cooked, sliced and plated, and the added extra cheese bubbling away on top, I place it on the tray along with the wine bottle and a glass before heading to my room to relax.

Sitting alone, eating my pizza and drinking my wine, I am replying to a barrage of text messages that I've received throughout the day. All well-wishers asking me how it went. It is lovely to have so many wonderful friends who genuinely care if I'm OK, and I find myself smiling as I type my responses to them. After the second glass of wine, I am struggling to keep my eyes open. It's only ten o'clock but it's been a long day and I need to get up early tomorrow. I'm heading out on Ozzy to a bike meet with some friends. Ozzy is polished and ready to ride but I won't be if I don't get a good night's sleep.

With my makeup removed, teeth brushed, HRT gel and moisturiser applied, I slip into my nightie and pull back the duvet. I love the feel of a cold bed as I sink into it, pulling the covers over me, making me feel all snuggly. I give Barney bear a little hug and kiss his forehead before turning out the light and closing my eyes. As sleep comes for me, I hope for another sex dream about Chris Hemsworth (what? I'm only human). I also think about the day and what it means to me. The significance may seem trivial to many but that appointment, that short period in time in that tiny office at the hospital was a defining moment not only in my transition, but in my life. Freedom from the process of transition is of course a wonderful thing and I'm sure in time I will appreciate it. But like a prisoner who has done hard time can often have trouble adapting to the world once released, I'm still grieving for what I'm going to miss so much.

Sleep is closing in fast now; my thoughts are no longer clear or lucid. One final thought enters my foggy, tired brain. What will tomorrow bring? After all, the possibilities are endless.

How to be a trans ally

Now that you have read the book, I hope you have a better understanding of what living with gender dysphoria is like, and what a huge undertaking transition is for a person. Transition is hard enough without the added abuse that people from the trans community face. As a transgender woman, I face abuse on a fairly regular basis. I even receive abuse from other members of the LGBTQ+ community at times. If you are not swayed by my story and remain unconvinced that transgender people are equally valid human beings, deserving the same rights and opportunities as cisgender people, then that's OK. I respect your opinion and I wish you well. If on the other hand you would like to become an ally of trans people, or perhaps you already consider yourself an ally but would like to know more, read on.

Of course, this guide is not exhaustive, and I may not have included all the "correct" things to do or say because there isn't always a definitive answer to every situation you might encounter. When you become an ally of transgender people, your actions will help to make society a better, safer place for transgender people and for all people who are "different", whether trans or not.

'He just looks transgender'

I hear this a lot. While it might be true that in some cases you might spot some differences in some individuals that "out" them as trans, it is not true of everyone. Most importantly, not every trans person has transitioned. Some may not be able to because of religious beliefs, family or financial implications. They may be desperately unhappy, living day to day with gender dysphoria and with no way to relieve that suffering. Being trans isn't always visible, it could be your best friend or your closest relative. Be kind.

Gender identity vs sexual orientation

Gender identity is not directly linked to sexual orientation. Sexual orientation is about who we're attracted to. Gender identity is our subconscious sense of gender, either male/female or neither of the gender binaries. Transgender people could be straight, gay, lesbian, bi, pansexual, who knows? I was once asked, 'so now that you're a woman, are you going to start sleeping with blokes?' Not only was this question wildly offensive and inappropriate; it was also very misguided. Our gender identity is who we go to bed *as*. Our sexual orientation is who we go to bed *with*.

It's all about the pronouns baby

I am misgendered on a fairly regular basis. It mostly happens when I make phone calls and is the reason why I will go to great lengths to avoid using the phone if I can. Misgendering is when a person uses the wrong pronoun to address someone. This may not always be a trans person. Quite a few of my lesbian and non-binary friends have reported being gendered male in public spaces because they dress a certain way or wear their hair short. It can be either malicious, said on purpose to provoke or hurt a person, or an honest mistake. If you're unsure which pronoun a person uses, either try to pick up on the pronoun other people use when referring to them, or simply ask which pronoun the person uses, starting with your own. For example, "Hi, I'm Amy Kate, my pronouns are she and her. What about you?" Then use that person's pronoun and encourage others to do so. If you accidently use the wrong pronoun, apologise quickly but sincerely, then move on. The more you make an issue of the situation, the more uncomfortable it is for everyone. Social media platforms such as Instagram are starting to add the option to display your preferred pronouns which can be really helpful. If in doubt, you can always check their Instagram account. Gender fluid, gender queer and non-binary people often use neutral pronouns such as they/them. This might seem confusing at first but these pronouns are no less valid than she/her and he/him. Imagine your friend tells you that they have been to see their doctor. If you were unaware of the doctor's name or gender you might ask 'how did your appointment go? what did they say?' We automatically assign a gender to a person when we meet them or hear their voice, whether it is the right one or not. Scientists suggest that this is part of our "fight or flight" reflex, in order to identify our enemies. When we have no data about a person's gender or name, we easily adopt a neutral pronoun as seen in the example above. Also, did you spot that I used "they" and "their" to describe your friend, because I do not know their gender or non-binary status. In recent times, many trans and non-binary people have started to use pronoun badges in workplaces, especially if they face the public or are part of a large workforce and often come into contact with co-workers who have never met them.

'What's your *real* name?'

For some transgender people, even hearing their birth name is a tremendous source of anxiety. At the very least, it is a part of their life that they wish to leave behind. Respect the name a transgender person is currently using. If you happen to know a trans person's birth name, don't share it without the person's explicit permission. Referring to a trans person by their birth name, either in person or in their absence is called "deadnaming". It is not only offensive, but it could cause the person to be traced, and could lead to physical abuse or even death. Similarly, don't share photos of someone from before their transition unless you have their full permission.

"Coming out" as a different sexual orientation other than "straight" isn't the same as coming out as transgender

"Coming out" to other people as a different sexual orientation such as gay, lesbian, bi or pansexual is typically seen as revealing a truth that allows other people to know your true authentic self. The LGB community places a great emphasis on being "out", with the suggestion that until a person is open about their sexuality, they cannot be truly happy. When a transgender person has transitioned and is living their life as their true authentic self, the world now sees who they truly are. Sadly, in some cases when a trans person "comes out", people no longer see the person as "real". Like me, some people may choose to publicly discuss their gender history in an effort to educate and raise awareness in the hope for cultural change, but don't assume that every transgender person owes you disclosure; their gender history is nobody's business but theirs.

Common sense is not that common

Even though many transgender people are proud of their achievements in transition, they wouldn't necessarily share them with a pub or restaurant full of strangers. A few years ago, I was quietly enjoying a meal and drinks with some colleagues from work when a former colleague who I hadn't seen since early transition spotted me. It was clear she'd had a few glasses of vino from the wobble in her walk and the lack of volume control in her voice. She stood above me, proclaiming at the top of her voice, 'AMY! Haven't seen you in ages. How's your transition going? Oh my God, your tits are huge!' As if that wasn't enough, she then explained to her friend that she used to know me as Ian before I transitioned, and that we had worked together for several years without her knowing I was trans. Until that point, no-one in the pub dining area had even looked at me, I had completely blended in. Now, everyone was looking at me. Thanks for that…

Terminology is important stuff

Transgender people use many different terms to describe themselves and their lived experiences.

Respect the terms they use such as transgender, transsexual, non-binary, genderqueer etc. If a person is not sure which label fits them best, give them the space to work it out for themselves. They've spent their lives up to this point conforming to a gender they didn't ask for; they don't need you to tell them which term you think they should use. You wouldn't like your identity to be defined by others, so please allow others to define themselves as they see fit.

Patience is a virtue

A person who is questioning or exploring their gender identity may take some time to figure out what's right for them. For example, they may use a particular name or pronoun, and then decide at a later time to change that name or pronoun if it doesn't feel right. I have a friend who transitioned from female to male and was happy for a while but then realised that they still didn't feel right about their gender identity. They changed direction, identifying as non-binary. This decision took some time, but it was the right one. They now live happily in the right identity for them. Do your best to be respectful and use their preferred name and pronouns. Non-binary and gender fluid people are just as valid as trans people who go from one binary to the other.

There is no "right" or "wrong" way to transition; it's different for everyone

Some transgender people require hormones and surgeries as part of their transition to align their bodies with their gender identity. Some transgender people transition without hormones or surgeries. Some cannot have surgeries due to health or financial reasons. A transgender person's identity is not dependent on whether or not they have had surgeries or they're taking HRT. Accept that if someone tells you they are transgender, they are, regardless of what path their transition took.

Questions questions...

You would never ask a cisgender person what's lurking in their underwear. It is equally inappropriate to ask a transgender person that question. Don't ask if a transgender person has had surgery or, "the op" or if they are "pre-op" or "post-op.". If they choose to disclose that information, it is their choice. The creation of a vagina in a trans woman does not define her as a woman and the creation of a penis in a trans man does not define them as a man. I was once asked by a friend, 'so when you recovered from surgery, how did it feel to be a woman? You know, fully?' The implication that a woman is defined only by the presence of a vagina is quite problematic, especially when you take into account that the question was asked by a woman.

Compliments aren't always welcome

While you may intend to be supportive, comments like these can be hurtful or even insulting:

'I would have never known you were transgender. You look so pretty.'

'You look just like a real woman.'

'She's so gorgeous, I would have never guessed she was transgender.'

'You're so brave.'

'You'd pass so much better if you wore makeup'

'Have you considered a voice coach?'

"You look just like a real woman" is a terrible thing to say to a transgender woman. They *are* real women, regardless of how they look. "I would never have guessed she was trans" also implies that someone who is trans could never look that pretty. While on the surface it seems like a compliment, but to the recipient, it most definitely isn't.

Being called "brave", while it's meant as a compliment, is high on most trans people's list of "pet peeves". The reason is because society, the same cisgender people who are calling us brave, are the reason we have to be brave in the first place. People who call us brave understand that people in society treat us awfully. They know we are always at risk, vulnerable and open to abuse. They see the red tape that we have to go through to access healthcare and legal recognition of our gender. They see the insults, the stares, the online abusive comments from nasty little trolls. And then they gloss over that to talk about how brave we are for living through it. No trans person should have to be brave. We don't want to be brave, we don't want to be warriors, but we have to learn how to fight and how to survive. All we really want to do is live our lives peacefully and quietly without fear of attack.

Don't let it slide

You may hear anti-transgender comments from transphobic people, including anti-LGBTQ+ activists, but you may also hear them from LGB people. Someone may think that because they're gay, lesbian or bisexual, it's OK for them to use certain words or tell jokes about transgender people. It's important to challenge anti-transgender remarks or jokes whenever they are said, no matter who says them.

I just wanna pee...

In a perfect world, every public toilet would be gender neutral. Obviously, this is not the case, so trans people often receive abuse or discrimination for using the toilet that aligns with their gender identity. I have personally been verbally abused in female toilets, by women who claimed that I should have used the male toilets. I'm a woman, what business would I have in a male toilet? A while back, I approached four of the popular budget gyms to ask about joining. My main query was whether I would be able to use the female changing rooms, as I identify and live as a female. The answer, from all four of them, was that I could only use the female changing rooms if I'd had gender affirmation surgery. I asked how they police that? None of them could answer. Should I drop my knickers as I enter the gym to confirm that I have a vagina? Maybe they employ someone who is in charge of vagina security? In any case it is an unworkable, ridiculous and discriminatory policy. Needless to say, I didn't join any of the gyms. As an ally, if you are out with a trans friend, it can be a good idea to ask if they would like you to accompany them to the toilet, so that they don't have to go in alone. They may politely refuse, but they will be grateful for the thought.

Listen to transgender people

The best way to be an ally is to listen with an open mind to transgender people. Check out books, films, YouTube channels, blogs and podcasts to find out more about transgender people and the issues people within the community face.

Don't be a hero

Don't be afraid to admit when you don't know something. It is better to admit you don't know something than to make assumptions or say something that may be incorrect or even potentially hurtful. Find the appropriate resources that will help you to learn more. Places like Stonewall, GLAAD, and Mermaids are great places to start.

Pride

Be proud to be an ally, enjoy it, embrace it. The LGBTQ+ community can be a wonderfully inclusive and open place to be. You don't have to be part of the community to enjoy it either. Have fun, make interesting new friends and explore the diversity of our community. Go to a PRIDE event and release your inner Unicorn, you won't regret it.

You can change:
Your body
Your behaviour
Your beliefs
Your mind

You can't change:
Who you are

About the author

Amy Kate Carter was born in Leicester in 1972. Growing up around cars, she worked on them with her father, learning valuable skills from him. Amy left school at the age of sixteen with very few qualifications. She studied at Leicester college to become a motor mechanic and later went on to become a technical trainer in the motor industry. Amy carried a secret with her for many years before making the decision to transition from male to female in 2015. The five years that followed were some of the hardest she has ever faced, and now, with transition in her rear-view mirror, she is able to reflect on the experience. The result is her first book, ***Hello world, I'm Amy Kate***.

Printed in Great Britain
by Amazon